Men, Women, Messages, and Media

UNDERSTANDING HUMAN COMMUNICATION

Second Edition

Wilbur Schramm

EAST-WEST COMMUNICATION INSTITUTE

William E. Porter

UNIVERSITY OF MICHIGAN

1817

HARPER & ROW, PUBLISHERS, New York
Cambridge, Philadelphia, San Francisco,
London, Mexico City, São Paulo, Sydney

Sponsoring Editor: Phillip Leininger
Project Editor: Eleanor Castellano
Designer: Robert Sugar
Production Manager: Marion A. Palen
Compositor: Maryland Linotype Co.

Art Studio: J & R Art Services, Inc.

This book was originally published under the title *Men, Messages, and Media: A Look at Human Communication.* Copyright © 1973 by Wilbur Schramm.

Men, Women, Messages, and Media:
Understanding Human Communication, Second Edition

Copyright © 1982 by Wilbur Schramm and William E. Porter

Library of Congress Cataloging in Publication Data
Schramm, Wilbur Lang, 1907–
  Men, women, messages, and media.

  Rev. ed. of: Men, messages, and media. 1973.
  Includes index.
  1. Communication. 2. Mass media. I. Porter,
William Earl. II. Title.
P90.S375 1982   001.51   81–20123
ISBN 0-06-045798-8   AACR2

CONTENTS

PREFACE

This is a revision of a book written by Wilbur Schramm and published in 1973 under the title *Men, Messages, and Media*. This new edition, the preparation of which was shared by the two authors, carries a slightly different title, reflecting a change in social norms that has taken place in the past decade. The language of our revision takes into account these new norms.

The design of the first edition, as well as this one, represents an attempt to introduce the reader to the communication process, a term that covers acts ranging from a driver's reacting to the painted letters of a stop sign through a news story in *The New York Times* to a computer scientist's instructing a machine on how to correct its own errors.

This is not the conventional way to approach the study of communication. Since long before the First World War, universities have had departments called "journalism" and "speech." Both originally were concerned with presentation—the art of writing well, in the one case, and in the other, the art of speaking effectively. Inevitably, the drive to know more led these departments in different directions.

Teachers of journalism began to analyze the magazines and newspapers—and, in time, the broadcasts—in which the craft they were
teaching appeared; teachers of speech began to examine such matters
as the psychological aspects of public address. Eventually, both (along
with scholars from the psychology, sociology, political science, linguistics, and other fields) became interested in the effects of communication and the systematic analysis of what goes on when people
communicate with each other.

As such patterns of study developed, they inevitably overlapped;
academics began to look over one another's shoulders. But the business
of introducing students into the field remained essentially divided in
two. Study in journalism schools and departments has generally begun
with a survey of the media of mass communication, based upon detailed description of each of the major media, and then moved on in
succeeding courses to the basics of newswriting and editing. The
traditional speech department has usually reversed this procedure,
beginning with practice in the essential skills of public speaking and
moving—in later courses—into the analysis of the elements of con-
struction, exposition, and persuasion.

These are good patterns, and they work. They serve particularly
well the nascent professional—the student who wants a career in a
field based upon writing, such as newspaper reporting, or upon the
spoken word, such as broadcasting.

Still, a single act, however modified by circumstances or equipment, is the foundation of all such study, and the first edition of this
book tried to present it from a new and comprehensive point of view,
by providing an introduction to mass communication as a part of
human life and society, reflecting modern knowledge of the field but
still readable without advanced knowledge of social science or research
methods. This new edition follows the same pattern, with revisions to
reflect the growth of knowledge and experience in teaching with the
book. The beginning sections dealing with the nature of language, for
example, have been revised to reflect the present state of theory
about language origins. The section on the mass media, while it
makes no attempt to describe all the dimensions and aspects of these
great social institutions, does concentrate on what seem to us the
most important parts of introductory media study—the makeup of
audiences, the nature of their exposure to television and print, and
the process through which news, in particular, is highlighted. Material dealing with social control of the mass media has been elaborated
and updated.

The most substantial change, however, has been in the section that
deals with the effects of communication. The major theories of effects

are reviewed and some of the context of their historical development set out.

The final chapter deals with our communication tomorrow, which promises an age geared to computers, recorders, individualized and interactive broadcasting, and new systems for storing and exchanging information. It has become fairly clear that we are now in the first years of such an age. Some historians are already referring to it as the Age of Information, others as the Information Revolution. The name matters less than what seems likely to happen. New communication technology—notably the computer, the communication satellite, and microelectronics—promises to increase greatly the flow and power of communication. Indeed, the computer may become the great communication machine of the remainder of this century because it is the only machine able to handle the tide of information that is likely to flow. It may be that the ability to have access to this mass of information, to be able to sort it out and store it for use, will prove to be a source of national strength comparable to natural resources, industrial development, and military capability. We have concluded the book with a new section on what these dramatic developments may mean to all of us.

In addition to these content changes, to make this new edition more useful to both teacher and students, we have added to each chapter a group of topics for further thought and some suggestions for further reading.

Finally, this is a revision of the book originally written by Wilbur Schramm without a collaborator, in which a good many illustrative passages were set out in the first person. This edition seeks to retain that quality; thus, it is Wilbur Schramm behind the "I" when it appears in the following pages.

For suggestions out of which changes in this second edition have grown, we are deeply grateful to more people than we can name. Among them are Paul Lazarsfeld, Harold Lasswell, Ithiel de Sola Pool, Daniel Lerner, Elihu Katz, Alex Edelstein, F. Gerald Kline, Steven Chaffee, Donald Roberts, and, of course, the staff of Harper & Row. To the students who wrote or talked to us about their experiences with the first edition, we owe a deep debt of gratitude. All these and others have helped to make this second edition better.

WILBUR SCHRAMM
WILLIAM E. PORTER

1/
HOW COMMUNICATION DEVELOPED

As I write these lines I can look up from my paper at the jagged green mountains of Hawaii. If I look down the horizon to the seacoast, I can pick out the place where the first inhabitants are supposed to have stepped ashore on these islands. They came out of the Stone Age, twelve hundred years ago, riding in an outrigger canoe fashioned with the crudest of instruments. They came to Hawaii at the end of an incredible 5000-year journey from Southeast Asia, carrying their gods, their children, their foods with them, hopping from island to island over thousands of miles of open sea, living in a rapport with wind, water, and earth such as we could hardly expect of ourselves today. They landed on a lava island, planted their seeds and their culture, and made the land theirs.

Those first Hawaiians were already skillful communicators. They could read information in the skies and in the waves, and use it to navigate. They had a well-developed language. True, they could not write it, although they recorded some information in pictures and carvings. But they used their spoken language as a powerful instrument. With it they created a viable government and a pleasant family life. They expressed wonderfully subtle ideas and relationships. They persuaded others to accompany them on voyages over the horizon and reassured them in moments of discouragement. They carried with them all the lore of ocean sailing, the beliefs and rituals and customs of life as they wanted to live it, and passed all this on to their children, without writing. When they landed on Hawaii and felt the earth shake and saw smoke and fire in the mountains, they had information that helped them recognize Madam Pele, the Goddess of Fire; and they knew how to communicate with her, too, with prayer and offerings and dances.

THE MEANING OF "COMMUNICATION"

But pause here a moment. "He knew how to communicate with her." What does that mean?

When the critic and philosopher Kenneth Burke sent a book to press in 1935, he proposed the title *Treatise on Communication*. The publisher vetoed the name because, so he said, readers would expect a book on telephone wires! That is how one of Burke's most important volumes came to be called *Permanence and Change*.

We cannot quarrel with multiple uses for a term that is so pervasive in our thinking and our behavior, but we must at least make clear what it is we are talking about when we use the term *communication*. This book is not—at least not directly—about telephone wires, nor transportation (as it might be if it had been written by an economist), nor Reading and Writing (which is what our children studied under the name Communication in primary school), nor freshman English and Speech (which their baby-sitter was studying at the same time in a college course called Communication), nor *successful* communication (which we are talking about when we say, "Harry really communicates!"). Indeed, we will find some of the failures of communication as instructive as the successes.

This book is about the fundamental human social process. Communication is the tool that makes societies possible. It is no accident that *communication* and *community* have the same word root. Without communication, there would be no communities; and without community, there could be no communication. The particular qualities of human communication are what chiefly distinguished human from other societies.

In an eloquent chapter written 70 years ago, the sociologist Charles Cooley called communication "the mechanism through which human relations exist and develop—all the symbols of the mind, together with the means of conveying them through space and preserving them in time."[1] And the anthropologist Edward Sapir wrote with great insight in the first edition of the *Encyclopedia of the Social Sciences*.

> While we often speak of society as though it were a static structure defined by tradition, it is, in the more intimate sense, nothing of the kind, but a highly intricate network of partial or complete understandings between the members of organizational units of every degree of size and complexity, ranging from a pair of lovers or a family to a league of nations or that ever increasing portion of humanity which can be reached by the press, through all its transnational ramifications. It is only apparently a static sum of social institutions; actually, it is being reanimated or creatively affirmed by particular acts of a communicative nature which obtain among individuals participating in it. Thus the Republican party cannot be said to exist as such, but only to the extent that its tradition is being constantly upheld by such simple acts of communication as that John Doe votes the Republican ticket, thereby communicating a certain kind of message, or that a half dozen individuals meet at a certain time or place, formally or informally, in order to communicate ideas to one another and eventually to decide what points of national interest, real or supposed, are to be allowed to come up many months later in a gathering of members of the party. The Republican party as a historical entity is merely abstracted from thousands upon thousands of such single acts of communication, which have in common certain persistent features of reference. If we extend this example into every conceivable held we soon realize that every cultural pattern and every single act of social behavior involve communication in either an explicit or implicit sense.[2]

Society is a sum of relationships in which information of some kind is shared. Let us understand clearly one thing about it: Human communication is *something people do*. It has no life of its own. There is no magic about it except what people in the communication relationship put into it. There is no meaning in a message except what people put into it. When we study communication, therefore, we study people—relating to one another and to their groups, organizations, and societies; influencing one another; being influenced; informing and being informed; teaching and being taught; entertaining and being entertained. To understand human communication we must understand how people relate to one another.

Two or more people come together, trying to share some information. They are likely to be very different people. Because their life experiences have been different, the signs that carry the information are likely to look different to them. The more different the experiences, the more different the information that is likely to be read into them. Ideas like "pain" and "hunger" have a fairly good chance of being understood in common because all of us have experienced these things—though even in this case, the "stiff upper lip" tradition of one culture is likely to be misinterpreted in a culture where feelings are more openly expressed. But words like *freedom, communism,* and *apologize* obviously are going to cause trouble when people come from different life patterns, especially if they come from different cultures.

Note carefully, however, that communication is not conducted entirely, or even mostly, in words. A gesture, a facial expression, a pitch pattern, a level of loudness, an emphasis, a kiss, a hand on the shoulder, a haircut or lack of one, the octagonal shape of a stop sign—all these carry information.

It is not a simple relationship. Kingsley Davis wrote, as long ago as 1949, about the indirectness of the communication relationship, in which "one person infers from the behavior of another . . . [the] idea or feeling the other person is trying to convey. He then reacts not to the behavior as such but to the inferred idea or feeling. The other person then reacts to his response in terms of the idea or feeling—the meaning—behind it."[3] All there is to go on are the signs—the print or sounds or movements—and it is always necessary to infer what lies behind them. Not what *they* mean but what *the person* means. Or, to put it more precisely, what is *inferred* from what they mean as to what the person means. And, therefore, in the communication relationship one always listens with a "third ear."

When this relationship works well, it results in a kind of "in-tune-ness" that is one of the remarkable human experiences. When it works poorly, it results in misunderstanding, sometimes in hostility, and often in behavior far different from what was intended. However it works, this is the process that allows us to form the images in our heads that map our environments and guide our behavior.

This process, the way we use it, and its effects upon us and our society are what this book is about.

THE DAWN OF COMMUNICATION

Now back to those first of all Hawaiians, who landed from their outrigger canoe sometime between A.D. 750 and 800, liked what they saw, and decided to make it their home. They were relatively far advanced in the long history of communication. They were, let us say, at about 23:59 on the 24-hour communication clock running from one-celled animals to Alfred North Whitehead or Albert Einstein.

It may be stretching the point to say that communication began with primitive one-celled creatures, yet these too could process some information—which is the essence of communication. They could at least map their environments in terms of what was nutrient and what was not. But their messages were chemical. Nobody has recorded the communication history of the great leap upward from the level of chemical information to the level of animals able to take in information with their sense organs and give signals with their bodies. Yet compared to the greatest of Olympic high jumps, that leap—from information-processing bacteria, as we see them in a petri dish, to animals capable of two-way communication by means of sense organs, central nervous systems, and musculatures—required a run down a cinder path for hundreds of millions of years; it cleared the great barriers of self-identity, processing information from the environment, and establishing relationships with other identities. And when that height was cleared, living creatures were still only at the threshold of what we think of as modern communication.

None of us doubt that a dog can communicate. But, as Kenneth Boulding said in his wonderfully wise and witty book *The Image*, so far as we know a dog is not aware that there were dogs before him and that there will be dogs after he is gone. Dogs certainly communicate messages while chasing a cat, but so far as we know they never stand around afterward and say, "That was a fine chase, but not so good as yesterday's." Or, "If you had blocked that alley, he wouldn't have got away!"[4] But the Stone Age people who came to Hawaii could do all that. They could process information so as to criticize and improve their own behavior. They could conceive of a past in which they had not lived and a future in which they would not participate. They could deal with abstract notions like goodness, evil, power, and justice. Furthermore, their skill with communication was such that they could make an image of their environment in terms that were relevant to their needs and goals, and tinker with that image in their heads until the image would help change the environment while the changing environment altered the image.

What happened between the first two-way-communicating animal and the first communicating people who landed on Hawaii was a continuing process of extending the senses farther and farther so as to command more information; extending the voice and gestures farther and farther so as to deliver more information; making one's messages always more portable, more separable from oneself both in space and time. Considered that way, Marshall McLuhan's metaphor of the media as extensions of man is sound history, although the process was under way long before there were any media as we now know them.[5]

THE BEGINNINGS OF LANGUAGE

Somehow, somewhere, in the primeval shadows, human animals took doubtless hesitant but gigantic steps. They developed language. Animals must have communicated with one another for millions of years before any of them developed an ability to generalize on the signals they had learned to give. When animals growl, they can communicate dislike of or warning about something at hand. But at some magical moment, some animal learned to make that signal portable, so that it would apply not only to the particular creature being growled at but to a whole class of creatures or events or things. That is, they learned to say, "I don't like cats" or "Stay away from my cave," without having to point at a cat or a cave.

How did language start? We can only guess. As with many other great events, we can be fairly sure that no one recognized it at the time as a great event. But somehow, somewhere, humanizing animals developed sound-signs that could be carried around and used to mean the same thing everywhere, without having to point at the subject or stand next to it or snarl at it. Word-signs began to supplement signals. How? We have only speculation to go on.

Some of the speculations have given rise to ingenious and amusing names. There is the "bow-wow" theory, for example, which suggests that words came into being through the imitation of natural sounds like the barking of a dog or thunder or the waves. There is the "poo-poo" theory, which seeks to explain speech as growing out of involuntary expressions of emotions—pain, pleasure, fear, satisfaction. There is a whole set of theories based on the supposition that words came into being in close association with other movements of the body. A Soviet scholar speculates that the first word-sounds were merely accompaniments to gestures; when the sounds became detachable they retained the meanings of the gestures.

Other theorists have advanced a "sing-song" theory—that words grew out of primitive and wordless chants communicating emotions and celebrating events. Still others have suggested the "yo-heave-ho" theory, in which words developed from the grunts of physical exertion. There is also the "yuk-yuk" theory—that words arose from chance sounds that happened to be associated with events of special importance or excitement. For example, perhaps a humanizing animal happened to be making the sound *yuk*—playing with his vocal system as he did with other parts of his body—when he bit into an especially tasty clam, and thereafter *yuk* came to be associated in his memory with a clam or with something good to eat.[6]

One concept of the birth of language few linguists argue with— that it was somehow related to the development of tools. Crude tools, such as sharp stones for cutting or scraping, may have existed as long as a million years ago. When an early hunter had a tool in his hands, he must have found it very hard to make the gestures that were such an important part of the nonverbal communication that preceded language. When he made spears or knives he could go hunting. Hunting by night, living in dark caves, he must have discovered that voice signals, instead of being incidental to his main activities, could take over many of the functions of visual signals and gestures. And so he learned to be as skillful with his vocal mechanism as with his hands.

There is no way of being sure about this prehistory. The facts are buried too deep in the past. And it is not really necessary to choose among the different theories, because essentially they are all the same. They all say that certain humanizing animals began to associate certain sounds with certain experiences or behaviors. These sounds picked up some of the meaning of the original experience they were associated with. This makes sense to us because it is the way children acquire many word-meanings today. They see an animal and pet it, listen to it, perhaps smell it. Someone says "dog," and when that occurs often enough, the sound *dog* calls up in their minds the animal they have seen, touched, heard, and smelled. In the same way, at the dawn of civilization human animals must have gone around the world associating spoken sounds with elements of their environment.

How did they learn to abstract from these first associations so that *yuk* or something like it began to refer to *all* tasty clams rather than one? How did they then find a sound to mean "eat" or "things to eat" rather than just one kind of food? How did they find a sound to refer to all good things rather than one kind of good thing? How did they learn to string sounds together so as to fasten actions and relationships to names? How did they learn to express highly subtle relationships such as those that distinguish what was from what is or will be? The point is they did. Slowly and painfully, over many thousands of years, they must have added to their repertoires the basic conventions of language that any child now learns in three years. It must have been this humanizing skill, and the intellectual growth related to it, that enabled one group of animals to gain an advantage in the race for survival. With their new linguistic tools they could survey and catalog their environment more efficiently, bring reports back for decision and make decisions in terms of information previously stored, organize their social relationships more efficiently, pass what they had learned on to new members of the society—in other words, process information more efficiently than other animals.

There are no fewer than 3000 languages and major dialects still spoken in the world. No matter how many starting points there were, languages must have been evolving in countless tribes and tribal groups that had little contact with one another and therefore little need to develop compatible languages. Each of these tribal languages must necessarily have mirrored the experience and the developing culture of the people who spoke it.

How did all these separate forms shake down to the 3000 used today and to the dozen or so, like English and Chinese, that are understood by large portions of the world's people? It must have been the effect of increasing contact among peoples: easier travel, the growth of trade and commerce, the development of cities and later of city-states and nations, conquest, empire, and the more subtle influences of power and ideas and prestige. This process made it necessary to find common languages, and the process continues, inevitably though slowly, toward a single world language.

THE BEGINNINGS OF WRITING

Along the path of history, up the long incline, perhaps hundreds of thousands of years beyond the beginnings of language, lay another landmark: writing. Having learned to separate sounds from their referents, humans now learned to separate them from the speaker as well and consequently made them even more portable.

We know approximately when writing was first introduced—in the fourth millennium B.C.—but little more about how it was introduced than we know about language. We are confident that it developed in more than one place, grew out of trial and error with a number of visual devices, and doubtless came from the older experience in drawing pictures. No animals except humans have ever been known to draw unaided a picture of their environment, although some chimpanzees, given human encouragement and materials, have produced abstract paintings. These have quite deservedly been sold and exhibited, though they are not representational pictures but only abstract patterns of line and color. But for thousands of years before they could write, humans covered cave walls and tools and ornaments with pictorial designs and representational pictures that showed high skill and were sometimes very beautiful.

This skill was not restricted to any tribe or place. Excitingly beautiful pictures of hunters and animals have been discovered as far apart as the caves of southern France, the inner Sahara, and the aboriginal areas of Australia. Many of these pictures must have had a magical purpose; they served as totems or were intended to ensure that the animal painted in the cave would also be available on the hunting grounds. Perhaps some of the pictures recorded great achievements, and some may have been left behind by unknown early Van Goghs and Cézannes who wanted to set down some of the beauty they saw in the world around them. Whatever their uses, these pictures may be thought of as the first written communications, and if so, the dawn of writing may be set at 20,000 to 30,000, rather than 5,000 to 6,000 years ago.

As language arose from the need to abstract upon events and experience, so must writing have come from the need to abstract upon
pictures and to make word-signs last longer than the fleeting second
during which they could be heard. Many devices apparently were
tried for this purpose. The custom of tying a piece of string around
a finger to remind oneself of something to be done reaches back
thousands of years to the time when people tied knots in string in
order to count and keep records. Darius the Persian, for example, gave
his commanders a string with 60 knots in it and said to them, "Men
of Ionia: Every day from the day you see me march against the
Scythians, undo one of these knots. If I do not return before the last
knot is undone, gather your supplies and sail home. . . ." Just as we
pound stakes into the ground to mark off a mining claim, so did
ancient peoples use stones or wood, often marked with an individual
sign of identification, to indicate the boundaries of their land. Stones
were used to mark the shadow of the sun at its most northerly and
most southerly points, and the days of the sun and moon cycles were
checked off with scratches on a rock, much as we count ⫫⫫ or 正
today. Thus a calendar was made. And the word-symbols apparently
made use of these counting signs and of the pictures.

The hieroglyphs of Egypt and Crete were mostly pictures, although
each one stood for a word-sound. Some 600 Chinese ideographs are
mostly pictorial and representational, and many others show signs of
pictorial origins (Figure 1). The ancient Maya writing is largely pictorial in style. It is difficult to trace modern written signs back to
pictorial origins because there must have been a constant effort to
simplify the pictures, conventionalize them, and make them widely
applicable and easily portable. To write a sentence in pictorial form
required an artist and a great deal of time. What was needed was something that could be written quickly and economically, and that would
relate to the sophisticated spoken language already in use rather than
going back to the direct representation of reality. Gradually, therefore,
the pictorial signs must have come to stand for sounds rather than a
scene or an event.

The hieroglyphs did just that. They were abstracted and conven-
tionalized. A writer had merely to set down a series of sound-signs,
not paint a mural or draw a story-board. When writing emerges into
history, it is already stylized in this way, although in many cases it
retains some additional meaning from its pictorial form. Thus, in a
language like Chinese there are more ideographs than sounds, and the
pictorial nature of one ideograph helps distinguish it from others.
Many Chinese, Japanese, and Korean names, for example, sound alike
but carry personally identifying characteristics in their appearance.

Styles	Uniform	Tiger	Rain	Mountain	Sun
Primitive					
Very ancient					
Ancient					
Offical					
Modern Cursive					
Regular					

Figure 1   How Chinese characters developed from stylized pictures.
(Source: Lancelot Hogben, *From Cave Painting to Comic Strip*, New York:
Chanticleer Press, 1949.)

Because writing came when there was already more travel and more
frequent contact among peoples, and also because many spoken languages to this day have never developed their own written languages,
there were fewer types of writing than of spoken language. Nevertheless, the written languages, like the spoken ones, reflect not only
the flow of human contact and the effects of conquest and ideas and
larger social groupings but also, and much more important, the cultures out of which they came. Even the basic worldwide division
among writing systems—the sign-syllabic systems that probably originated in the Fertile Crescent of the Middle East and spread over the
Western world and the word-ideographic systems that originated in

eastern Asia and spread through China, Japan, and other Asian coutries—seems to reflect cultural differences, or at least we can speculate that it does. The sign-syllabic system, in which every sound in a word has a different written symbol, is easier to learn, easier to use, easier to change, and may well represent the Western concern with change and growth. The word-ideographic system, on the other hand, in which every word has a different symbol and which requires children to master about a thousand signs (rather than 26 or 30) before they can read relatively simple prose, seems to go with a need for stability and a deep sense of the past. Perhaps as some scholars have suggested, the serene atmosphere of the long Chinese dynasties was conducive to such a system. And certainly the language helped preserve the Chinese dynasties, for in China the written language did not change with the spoken language, as it did, for example, in Europe, where the French, Germans, Scandinavians, Dutch, and Spanish neither understand nor read one another's languages, although they all came from a common Indoeuropean tongue. By contrast, all Chinese have for more than 4000 years been able to read the same language, although the spoken languages of Peking and Canton, Shanghai and Hunan, sound quite different.

Be that as it may, the invention of writing, which was probably taken for granted in its own time, seems in retrospect to be one of the earthshaking events of history. It made it possible to carry information over the curve of earth, farther than a speaker could go, or smoke signals or pennants or monuments could be seen, or drums could be heard. It preserved events and agreements for later times so that people could store some of their experience without having to strain to remember it. Therefore they were able to spend more time processing current information and planning for the future. And it must have speeded up enormously a people's ability to change their way of living when they so wished.

The ancient civilizations typically credited the invention of writing to one of their gods—the Egyptians to Thoth, God of Wisdom; the Babylonians to Nebo, God of Destiny; the Greeks to Hermes, herald and messenger of Olympus. So much they valued it.

THE BEGINNINGS OF MASS MEDIA

Animals communicated with one another for millions of years before any of them developed language. Human animals spoke to one another for tens of thousands of years before any of them learned to write. Knowledge and ideas were shared and preserved in writing for thousands of years before there were mass media.

When did the mass media come into being? The Acta Diurna, writ-

d posted after every meeting of the Roman senate,
been the first newspaper, although it appeared in
Acta Diurna was on stone, but the people around
usually wrote on papyrus, later on vellum. Then
paper and ink were invented in China by the second century A.D.
Books were block printed there by the eighth century, and even movable metal type was developed in China and Korea at least a century before it came into use in Europe. Gradually the superior type of printing paper and ink, the art of printing from wood block, and other Asian developments moved westward. Block printing was available there at least half a millennium before Gutenberg. One of the most common products of the new methods in the later Middle Ages was playing cards. But long before "printing" (meaning printing from movable metal type of the kind we associate with Gutenberg), any rich person in Western Europe could have a handwritten and illustrated book if he or she could pay a scribe to make it. We know what some of these handwritten books cost. In the early thirteenth century, for example, it took the equivalent of about $3000 in modern currency to copy a thin volume as a birthday gift for a French princess.

What happened in the mid-fifteenth century in the city of Mainz, Germany, was that a man named Johann Gensfleisch, commonly known as Gutenberg, put together some materials and procedures that were already generally available and produced religious documents in numerous copies. He used ink and paper that depended on skills developed first in East Asia. The press he used was adapted from the wine press of Western Europe. The movable metal type from which he set his text by hand was not really new either, because the Koreans had used something of the same kind, but he had found an efficient way to cast it, and he had a syllabic rather than an ideographic language with which to work. Putting all of these elements together, he created a viable way of making multiple copies of written texts, often very beautiful copies, at relatively low cost. And thus the early 1540s (for printed documents) or about 1456 (for the Gutenberg Bible) is as good a date as any to celebrate as the beginning of mass communication.

Technically what Gutenberg did, and what all the mass media have done since his time, was to put a machine into the communication process in such a way as to duplicate information and to extend almost indefinitely a person's ability to share it. The communication process was little changed, but because people live by information this new ability to share it had a profound effect on human life.

In some of the new countries that are just now emerging from an oral into a media culture, we can see 500 years of mass media de-

velopment foreshortened. There are still many villa
where roads do not reach, where no one reads, and
not penetrated. Life in these villages often seems to
unhurried quality. Time tends to be measured by th
needs rather than by a clock. Even though life is sometimes harsh and
brief in a traditional village of this kind, still we can see farmers on
their way to the fields or fishermen on the way to their nets stop to
watch the antics of a young animal or enjoy the early sun on a mountainside if they feel so inclined—and we think rather ruefully about
commuter trains, appointment calendars, class schedules, and other
modern devices that keep us hurrying around the modernized world.

Knowledge is power in a traditional village as elsewhere, but in a
premedia culture that form of power tends to reside with the old
people who can remember the wisdom of the past, the sacred writings,
the laws, customs, and family histories. When radio and print enter
a traditional village, or even when a road is built, the change is often
spectacular. For one thing, the amount of available information is
enormously increased. Communication comes from farther away. Almost overnight, horizons move back. The world stretches farther than
the nearest hill or the immediate horizon. Villagers concern themselves
with how other people live. Power passes from those with long memories to those who command relevant information from distant places.
When it is written down, the past becomes common property. Attention turns to information that might be used to bring about change
rather than to preserve changelessness. New concepts and images flow
through the communication channels—crop rotation, insecticides, vac-
cinations, elections, family planning, engineering. Thus, as Harold
Innis has so brilliantly pointed out, the life of the village, when it
passes from an oral to a media culture, comes to center on space
rather than on time, what can be rather than what has been, and the
wheels of change are set in motion.

The mass media are both great multipliers of information and long
pipelines for information; we will have more to say about them in
later chapters. Here let us merely note that they also become powerful
gatekeepers along the pathways of information, with a great deal of
power over what travels along those pathways. Thus they supplement
or replace the personal gatekeepers—the priest, the traveler, the old
people—who performed this function before the development of media. But the communicating machines are able to gather so much
information, multiply it so fast, and come into use so pervasively that
they represent a quantum jump in the ability to control and circulate
information and focus the attention of human beings.

Mass media have come into use only in the last second of the long ay of life on earth. Yet in that time, printing and reading have reached every corner of the earth. The airwaves over every populated part of the earth are full of radio signals. More than 60 countries have television. Hardly a country in the world is still unacquainted with film. In the cities these media are taken for granted, but anyone who has seen African boys running through the bush shouting the news that the film van has come or watched a father proudly urging his son to write his name for a visitor, thus demonstrating that for the first time in that family a child has learned to write—anyone who has seen sights like these will never doubt the phenomenal appeal of mass communication.

Where the mass media are readily available today, people typically spend more time on them than on any other daily activity except work and sleep. Many children in North America devote as much time to television in their first 12 years of life as they spend in school. Almost all news comes through the mass media, and consequently, almost all of our images of our distant environment. A high portion of the entertainment in a media-rich society is delivered by these channels. The mercantile systems are geared to advertising in the mass media, and tastes are at least to some extent shaped by media offerings.

Thus, the communicating organizations that grow around the communicating machines—news agencies, newspaper and magazine staffs, broadcasting stations, publishing houses, film studios—have come to be extraordinarily powerful gatekeepers on the information pathways. Knowing as we do that only perhaps 2 or 3 percent of all the news that starts from India ever gets to a reader in Indiana, and holding some doubts about the completeness, accuracy, and depth of the news coverage in the first place, we have reason to be justifiably concerned about the images we form of our faraway but important environments. When we consider the power of the media to focus our attention on one subject or one person rather than on others that might concern us, we have good reason to ask how these gatekeeping decisions are made and under what controls. For the modern media are inextricably intertwined with modern life.

Whether the Revival of Learning stimulated the development of printed media or printing stimulated the thoughts and ideas of the Revival is not a very important question. Neither is the question of whether mass media stimulate change in the traditional village or change in the village stimulates the introduction of media. There are a series of interactions. The book and the newspaper moved hand in hand with the Enlightenment. The newspaper and the political tract were involved in all of the political movements and popular revolutions of the seventeenth and eighteenth centuries. The textbook made public

education possible on a wide scale at a time when there was a growing hunger for knowledge. The news sheet first, and the electronic
media later, made it possible for ordinary people to be informed about
politics and to participate in government at a time when there was
widespread dissatisfaction with the locus of power.

Without channels of mass communication the Industrial Revolution of the nineteenth century could hardly have transformed our way
of life as it did. This technical revolution, in turn, added the camera,
the projector, the microphone, the tape and disk recorders, the transmitter, and the computer to the available tools of communication—
all within a little over a hundred years. And in the developing regions
today, where, as we have pointed out, this entire process has been
foreshortened, the information media have stimulated a revolution of
rising aspirations and are themselves among the goals of these aspirations.

It is no accident that we have used the word *revolution* in talking
about social interactions with mass communication. The media have
been involved in every significant social change since they came into
existence—intellectual revolutions, political revolutions, industrial revolutions, and revolutions in tastes, aspirations, and values. They have
taught us a basic precept: Because communication is the fundamental
social process, because humans are above all information-processing
animals, a major change in the state of information, a major involvement of communication, always accompanies any major social change.

The rate of change in the style and form of human communication is therefore itself a social datum of importance; from language
to writing: tens of thousands of years; from writing to printing:
thousands of years; from printing to films and broadcasting: 400
years; from the first experiments with television to live television
from the moon: 50 years.

What comes next? Some new forms of media are on the horizon,
and we will say more about them in later chapters. But it is rather
clearly evident that we are entering an age of information, in which
knowledge rather than natural resources may become the chief resource of mankind and the prime requisite of power and well-being.
Peter Drucker points out that as many books have been published in
the past 25 years as in the 500 years before 1950; that perhaps 90
percent of all the scientists about whom we have records are alive
today; and that in the United States, workers engaged in providing
knowledge to the public now outnumber farmers and industrial workers. During the next half-century, people will finally have to come
to terms with their extraordinary ability to process and share information. They will have to learn to use it for their own good rather

than for their own destruction, and for further humanization and socialization rather than for alienation or regression. At this moment in history, therefore, it seems reasonable to take stock of what we know about human communication.

For Further Consideration

1. Families and tribes lived together long before they had language, and yet they must have communicated all that time. What must communication have been like before language?
2. "Communication shapes society, and society shapes communication." How does this process work?
3. What would you expect to be the advantages of a language (like English) with an alphabet as compared to the advantages of a language (like Chinese) that has no alphabet but uses a different character for each word?
4. The first great step in the development of human communication was language. The second was writing. Have any developments since then been comparable in importance to these two? Which ones, and why?

References

1. C. Cooley. *Social Organization.* New York: Scribner, 1909, p. 61.
2. E. Sapir. "Communication." In *Encyclopedia of the Social Sciences,* 1st ed. New York: Macmillan, 1935, vol. IV, p. 78.
3. K. Davis. *Human Society.* New York: Macmillan, 1949.
4. K. Boulding: *The Image: Knowledge in Life and Society.* Ann Arbor: University of Michigan Press, 1956, esp. pp. 15 ff.
5. M. McLuhan. *Understanding Media: The Extensions of Man.* New York: McGraw-Hill, 1966.
6. For an interesting, brief treatment of this material, see M. Fabre, *The History of Communications, The New Illustrated Library of Science and Inventions.* New York: Hawthorne Books, 1963, vol. 9, pp. 12 ff.

2/
WHAT COMMUNICATION DOES

We are communicating animals; communication pervades everything we do. It is the stuff of which human relations are made. It is a current that has flowed through all human history, constantly extending our senses and our channels of information. Now that we have achieved broad-band communication from the moon, we are looking around for other creatures on other worlds to talk to. Communication is the most human of skills.

But let us look a little harder at this idea. What does communication actually *do* for us, and what do we actually *do* with it?

The question may sound as silly as "Why eat?" or "Why sleep?" We eat because we are hungry. We sleep because we are weary. We shout "fire!" because the house is burning. We say "Pardon me!" because we have bumped into someone.

To all of us, communication is a natural, necessary, omnipresent activity. We enter into communication relationships because we want to relate to the environment, especially the human environment, around us. As Sapir wrote in the passage quoted earlier, society is a network of such relationships maintained chiefly by communication.[1]

To an observer, communication seems to flow through the social system like blood through the individual cardiovascular system, serving the whole organism, concentrating now on one part, now on another according to need, maintaining contact and balance and health. We are so accustomed to living in an ocean of communication that we can hardly imagine living without it.

Try to think of a society existing without communication. A world society? During recent years a stony official silence was maintained between the United States and China, but communication went forward through many channels: statements through the mass media, political action obviously intended to convey messages, third countries, intelligence-gathering on both sides. It even proved necessary to arrange "unofficial" meetings at the ambassadorial level in a neutral country. An extraordinary set of ambassadors was exchanged—Ping-Pong players—through whom the high officials of one country were able to speak with remarkable openness to the people of the other.

A group society? A "silent" Trappist monastery prohibits conversation but not communication. The monks depend on countless acts of communication: a glance or a smile, administrative actions, adherence to a schedule, the kind of commitment and solidarity that members communicate through acts of devotion.

Suppose a hermit retires from the world to meditate in his cave on a mountainside. He is trying to avoid communication with other human beings—unless they come to seek his wisdom. But the very act of meditation implies internal communication. The hermit is dredging up stored information from his past, adding information from his nonhuman environment, thinking, talking it over with himself. He is in communication with his breviary and his books—and, in a sense, with all those whose ideas have influenced him. He is communicating a message to mankind in general by retiring to his cave. And like St. Francis, he may talk to the birds.

Even in extreme cases, therefore, communication goes on. For most of us most of the time it is largely unconscious, until we become self-conscious about it. A professional may be highly self-conscious and self-critical about the article being written for a magazine. A politician may be self-conscious about the speech being rehearsed. But children wander through life sending and receiving messages naturally, behaving with their whole organism, not thinking much about how they do it. They know their parents reward them for saying "Daddy" and later for saying "Please," but even these behaviors merge into natural patterns. They enjoy watching television and go back to programs they enjoy more than others. They go to school and become a bit self-conscious about the themes they have to write or in the case of a boy, the first telephone call to a girl. But unless they develop a speech defect or deafness or some other painful difficulty, they simply communicate in the ways that come naturally to them, using the behaviors they learn by trial and error to bring about the results they want.

Even when children grow to adulthood and become more conscious of the effects of communication and the consequences of doing it in different ways, they still find it hard to verbalize why they communicate as they do. Some years ago, when New York newspapers were on strike, Bernard Berelson took advantage of the opportunity to ask a sample of New Yorkers what they missed in the newspapers they were not receiving. His purpose, of course, was to try to find out why they read what they did. But they had extreme difficulty saying even what they missed. They could tick off some information services they were no longer receiving—the weather forecasts, the movie schedules, the evening broadcast lineups—but missing these was not what chiefly bothered them.

Many were afraid they were missing some specific information of importance to them: Several elderly respondents thought that some of their friends might have died and been buried without the respondents knowing anything about it. Still more bothersome was a vague sense of something absent in their lives: "Contact with the world," some said, "a feeling of being in touch," or simply "something I did every day." Perhaps the most significant finding of the study was how fully the act of reading the newspaper had been incorporated into people's daily lives, how natural this communication behavior had become, and how deeply the reasons for adopting it in the first place had disappeared into the shadows of the past.[2]

This is one reason why "what communication does" is hard to verbalize. Another is that the reasons for using communication are often highly complex and not necessarily on the surface. Still another is that the *manifest* (intended) functions of communication do not always take account of the *latent* (unintended) functions.[3] The language is Robert Merton's, and he is saying, in effect, that the actual consequences of communication are not always the intended ones. For example, a warning about cancer may result not in sending people to seek a medical checkup but rather in frightening them away from the clinic. A cheery good-morning could lead not to good fellowship but to a suspicion that the speaker is going to try to borrow money. And finally, since most of our analysis of communication functions has to be done from the outside, we find ourselves always trying to look into the black box.

But we have access to at least one black box each: our own. For what purposes do *you* communicate? Why do *I* communicate?

I came out of my house this morning, saw a man in a sport shirt smiled, and said, "Good morning." Someone translating that literally into a tribal language of New Guinea might have difficulty. Was saying it was a "good"—that is, a fair—morning? No, it was a fou morning, with rain squalls scudding down from the mountains and threatening to soak me. Was I commenting on the goodness of the morning in a moral sense, as we say "Good Friday"? No, it was day like other days. Was I wishing him a "good"—i.e., a pleasant— morning? To some extent, but he looked perfectly competent to man age his own morning, and as a matter of fact I felt rather irritated because he could spend this morning beside the sea while I had to go to work. What was I really saying to him? The most reasonable explanation I can give is that I was conducting our own tribal ritual I was communicating that I belonged to his group and his culture, and was not an outlander or a rebel or a threat. In other words, I was confirming a comfortable relationship.

He said to me, "How are you this morning?" I doubt that he was much concerned about my health. He was doing what I was—com municating social membership and a certain degree of friendship. He expected me to say "Fine," and I did. In effect, we seemed to be cast ing around us our social radar beams, as ships do in the fog or air planes on instruments, confirming our identity and that of the othe person who appears on the radar screen, confirming our membership in a friendly culture group, doing what we had long ago learned wa expected of us. The authors who have written about human relation ships as "ships passing in the night" were not writing about ou closest and most intimate relationships but rather about the kinds o contact I have just described, which constitute a large portion of th contacts we have in life. And for all of these, communication serve us as radar, identity signal, and early warning. Or at least that is how it looks to an observer.

Another example: Amid the smoke and chatter of a cocktail party a young man says to a pretty girl, "Cigarette?" On the surface, h is inviting her to take one of his cigarettes. Actually, he is commu nicating interest and doubtless hoping she will respond in the sam way. He is communicating membership in a culture by offering her cigarette, and he probably hopes she will confirm her membership by taking a cigarette or at least rejecting it with a smile rather tha slapping his face because she doesn't believe in smoking or doesn' think a boy should speak to a girl without an introduction. In othe words, it is the same situation as the one we have just described radar, identification, early warning. If the girl responds favorably, h next question is likely to be, "Haven't I seen you somewhere?"—whic really has nothing to do with whether he has actually seen her; rather, it is an opening move to find out a little more about her, perhaps to estimate whether this chance acquaintance might become a more lasting one. In other words, radar behavior merging into tool behavior.

Still another example: I usually hear church bells at about six every evening. I listen to them because it is hard to ignore them but even more because they have a pleasant tone and blend well with sunset or late-afternoon shadows. They give me a sense of pleasure and warmth. Moreover, they tell me the time. If I am still working, it is time to begin thinking about a late-afternoon swim and a cocktail. The evening is beginning; it is time to recall the plans or engagements I have made. In addition, the bells remind me that religion is part of my culture and that some of my fellow residents are at that moment practicing it. And they raise pleasing pictures in my mind of a church and candles and an organ and plainsong and people in humble postures.

What is St. Mary's Church trying to communicate by means of those bells? It is calling the faithful to worship. But most of the people at that particular service would probably come with or without a bell. The bells are perhaps meant to communicate a presence, an availability in case someone needs the kind of spiritual assistance the bells symbolize. Perhaps they are intended to reach sinners like me and remind us of our religious obligations, even though we have seldom been inside St. Mary's. And perhaps St. Mary's is communicating its own membership in an ancient and honorable tradition in which bells have served as a sign for centuries.

Thus, the full significance of acts of communication is seldom on the surface. Every act of communication, every communicator and receiver, has an individual set of purposes and reasons. But we cannot be satisfied with that explanation. Acts of communication are more similar than they are different. Human communication deserves a more systematic explanation of what it does.

HUMAN COMMUNICATION—EXPLAINED
BY THREE PSYCHOLOGISTS

Some very able men have written about the functions of communication. Jean Piaget, a Swiss child-development psychologist, distinguished between what he called social and egocentric speech in a child. When a child uses speech socially, Piaget said, "the child addresses his hearer, considers his point of view, tries to influence him or actually exchange ideas with him. . . ." In the other kind of speech, "the child does not bother to know to whom he is speaking, nor whether he is being listened to. He talks either for himself or for the pleasure of associating with anyone who happens to be there."[4] Later research, however, has indicated that much more of a child's speech than Piaget thought—perhaps 90 percent—is apparently socially intended. And although children play with their vocal mechanisms as they do with other parts of the body, there is little agreement with Piaget's conclusion that social communication usually appears around the age of seven. It actually appears much earlier. Very early, children discover that their vocal behavior can be used as a tool. They learn what kind of vocal behavior is rewarded and soon discriminate among kinds of behavior and kinds of rewards.

Nevertheless, if we analyze our own supposedly adult communication behavior we find that a rather surprising amount of it is largely for our own satisfaction. We hit our fingers with a hammer and say some strong words until the pain begins to go away. We sing in the shower, enjoying it thoroughly and rather hoping no one else will hear. We get a quiet enjoyment out of recalling an incident that we could probably never communicate fully to anyone else. All of these actions are using communication as a tool for our own satisfaction without intentionally involving anyone else.

A number of psychologists have recognized that much communication is tool behavior. Edward Tolman, a psychologist of learning, once described human speech as nothing but "a 'high-faluting' 'tool' not differing in essence from other tools such as strings, sticks, boxes, and the like." For example, he wrote, "this is quite obvious in the case of a command. What happens in a command . . . is that by means of it the speaker causes one of his fellows to do something. Instead of the former having to take the latter by the scruff of the neck and actually push him through the desired act, the speaker by means of a command accomplishes the same result."[5] Children learn this without difficulty. When they cry, they are likely to be picked up and fondled; if they are not, they make less use of that particular communicative act. A smile gets them a smile. Certain sounds earn them food or a toy to play with. They learn names and find not only that this brings social approval but also that it replaces harder physical labor.

As we have suggested, even talking aloud to oneself often has a tool use. The spicy words one says after hitting a finger are functional not only in relieving tension but also in avoiding other, less acceptable ways of expressing feeling, such as weeping. All of us know that inner discussion, inner talk, plays a part in many difficult decisions. Lorimer wrote about an 18-month-old child he observed in a verbal battle between a command not to touch some objects in a chest and an understandable curiosity as to what was in the chest.

"For ten enormous minutes," he said, "I watched with fascination the battle between the impulse and the inhibition, as the little hand reached toward the things in the chest and withdrew to the verbal accompaniment 'no! no! no!' uttered by the child herself. Then the battle subsided, called to close by the distraction of other interests."[6] Thus, even the most apparently egocentric communication often has a tool purpose also.

In some contrast with this is William Stephenson's approach in *The Play Theory of Communication*. He concentrates not on the communication tool behavior intended to bring about change but rather on the part of communication that is not intended to accomplish anything except a sense of satisfaction and well-being.[7] Following the Dutch scholar Huizinga (in a book entitled *Homo Ludens*[8]—Man Playing) and the pleasure theories of the Hungarian psychiatrist Szasz,[9] Stephenson bases his thinking on a sharp distinction between play and work: "Work deals with reality, with earning a living, with production. Play, on the contrary, is largely unproductive except for the self-satisfaction it provides."[10] Corresponding to these are two kinds of communication behavior. One is illustrated by a conversation between two people that seems to serve no apparent purpose: Neither is trying to convince or put down or get anything out of the other; they expect nothing of each other except conversation. But they enjoy the experience. The result, in Stephenson's words, is communication-pleasure. Quite different is communication that is intended to bring about action—for example, a command, a cry for help, persuasion, demand. Stephenson calls the effect of this communication-*un*pleasure, communication-pain. It takes work to get something done; play is just fun—in communication as in other behavior. Social control (of which an example might be the formation of public opinion) is work. Work is a function, he says, of all social institutions, but the central concern of the mass media is not with work but rather with communication-pleasure: making it possible for people to free themselves from social control and withdraw into the land of play.

"Playing is *pretending*," he says,

> a stepping outside the world of duty and responsibility. Play is an *interlude* in the day. It is not ordinary or real. It is voluntary and not a task or a moral duty. It is in some sense disinterested, providing temporary satisfaction. . . . Play is secluded, taking place in a particular place set off for the purpose in time or space. The child goes into a corner to play house. And play is a free activity, yet it absorbs the players completely.[11]

This description is very much like what others have written about television-viewing behavior. Yet Stephenson does not credit work-communication and debit play-communication. Quite the contrary. He feels that communication-pleasure is psychologically useful. It is "an enrichment of individual aspects of self." It is "self-developing and self-enhancing." It provides "opportunities to exist for ourselves, to please ourselves, free to a degree from social control." When mass communication is used for social control, it has to face firmly embedded beliefs and attitudes that are very difficult to change; when it is used for play it can "suggest to the masses certain standards of conduct, . . . provide for the leisure of such peoples, . . . make life easier for them." He feels that other theorists have tended to approach the mass media with "heavy loads of conscience . . . bent on doing good in terms of their own values," and therefore tending to view with alarm the trivia, the violence, the invitation to "escape" from real problems provided by the entertainment media. He emphasizes that he sees nothing nefarious in this. He feels that mass media play behavior is useful and that it has been a mistake to study mass communication largely in terms of persuasion and social effect; it should rather have been studied in terms of its play and pleasure elements. For this reason, he chose to develop "a play theory and not an information theory of mass communication."[12]

If Stephenson's book had been easier to read, and if he, like McLuhan, had been a coiner of phrases, the commercial entertainment media might have chosen to lionize him rather than McLuhan. His play theory presents a better justification for prevailing media content than does McLuhan's global village.[13] After once exposing oneself to this brillantly conceived theory, one can never again ignore the importance of the play-pleasure elements in communication. And yet this theory leaves something to be desired as a general explanation of communication functions.

Undoubtedly a considerable portion of communication behavior can be described as play, just as other considerable portions can be described as tool behavior and still others as egocentric behavior. The distinctions among these are far from sharp. Much egocentric communication is play, and it is not hard to conceive of certain play as tool behavior also. A little scene from Mark Twain's biography combines them all. Twain was known for outbursts of colorful profanity, into which he put the same imaginative quality that readers found in his writing. His demure little wife tried to shame him by repeating some of his language. Twain listened in some surprise and then realized what was missing. She wasn't relieving inner tensions by saying what she said; she wasn't talking to herself; she wasn't enjoying, as any writer would, the flow of words and imagery that he could put into a few well-turned and thunderous phrases. Twain chuckled, and told his wife that she had the words but not the tune!

These are single-factor approaches. Each one helps illuminate a *part* of communication behavior. By choosing to detour attention from the information function, Stephenson ignores the quality that chiefly distinguishes communication from other behavior. His chief interest is in the use of the mass media; consequently, he plays less attention than we might wish to interpersonal communication or to the use of the media for such tool purposes as instruction. His existential position toward the entertainment media is doubtless highly congenial to the media because it tends to sidestep the critics who come with "heavy loads of conscience," yet this too leaves out an important part of thinking about the functions of the communication system. In other words, it is a useful, but partial, theory, which ought to generate important propositions for future research on communication effects.

The trouble with most such single-factor theories is that they may explain so much that they explain nothing. Explaining the function of communication in terms of work and play runs into the fact that these categories blur into each other. For example, people can enjoy saying "Good morning!" and at the same time meet their social obligations. The very hard work of creative writing also has important components of play. The really interesting distinctions may be within rather than between such very broad categories. Is there not possibly an important difference between the kind of play-pleasure to be derived from, say, passing the time of day with a friend, escaping into a Walter Mitty fantasy life, allowing oneself to be massaged by the words of an orator, experiencing the catharsis that Aristotle felt was the chief reward of a Greek tragedy, agonizing or weeping over a football game, enjoying the aesthetic beauty of the Bolshoi ballet, or playing with the sounds and images of a poem one is writing? Is it not possible that there may be a useful distinction between the kinds of pleasure derived from playing with the medium—reading, speaking, viewing, listening, simply filling in time, or the like—and the pleasure derived from playing with the message—for example, enjoying a particular bit of writing, turning a particular phrase, or capturing a particular idea? Stephenson concludes, after some impressive arguments, that "newsreading is a communication-pleasure, sans reward." But is it really helpful to fit into his category of newsreading as play behavior, without differentiation, such different sub-behaviors as reading the grocery ads, reading about the pollution of one's swimming place, reading about a public boner by an elected official, reading a humorous feature story, reading the Pentagon papers, reading about the assassination of a leader, reading about the death of a friend, reading an interpretation of a Supreme Court decision—and to consider that play is a sufficient umbrella to cover all of their different functions and consequences?

THE SOCIAL FUNCTIONS OF COMMUNICATION

When we try to understand what communication does, we tend to shift back and forth between the individual and society like a zoom camera alternating between wide-angle and close-up pictures.

Piaget, Tolman, and Stephenson were all writing as psychologists concerned primarily with individual functions of communication. When we turn to the wide-angle lens and look at what political scientists, sociologists, and economists have written about the functions of communication, we find somewhat more differentiated theories.

In a classic essay, Harold Lasswell, a political scientist and a pioneer in communication study, identified three social functions of communication: (1) surveillance of the environment, (2) correlation of the different parts of society in responding to environment, and (3) transmission of the social heritage from one generation to the next.[14] Three groups of specialists, he says, are important in carrying out these functions. "Diplomats, attachés, and foreign correspondents are representatives of those who specialize in the environment. Editors, journalists, and speakers are correlators of the internal response. Educators in family and school transmit the social inheritance."[15]

Translate this picture of political communication back to Stone Age people in their caves. They station a watchman to survey the environment for dangers and opportunities. When the sentinel brings back his report (an approaching war party, a herd of game animals), there may be a council of war or a meeting of the best hunters to make plans. The decision is passed along. These uses of communication are timely, centered on events as they occur. But there is a continuing need to teach the children of the community to play their part in it. The boys must learn to hunt and to read a footprint; the girls, to sew and to prepare food. So the best hunter becomes a teacher, while the girls learn at their mothers' knee. In our time much of the task of surveillance is taken over by the news media; much of the coordination by government, political leaders, political reporters and analysts, and pressure groups; and much of the transmission of heritage by the schools.

Charles Wright, sketching a sociological perspective on communication (*Mass Communications: A Functional Approach*), added a fourth function to the Lasswell categories—entertainment. Lasswell had doubtless omitted that function as not an essential part of the political process, although history might argue with him. Wright called the second category, coordination, "interpretation and prescription," and the third one, transmission of the social heritage, by its sociological name, "socialization."[16]

In his book *Theories of Mass Communication*, Melvin DeFleur, another sociologist, added to these categories although not essentially changing them. The communication act, he said, is "the means by which a group's norms are expressed, by means of which social control is exerted, roles are allocated, coordination of effort is achieved, expectations are made manifest, and the entire social process is carried on. . . . Without such exchanges of influence human society would simply collapse."[17]

No economist has written with comparable specificity about communication functions in the economic system, yet it is possible to put together a set of economic functions from the work of economists like Boulding. For one thing, communication must meet the need for an economic map of the environment so that each individual and organization can form its own image of buying and selling opportunities at a given moment. Some of this will be done through advertising, some by means of price lists and business analysis. For another, there must be a correlation of economic policy, whether by the individual, the organization, or the nation. The market must be managed and controlled, and manufacturers, merchants, investors, and consumers must decide how to enter it. Finally, instruction in the skills and expectations of economic behavior must be available. The social scientists' maps, therefore, look like Table 1 at the top of the next page.

These are no more satisfying than the single-factor approaches previously examined. The categories blur. And it is rather startling that no more attention has been given to the social function of entertainment. Perhaps the most encouraging feature of these social science approaches is the degree of agreement among them.

Social functions of communication as applied to the individual

Let us go back to the high-definition lens and see what kind of individual map we might construct on the basis of the social functions just enumerated. We might think of four basic functions—no more perfect, no more mutually exclusive than the classes of functions we have been reviewing but taking more account of the fact that human communication is both an individual behavior and a social relationship.

Table 1 THE SOCIETAL FUNCTIONS OF COMMUNICATIONS

WHAT COMMUNICATION DOES		
Political system	*Economic system*	*Social system in general*
Surveillance (gathering intelligence)	Information on resources and buying-selling opportunities	Information on social norms, roles, etc.; acceptance or rejection of them
Coordination (interpretation of intelligence; making, disseminating, enforcing policy)	Interpretation of this information; making of economic policy; operation and control of market	Coordination of public understanding and will; operation of social control
Transmission of social heritage, laws, and customs	Initiation into economic behavior	Transmission of social norms and role prescriptions to new members of society
		Entertainment (leisure activity, relief from work and realistic problems, incidental learning, and socialization)

Each of these functions has an outward and an inward aspect, like all communication: One seeks or gives information, one receives and processes information. And therefore we might construct a sort of index to our map, like Table 2:

Table 2 THE ASPECTS OF COMMUNICATION

Function	*Outward aspect*	*Inward aspect*
Social radar	Seek information, inform	Receive information
Manipulation, decision-management	Persuade, command	Interpret, decide
Instruction	Seek knowledge, teach	Learn
Entertainment	Entertain	Enjoy

The analogy to social radar is not bad. The captain of a ship in a fog at night must know where it is: Who is out there? Where are the rocks and shoals? Where are the sea-lanes to safe harbors? All of us, too, must maintain continuing surveillance of an environment that grows more complex year by year. Who's there? Friend or foe? Local or stranger? Danger or opportunity? We have a deep need for a sense of belonging, for being part of our culture and our society, feeling a degree of stability and familiarity in our surroundings and life patterns. The historian Arnold Toynbee often exhibited acute unease in a new place until he had a map in his hands and could locate himself on it. And so every day we revise and update our working maps; the more unfamiliar the location or the experience, the more we depend on our social radar.

Primitive peoples, huddled together in their caves against cold and danger, asked the same questions: Where are we? Who or what is out there? They wanted to know what dangers and opportunities and threats were hidden in the dark. Were there enemies? Were there game animals? We ask the same things as we grow up or when we move into a new town. We seek friends and allies. We try to locate the points where we are in danger or where we can find rewards. We interpret the radar blips and make our maps. Stone Age people, as we have said, stationed a watchman on a hill; today we depend on interpersonal communication to make our close-by maps and on the mass media to look over the hill.

At one end of the scale, social radar behavior is very specific. The merchant wants to know the prices in a city. The farmer wants to know whether it is going to rain on the day he intends to plant. The boy wants to know whether a new girl is one he could try to date. At the other end, it is very general. Berelson found a great deal of this in the people he talked to about missing the newspaper. Some individuals were uneasy because their radar was not registering its customary blips. One husband complained he had to look at his wife instead of at the news; several wives complained that they had to look at their husbands rather than at the crossword puzzle. When interviewers probed below that level, they found that a sensation of unease came from a feeling that one was closed off from the world—wondering what was happening, even though when they had access to a newspaper, they barely scanned the headlines and seldom found a story of great interest. Old people whose families have moved away and who have lived beyond their friends in their own generation and consequently have few individuals to talk to, often turn to the mass media for a sense of belonging to the events and society around them. By keeping up with the news and the battle of ideas, even though they do not participate in any of those events, they combat the cold and dark of loneliness and alienation.

So all of us use communication in different ways as our social radar. We also use it for *manipulative* purposes. Think of all the times in the course of a day when we call upon communication in lieu of other methods to bring about behavior we desire in others. "Mrs. Miller, I want to dictate a letter." "Johnny, go outside and bring in the newspaper." "Please pass the sugar." "STOP." "No left turn between 3 and 6 P.M." "Vote Yes on Proposition A!" "Patronize your local merchants." "Don't be a litterbug." "Let's go to a movie." All of these substitute for physical force or more tangible rewards in getting people to do what we want them to do. This kind of tool behavior comes to a peak during a hot election campaign, when every channel of information and trick of persuasion is employed to manipulate decisions and voting in a desired direction. In every family it comes to a lower but significant peak at a time of decision: Should Johnny have the car tonight? Should Mary's allowance be raised? Should we go to the mountains or the seashore for this year's vacation?

For the other side of manipulative communication is *decision*. Sometimes this is very easy: No great effort is necessary to decide to pass the sugar. At other times it may be very difficult—for example, deciding whether to vote Yes or No on Proposition A, or whether or not to marry a particular person. A President decides to enter an undeclared war in Southeast Asia but then has the greatest difficulty manipulating the decisions and behaviors of the people to implement his policy.

Decision and manipulation are usually two sides of the same coin. Any decision of importance is usually the outcome of competitive manipulation; any decision involving others will require some manipulation to put it into effect. Together they constitute a kind of communication *management*.

There is another large class of communication uses that we call *instruction*. This includes what the teacher does in a class and what the students do—not only exposition but also guidance and practice and problem solving. It includes not only what happens in class but also instruction outside school. We explain to someone how to follow the best route to our house. We teach our children to say "Please," mow a lawn, make a bed. An extension agent instructs a farmer in the use of a new seed. Cuba sends out schoolchildren to teach mountain people how to read. By failing to laugh or respond, we teach an uncouth person that there are some places where one does not tell dirty jokes. (At a point like this instruction and manipulation are very close.) We read the directions before we use a new blender. We look at the road map before we drive across the island to the surfing beach. (At this point social radar and instruction are very close.) This process goes on all the time. As I wrote this paragraph I took part in three acts of instructional communication: (1) A young man appeared in the doorway and asked where he could read about communication satellites. (2) Another young man looked in to ask whether Dr. Lerner was here today. And (3) the mail brought a rather formidable brochure about how to make out the Hawaiian income tax.

These uses of communication tend to overlap. The income tax brochure was both instructive and manipulative: The tax collectors want to make sure I know how to pay so that I *will* pay. In particular, all of the tool behaviors are likely to have some entertainment mixed in. Public speakers know that they must lighten their message with humor or narrative. Teachers know, as Horace said, that they must both teach and please. Herta Herzog discovered by interviewing members of the audiences that soap operas, although intended for entertainment, are used by many listeners for advice, insight, and reassurance regarding their personal problems.

A startling percentage of mass communication is used primarily for entertainment. Almost all American commercial television, except news and advertising (much of which tries to entertain); most large-circulation magazines, except the advertising pages; most radio, except news, talk shows, and advertising; most commercial movies; and an increasing portion of newspaper content—all are aimed at entertaining rather than enlightening. And as Stephenson has argued convincingly, almost the entire content has a generalized function of play or pleasure. It may be significant that we use much of our everyday, interpersonal communication for orienting ourselves—answering the questions, Where am I? Who is out there? How shall I respond to my immediate environment?—and on the other hand fill our formalized and mediated communication pipelines largely with materials that relieve us at least temporarily from worrying about those questions.

It is likely that these functions have changed hardly at all since the birth of human society, although different institutions have come into use to do these jobs. Notable among them are enlarged and professionalized forms of government, formalized school systems, and the mass media. But the government is doing what government always has, the schools are socializing the young people as their parents and the skilled craftsmen used to, and the mass media are an extension of personal communication. Table 3 shows how the map changes.

SUMMARY: THE FUNCTIONS OF COMMUNICATION FOR HUMANS

What does such a map of communication functions tell us about ourselves as a communicating animal? We move through life always in touch with and touched by communication. We use it as our individual radar both to look for what is new and to seek reassurance and guidance concerning our relationship to the society around us, and at the same time to confirm to others our identity and our understanding of relationships. We use communication as our own management tool, for decision making and to persuade and manipulate

Table 3

Communication function	In oral society	In media society
Social radar	Personal contact, watch-men, town criers, travelers, meetings, bazaars, and so forth	Personal contact, the news media
Management	Personal influence, leaders, councils	Personal influence, leaders, institutions of government and law, opinion media
Instruction	Teaching in the family, by expert example, and by apprenticeship	Early socialization in family, educational system, instructional and reference media
Entertainment	Ballad singers, dancers, storytellers, group participation	Creative and performing arts, entertainment media

others. In our small way we join in society's larger program of decision making and then receive, interpret, and react to the signals that tell us what society has decided and expects of us. We are especially concerned with passing on knowledge, skills, and norms to the new members of our society—the new class of "barbarians" who enter the world each year and must be socialized within 20 years or so to become useful members of the social group, comfortable and safe to live with, prepared to take over the responsibilities they will be handed.

In seeming contrast to these tool uses of communication, we engage in much of our communication in a spirit of pleasure seeking and relaxation from the demands of social control. This spirit, as Stephenson points out, is a form of play. Indeed, we probably view a relatively small part of our communication behavior as "work" and are very unlikely ever to verbalize the ponderous functions we have credited to communication. We seek an enormous amount of entertainment in the mass media, and in our most serious public spokespeople, even in our most serious newspaper or newscast, we value a light touch.

Thus, as all philosophers from the Greeks to the French Academy have decided, we are neither entirely Godlike nor entirely animallike. Our communication behavior proves us to be really quite human.

For Further Consideration

1. Can you think of any relation between the way children learn language and the uses they learn to make of it?

2. Recall Berelson's article on what people miss when they miss the newspaper. Suppose you had to go without the newspaper for a month. What parts of it would you miss most? What would you miss most in television if you were without it for a month?

3. It has been said that each mass medium contributes to each of the principal communication functions of society. That is, it is a watchman, a leader and cooperator in policymaking, a teacher, and an entertainer. How do motion pictures, radio, television, and newspapers contribute to each of these functions? Is there any difference in how well each performs the function?

4. If humans were forced to give up one of the mass media, which, if it were to go out existence, would be hardest to replace with the other media?

References

A classic article in this area, "The Structure and Function of Communication in Society," was written by Harold D. Lasswell and first published in L. Bryson, (ed.), *The Communication of Ideas* (New York: Harper & Row, 1948). It is also reprinted in W. Schramm and D. F. Roberts, *The Process and Effects of Mass Communication*, rev. ed. (Urbana: University of Illinois Press, 1971), pp. 84 ff. Other useful general reading includes: M. DeFleur, *Theories of Mass Communication*, 2d ed. (New York: McKay, 1970); C. Wright, *Mass Communication: A Sociological Perspective* (New York: Random House, 1959); and W. Stephenson, *The Play Theory of Communication* (Chicago: University of Chicago Press, 1967).

1. E. Sapir. "Communication." In *Encyclopedia of the Social Sciences*, 1st ed. New York: Macmillan, 1935, vol. IV, p. 78.

2. B. Berelson. "What 'Missing the Newspaper' Means." In P. F. Lazarsfeld and F. Stanton (eds.), *Communications Research, 1948–1949*. New York: Harper & Row, 1949.

3. R. K. Merton. *Social Theory and Social Structure*, rev. ed. New York: Free Press, 1959, esp. pp. 51, 61–66.

4. J. Piaget. *The Language and Thought of the Child*. New York: Harcourt Brace Jovanovich, 1936.

5. E. C. Tolman. *Purposive Behavior in Animals and Men*. Englewood Cliffs, N.J.: Prentice-Hall, 1932.

6. F. Lorimer. *The Growth of Reason*. New York: Harcourt Brace Jovanovich, 1929.

7. W. Stephenson. *The Play Theory of Communication*. Chicago: University of Chicago Press, 1967, esp. chs. 4 and 11.

8. J. Huizinga. *Homo Ludens*. Boston: Beacon Press, 1950.

9. T. S. Szasz. *Pain and Pleasure*. New York: Basic Books, 1957.

10. Stephenson, *op. cit.*, p. 45.

11. *Ibid.*, p. 46.

12. *Ibid.*, pp. 48 ff.
13. See, for example, *ibid.*, pp. 45 ff.
14. H. D. Lasswell. "The Structure and Function of Communication in Society." Reprinted in W. Schramm and D. F. Roberts, *The Process and Effects of Mass Communication,* 2d ed. Urbana: University of Illinois Press, 1971, p. 87.
15. Lasswell, *ibid.*
16. C. Wright. *Mass Communication: A Sociological Perspective.* New York: Random House, 1959.
17. M. DeFleur. *Theories of Mass Communication,* 2d ed. New York: McKay, 1970.

3/
THE PROCESS OF
COMMUNICATION

We have just credited communication with performing some very important functions. How does it do these things? In other words, how does human communication work?

Let us begin with a few examples of everyday human communication and try to analyze what is going on:

A driver studies a road map.

A sentry's voice rings out in the night.

A traffic light changes from red to green.

A picture tube flickers on. We look over the shoulders of three newsmen who are asking polite questions of the President of the United States. The President speaks over their shoulders to us.

The girl is 13, blonde, blue-eyed, with a heart-shaped face. The boy is tall, lanky, with arms and legs that seem longer than necessary, as they usually do at age 13. He moves toward the girl; his face is rather red. He says, "Linda, would you like . . ." and stops in embarrassment. She smiles up at him. "I'd love to," she says.

A man buys a morning paper, climbs aboard a commuter train, finds a seat, and settles down to read the story under the black headlines.

These are all communication incidents, manifestations of the flow of communication through society. What is common to them all is *information*, a communication *relationship*, and the special kind of behavior that handles information and takes place only in communication relationships, which we call communication *acts*.

THE NATURE OF INFORMATION

Information is the stuff of communication. It is what distinguishes communication from, say, swimming or bouncing a ball (although information about one's watery environment and about the position of the ball one wants to bounce is a necessary part of each of those behaviors). All of the incidents just described exist for the purpose of conveying, sharing, or processing information in some way.

Precisely what do we mean by information? Obviously we are not just talking about "facts" or "truth" (if anyone can be sure of the truth in a given situation). We do not mean only news or instruction or the kind of data we find in an encyclopedia. We are using the term in a way not unlike that in which Shannon[1] and Wiener[2] used it when they wrote about information theory and cybernetics: anything that reduces the uncertainty in a situation. This is an idea that has influenced the thinking even of scholars who know very little about physics and engineering, and have never looked an information-theory formula in the face.

"Twenty Questions" is an information game. When one asks, "Animal, vegetable, or mineral?" the answer reduces the uncertainty about that particular question to zero and contributes to reducing the total uncertainty about what the game is supposed to discover. If one receives the answer "animal" and then proceeds to ask, "Human or nonhuman?" (answer: human), "A particular human or a kind of human?" (particular), "One human or a group of humans?" (one), "Male or female?" (male), "Living or dead?" and so forth, the questioner is progressively reducing the uncertainty in the system.

There are formulas in Shannon's mathematical information theory by which to calculate the entropy of a given system and the information required to eliminate uncertainty from it. In natural science entropy means "shuffledness," complexity, the opposite of simplicity or organization. When social scientists encounter the term *entropy*, they have reason to be excited, because this is one of the great general ideas used for a long time by natural scientists to describe the world. Eddington said that if it were possible to make a film of the developing universe, the only way a scientist could tell whether the film were running backward or forward would be to observe whether entropy increased or decreased. One of the great principles in evolutionary science is that *entropy always increases*. That is, more types appear. Separate types are mixed in different combinations. The universe becomes more complex. And inasmuch as information is the tool that reduces entropy, it would require more information today to describe the spaceship earth and its flora and fauna than would have been required, say, two billion years ago.[3]

The possibility of applying concepts like these to human communication is what made the publication of Shannon and Weaver's *The Mathematical Theory of Communication* and Wiener's *Cybernetics* at the end of the 1940s such an exciting event for communication scholars. And although it soon became clear that direct application of the mathematical treatment was limited because the universe of human information is less simple and less finite than the mathematical and electrical universe for which the formulas had been created, still the effect of the new electronic and mathematical approaches was to open a series of important new insights on human communication. One of the most important of these was on the subject we are now discussing: the nature of information.

The information individuals seek from most communication (if they are seeking information rather than the play that Stephenson describes) is whatever content will help them structure or organize some aspects of their environment that are relevant to a situation in which they must act. Consequently, information will make their decision easier. In locating point A, it helps them to know that A is southeast of B. If they can find out that it is 25 miles southeast of B, that is still more helpful. If they learn that it is near some mountains, that information contributes further. And if they can discover that it is on Route 37, they find that very useful indeed if they plan to go by automobile. All this information reduces the uncertainty of the situation. Note, however, that although it helps them make the decision, it does not make the decision for them. They still must decide such things as whether to go through C or D to A if there is a choice. They must decide whether to take the most direct route or the most scenic one. They must decide whether it is worth going at all, and if so, when. These decisions come out of their internal information processing, the other information (for example, their schedule, the condition of their automobile, and the like) they have stored up, and the values they have developed out of previous experience.

Take the case of the sentry who calls out in the night. He must have heard a footstep or seen something move. Thus, suddenly his picture of environment and situation has changed. Most communication arises, indeed, because our image of our environment or of our own needs changes. So the sentry calls upon whatever communication behavior he has learned that is appropriate for the new situation. If he were playing "Twenty Questions" he might have said, "animal, vegetable, or mineral," but he is on guard duty, so he calls, "Halt! Who goes there?" He is communicating by his words that this is a guarded place, that the intruder, if any, must respond or risk danger. If the intruder answers, "Friend," as they do in fiction, the sentry learns a certain amount of information. But he proceeds to try to reduce the uncertainty further. Perhaps he says, "Advance and identify yourself." If he then learns that the visitor is Sergeant Brown, Company A, serial number CZ14689732, he has a great deal of the information he needs. If the visitor moves into the light so that he can be recognized as a Marine sergeant with brown hair and brown eyes, about six feet tall, and dressed in field green, the uncertainty is reduced still further.

The boy who was so embarrassed got the information he was looking for. Suppose the girl had said, "I'm busy now—maybe tomorrow." That would have given him less information than if she had said Yes or No but more than he had before he asked. If she had said, "I'm busy now, but come by in an hour," that would have further reduced his uncertainty; he would have been fairly sure that she was not merely giving him a brush-off.

Consider a different kind of information. There was a boy who grew up on the plains and at the age of about 11 was taken for the first time to the mountains. He had seen pictures of mountains, read about them, heard about them, but as he rode toward them he became increasingly excited because he was going to see them for himself. And when he finally came to the place where he could look over a lake toward a snowy range, he gazed hard and said at last, "I thought they were higher, but I didn't know they were so beautiful!" The information he got, then, modified the image of mountains he had carried in his head.

We are talking about the most human skill—the ability to process information and share it with others. All animals process information to some extent, but we have developed the skill much more fully than has any other animal. We have learned to abstract information into language, to write language and store it and multiply it so that it can be carried around to be used in our absence and so that we will have information from other people available to us in their absence. We have learned to process information that sometimes does not proceed from any other person—for example, the nature of mountains—and to use that as a basis for communication with other people and to help govern our behavior. In other words, we are above all an information-processing animal.

The internal processing takes place in the black box, and we can only infer it. But the relationship and the acts are out in the open.

THE COMMUNICATION RELATIONSHIP

The relationship in which communication takes place seems simple: Two people (or more) come together over a set of informational signs that are of mutual interest to them.

What can we say about this relationship? Let us return again to the situation in which the boy is talking to the girl. Who are the participants in this event? A teenage boy and a teenage girl? Not really. The relationship is a matter of images. The boy, as he sees himself, is speaking to the girl as he sees her. The girl, as she sees herself, is responding to the boy as she sees him.

It is very likely that these images are by no means congruent. The boy's image of himself at that moment may be of an oafish, awkward creature whose arms are too long for his coat sleeves and who doesn't know what to do with his hands. Let's imagine that he sees the girl as beautiful, serene, queenly, and wonders how she could ever be persuaded to dance with someone like him. The girl, on the other hand, may very well be thinking of herself in quite different terms. She is perhaps wishing she were more popular with boys than she is, hoping that nobody will notice the little pimple on her chin. She may see the boy not as ungainly and awkward but as rather "cute," coming up to her as he does with his flushed cheeks and embarrassed speech. It is these images, rather than any objectively seen "boy" and "girl," that are operative in the relationship. And if we describe it from the outside, we can only describe what *we* see—a third set of images that are doubtless different from those held by either the boy or the girl.

In *The Republic* Plato wrote a beautiful description. People are in a cave, bound so that they face only a wall rather than the world outside. Behind them a bright fire burns. From time to time people move in front of the fire, and their shadows are cast on the wall of the cave. The watchers never see the people who know them only from their shadows in the flickering firelight.[4]

This is an excellent analogy to what happens in human communication. It is a shadow game. One participant never knows another as that person knows himself or knows herself as others know her. (As Robert Burns wrote, "Oh wad some power the giftie gie us to see oursels as others see us!") There is no objective fact or truth involved. Even between a husband and wife who have been married many years and doubtless feel that they know each other pretty well, even between a psychiatrist and a patient who has been studied through many sessions, even between a reader and a skilled writer like Proust, who spread his intimate thoughts and experiences over many volumes of *A la Recherche du Temps Perdu*, there is still no bridge over which one individual can walk to make contact directly with another. With communication and observation the shadowy figures may become sharper and clearer, but they are still abstracted from the reality. It is still a shadow play.

There are other shadowy figures in this relationship. There is the girl's mother, who taught her how a young lady should act. There is the boy's mother, who insists that he brush his hair carefully, straightens his tie, and occasionally gives him a few last-minute directions about manners with girls. There are the girl's friends and the boy's friends, from whom both of them have probably learned more than from their parents about how young people act in social situations, and who may now be watching to see what success the boy has with his invitation. And behind the family and peer groups stand a long line of still more shadowy figures, many of whom are forgotten but who have left an imprint on the images of behavior and values that the boy and the girl carry in their heads. These include the people they have admired enough to want to imitate, those who have taught them skills or beliefs, those who have rewarded them for a certain kind of behavior and thus helped teach them customs and habits.

Into the communication relationship, therefore, all participants bring a well-filled life space, funded and stored experience, against which they interpret the signals that come to them and decide how to respond to them. If two people are going to communicate effectively, their stored experiences have to intersect over some topic of common interest. If the circles below (Figure 2) represent A's and B's life's spaces, the overlapping area, AB, is the setting for their communication.

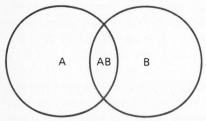

Figure 2   The setting of personal communication.

Both the boy and girl have sections of their life spaces devoted to social manners and behavior with the opposite sex. The motorist and the Department of Highway Safety have experience that intersects over the meaning of and expected responses to traffic lights. But if they did not—if, for example, one could imagine a motorist who came from a place where there were no traffic lights, who had never heard about traffic lights—the relationship would be a rather difficult one. And when one realizes that two life spaces are never perfectly congruent—meaning that no two individuals have ever had identical experiences and learned identical values and behaviors—it speaks well for the adaptability of the human organism that most communication relationships work out as well as they do for all of the participants.

THE TWO-WAY NATURE OF THE RELATIONSHIP

A moment ago we mentioned that the communication relationship involves a *sharing* of informational signs. This is too important to hurry over.

Most communication is two-way. The boy says something to the girl; the girl says something to the boy. In theory, this exchange may go on for a long time; they may sit all evening and converse, or they may see each other frequently and pick up the communication relationship with the additional understandings they have acquired from earlier exchanges. It is very hard to think of human communication that is really and solely one-way. Hamlet's soliloquy—"To be or not to be: that is the question"—has some qualities of one-way communication (if it were not given on a stage to be heard by an audience). But even if it were given in complete privacy, even if it were thought rather than spoken, still it would be a kind of talk with oneself. Hamlet is listening to his own arguments and doubtless considering them and judging them. That is what thinking is. We mentioned the Department of Highway Safety and traffic lights. Suppose we take an even less active communication from the department —a stop sign. Is that merely one-way communication—department to driver? The driver responds to it by stopping. If the driver does not stop, that fact will soon reach the department as a return link in the communication: if the driver does stop, the absence of reports to the contrary is itself a communication sign. Or watching television at home may be thought of as one-way communication, but turning on the set and selecting the station is itself a message (which the audience measurers have a certain probability of detecting), and often there is a more personal response, to the station by letter or telephone, or by talking to other potential viewers.

The most typical and frequent pattern of communication is therefore an extended two-way relationship, usually with the participants taking uneven parts in the exchange—a relationship in which signs are shared although they do not mean precisely the same thing to any two participants, but as a result of which the understanding is likely to grow closer and closer as the exchange continues. The result is never a completely congruent set of meanings because no two people are ever completely congruent (so far as we can tell from the outside). Furthermore, as the exchange of signs continues, new points of difference are almost certain to appear, and then they too must be resolved by further exchange.

But the process is best viewed as a *relationship* rather than as something A does to B or B to A, a relationship that involves *sharing* of signs that stand for information and that lead toward a convergence of understanding. Even if two people agree to disagree, still they have moved toward a common understanding of the situation as a result of talking it over. It is therefore quite proper to write of the sharing of communication, as some scholars have done, in terms of a "convergence process."

THE COMMUNICATION CONTRACT

In a sense, the participants enter into a communication relationship with a kind of contract governing their performance. Motorists, on their part, contract to stop when a traffic light is red, go when it is green, slow down when it is yellow. But they expect the light to go through that cycle so that all cars will have a fair chance to get through the intersection. If drivers wait for ten minutes while the light stays red, they will become frustrated and irritated because the motor vehicle department apparently is not living up to its side of the contract. The kind of radar behavior we described in the preceding chapter reflects a kind of social contract between individuals to identify themselves, to respond in the way expected, to confirm their social membership and sociability.

Social radar behavior is usually conducted under an implicit contract. That is, when we ask road directions we expect a simple and helpful answer. On the other hand, the person who is directing us expects us to listen carefully and to be grateful for what is told us. When we read the news in the newspaper, we expect full and accurate coverage and a selection of topics that will be interesting, perhaps important, to us. On the other hand, the newspaper staff members expect us to buy their paper and to know enough about it to comprehend the conventions of their craft—for example, the way headlines are written. A headline we saw recently would certainly have mystified any reader unfamiliar with headline style. It read: CONTRACT PLAN REPORT EYED. People who had studied English as a second language might well conclude that they had come upon a third.

Perhaps the best way to see the significance of these unwritten contracts is by looking at the expectations people bring to relationships established to serve the communication functions we described in the previous chapter. In informational relationships the unwritten contract calls for one party to be a good reporter and the other to come in a mood to seek and test reality. Entertainment, however, requires of one party a willing "suspension of disbelief." Entertainment seekers do not require of their communication partners full and accurate reporting; they do not come prepared to be skeptical of anything that checks poorly with their picture of reality. Rather, they are prepared to go along with a story or a spoof or a good joke, to identify and agonize with a character who never lived, perhaps never could live as described. Instead of expecting simple, clear, unambiguous writing, they expect a certain kind of artistic ambiguity and are prepared for latent meanings. Poetry, for example, often uses figures of speech and incidents that would never be accepted in news, because they can be, indeed need to be, interpreted variously by different readers. Poetry wouldn't be any fun if it were as clear and definite as a road sign.

News writers are expected to be clear and accurate; the form in which they write or speak is secondary to that requirement. But the way entertainers write or speak is itself expected to give pleasure. They should be imaginative rather than efficient, write richly rather than clearly, tell a good story, turn a phrase or build a scene expertly. Their part of the contract requires them to be, on their own level, artists. Even luncheon club storytellers must be artists—skillful at imitating dialects, knowing how long to string out a narrative, knowing how to put over a punch line.

The other parties to the entertainment relationship are expected to have a certain empathy with fictional characters, to go along with the conventions of films or broadcasts, to enjoy ambiguity and incompleteness rather than letting themselves be frustrated by it. The old primary school question, "What did the author mean?" is out of style and perhaps never was in style with sophisticated readers or teachers. The question is rather, "What does it mean to you?" In fact, it is in works of art that one can most easily appreciate that the signs of communication exist separately from the person who made them. For nearly 3000 years people have enjoyed the *Iliad* and the *Odyssey* without knowing much about Homer. For 400 years viewers of *La*

Gioconda (the Mona Lisa) have enjoyed the portrait and read their own interpretations into it without knowing what it meant to da Vinci, who painted it.

Consider the type of communication relationship in which persuasion is the main objective. Here the persuaders operate under no such contractual restrictions as informers or entertainers. They are on their own. To accomplish their purpose, they can select the information that fits their point and package it as they think best. They can use entertainment to attract attention to their messages (for example, television programs as showcases for commercials); they can try to preempt the perceptual field with large type, loud voices, parades, rallies, well-known names, and big events. They can argue, threaten, promise. They can even reward people on occasion for role playing, the way sponsors of some causes offer prizes for essays with a desired viewpoint. They are free to advance their ideas or sell their products. *Caveat emptor!*

But the other parties to the relationship are expected to come with their defenses up. They have faced persuasion before and should be prepared to be skeptical. They are expected to ask hard questions about the claims made, especially to ask what's in it for them. They are not even required to pay attention. If the other party is someone they respect, they may well subscribe to a social contract that requires them to give attention to the arguments; for example, our social norms encourage us to listen to the arguments of the presidential candidate of the opposing party. But we have no such obligation to listen to a salesman at the door, or to a telephone solicitor, or to read "junk" mail if we do not wish to. The contractual arrangement provides that persuasion is a buyer's market.

Persuasion is distinguished from, say, the use of force or a training process like operant conditioning by the fact that it is primarily a communication process. It consists simply of introducing some information with the intention of leading users to revise some of the pictures in their heads and consequently, perhaps, some of their behavior. Therefore, it is a shadow game like any other communication, and the enormous effort and budget expended by merchants and advertisers to find out more about their audiences shows how shadowy their perception of the other participants really is.

Let us consider one more type of relationship: instruction. This clearly presupposes a contract between teachers and pupils. On their part the teachers contract to give the pupils a systematic view of useful knowledge and to provide opportunities and guidance for them to practice what they need to learn. These days the contract would undoubtedly specify "relevant" knowledge. The pupils, on their part, contract to bring to the relationship a certain amount of trust in and respect for the teachers' guidance, and the willingness to engage in some learning activity. Supposedly, they come *wanting* to learn. But one of the teachers' responsibilities is to feed the pupils' motivation. If the pupils are not motivated to learn or the teachers are unable to motivate them, one or the other has abrogated the contract.

Thus, for each of these relationships the ground rules are different, and what happens in the relationship will also take a different form.

What brings people into a communication relationship? Many times it is chance. Whom does one see on the street? What member of the police force happens to be on duty when one needs to ask directions? What attractive girl is still available? What teacher is assigned to the seventh-grade science class? But it is also partly need—either a long-felt one or one that is aroused by a change in the situation. One needs to ask where 1044 Ala Moana is. One decides one needs a salable skill and signs up for a course in computer programming. One sees a tempting window display of baked goods and realizes one is hungry. And so on. Basically it is one's estimate of the probable reward of entering into a certain communication relationship as opposed to the difficulty of doing so. The reward of social radar behavior is often relatively slight—but then it is very easy to speak or nod to someone you see on the street, and it is socially expected. It might be very rewarding to own an encyclopedia, but if it costs $300 to $500 one might think hard before entering into that particular kind of communication. It would fit one's image of politeness to write a thank-you letter to Mrs. Parkman for her dinner party, but writing that kind of letter is difficult and a bit boring, and one must get ready for a lecture tomorrow, and besides it would be more fun to watch a program on television, and the pen is not working very well, and also one hates to write with pen rather than typewriter, and the typewriter is at the office, so. . . .

THE ACTS OF COMMUNICATION

What happens inside the communication relationship? There are communication acts and a set of informational signs. (A sign is the element of communication—a sound, a gesture, a written word, a picture— that stands for information. We will discuss signs at length in the next chapter.) One participant in the relationship puts out the signs. The other makes some use of them. That, in simplest terms, is the communication process.

But it is evident that some internal activity precedes and accompanies the offering of the signs. One must feel a reason for communicating in the first place. Then, inside the black box, there must occur some information processing that results in encoding a message and giving orders to the musculatures of the body that produce the signs— spoken words, written words, gestures, or whatever. For clarity, let us call this a Type A communication act.

Information processing is also required when someone makes use of the signs—which we will call a Type B communication act. That is, someone must direct attention to them, extract certain information from them through the sensory channels, and (in the black box) process that information, make what changes appear necessary in the stored images and the priority list of what needs doing.

When the late Wendell Johnson described this process from his psychological viewpoint, he said:

1. An event occurs . . .
2. which stimulates Mr. A through eyes, ears, or other sensory organs, and the resulting
3. nervous impulses travel to Mr. A's brain, and from there to his muscles and glands, producing tensions, preverbal "feelings," etc.,
4. which Mr. A then begins to translate into words according to his accustomed verbal patterns, and out of all the words he "thinks of"
5. he "selects," or abstracts, certain ones which he arranges in some fashion, and then
6. by means of sound waves and light waves, Mr. A speaks to Mr. B,
7. whose eyes and ears are stimulated by the sound waves and light waves respectively, and the resulting
8. nervous impulses travel to Mr. B's brain, and from there to his muscles and glands, producing tensions, preverbal "feelings," etc.,
9. which Mr. B then begins to translate into words, according to his accustomed verbal patterns, and out of all the words *he* "thinks of"
10. he "selects," or abstracts, certain ones, which he arranges in some fashion and then Mr. B speaks, or acts, accordingly, thereby stimulating Mr. A—or somebody else—and so the process of communication goes on, and on. . . .[5]

Johnson's beautifully simple exposition is aimed directly at describing what happens when two people talk together, but the process is the same whether it is a two-person group, a lecture session, a discussion group, a message carried by telephone or one of the mass media, or a President in a press conference. At the minimum there is a Type A communication act, a set of signs, and a Type B communication act. And one of the characteristics of the process is that at some instant the signs are completely separate from and out of the control of either participant. Thus the process has three distinct and separable components that can be observed, and to some extent analyzed, without having to go into the black box.

For a moment it may seem strange to think of the signs as being separate. Yet if we recall one of our common experiences with communication—mailing a letter or a manuscript and then wishing we had it back to make some changes or perhaps to reconsider whether to send it at all—we can understand this situation. When a word is said it cannot be unsaid. When a sentence is printed it cannot be unprinted. When one's facial expression conveys a certain emotion, one can't take it back. But suppose that the other person in the communication relationship has not yet noticed the expression or in the split second before the sound waves travel has not yet heard the spoken words, or that the sentence is on paper yet unread, or that the Dead Sea Scrolls are waiting in a cave for someone to find them. In this interval of time, long or short, there are only light waves or sound waves or ink on paper, quite separate from either participant in the relationship.

Sometimes the process of communication seems like coaching a football team and then sending it out to play without its coach, or training and equipping an army and sending it into battle without its general. The similes are not too far off. Communicators do all they can to prepare the signs they are going to send out. If they try to speak or write carefully, they will make use of all the strategies and skills they have learned. But then they can do no more about the signs. When the signs are sent out, they are on their own. And many a message has been sent—many a letter, for example, has been carefully written and posted—leaving the senders to wonder how it would fare. Like the general, they have wondered whether their soldiers would come home with their shields or on them, whether they would do what had been intended, whether they would even attack the intended objective.

Of course, football coaches can send in a substitute or an entire new team. Generals can order up reinforcements or air support. And this is also true of communicators. They can send more words after the first ones to change their tactics. They can write another letter. They can try to express the feeling that their facial expression or manner apparently did not convey. Just as the scoreboard or the tabulation of yards gained and lost tells coaches whether their game plan is succeeding, just as generals learn from field intelligence how their tactics are working, so communicators get "feedback" from the other person or persons in the relationship.

Feedback is another idea derived from engineering communication theory. It means a return flow from the message. In human communication, speakers hear their words at the same time, or practically the same time, that the other party hears them. They can then judge how well they have spoken. Moreover, even before they get a formal response from the other person they can derive some information from other behavior. If they are speaking to an audience, they can very quickly make a judgment as to how much interest is being shown and on that basis decide whether to tell a story or give an example or change their tactics in some other way. Then when the other party answers, it is rather easy to tell whether the message has been comprehended or has been persuasive. If they ask road directions and someone answers, "Yes, it is a nice day!" they have reason to think something has gone wrong, and they had better send another message to reinforce the first one. If they ask directions in English and the response is *"Je ne parle pas Anglais,"* they had better change languages. If a husband is talking to his wife at breakfast time and she keeps working on her crossword puzzle, he has evidence for concluding that his communication is not as compelling as it might be.

Feedback is thus a powerful tool. When it doesn't exist or is delayed or feeble—as, for example, in mass communication, when the audience is far away and personally unknown to the communicator, or when a class is required to listen to a lecture without the opportunity to ask questions—then the situation engenders doubt and concern in the communicator, and frustration and sometimes hostility in the audience. This is why the mass media and their advertising sponsors spend so much money ascertaining who is in the audience and what they think of the programs; why a few letters or telephone calls may have an effect on a broadcasting station or network quite out of proportion to their number; and why great efforts are made to supplement large lecture courses, when there must be large courses, with small discussion sections and office hours and other opportunities to question or clarify or object.

Note that feedback operates like any other communication process: It is merely a reversal of the flow, an opportunity for communicators to react quickly to signs resulting from the signs they have put out. In other words, having performed a Type A communication act, they are offered the opportunity for a Type B act. They can process the information they get from listening to their own words, rereading their own print, observing the person they are talking to, or finding out their program rating.

THE CIRCUIT AND THE ACTS

Studying communication behavior is like studying the sea: It may be done at any level and beyond a certain depth must be done in darkness. Yet what happens in the communication process does not have to be mysterious, nor does it need to be described in charts or diagrams. We have put later in this book a note on some of the models that have been influential in this field. Here, we are going to get along without any very great complexity.

Let us take as an analogy what happens in an electric light circuit.

A switch is turned, closing a circuit. This taps a source of energy, and electrons flow along a wire to a light bulb. They enter the filament and heat it, and it radiates energy that we see as light.

Is this communication behavior? Was it a *message* that flowed along the wire?

Fifty years ago many people would have described communication in just that way. They believed in a "hypodermic" theory of communication—that skillful communicators, especially if they could use the all-powerful mass media, could "inject" ideas or beliefs into an audience to directly control behavior. This long-abandoned belief is reflected in the term *thought transference,* which the Educational Resources Information Center (ERIC) of the U.S. Office of Education adopted to explain what it means by its index term *communication.* ERIC should know better, because thought transference is precisely what does *not* happen in communication. One's thoughts are personal and private. Some parts of them are abstracted into signs from which another person may stimulate his or her own thoughts.

If there is one thing we know about human communication, it is that nothing passes unchanged in the process, from person to person. Consider the difference between the electric light circuit and what happens when two people use a telephone.

When we turn on the light circuit, it is unbroken from the source of energy to the light filament. There is no coding or decoding, no interpretation, no change in physical nature. The energy that flows over the wire does not carry a message; it acts directly. The bulb is a passive partner. Until it wears out, it responds in the same way whenever a current of adequate size and nature reaches it.

But this does not describe human communication. True, it may be loud or obtrusive. It may have a startling effect. But it does not operate like an electric current. The sequence of cause and effect is not a simple transmission of motion from one body to another. Rather, it is a triggering effect, a catalytic process. A tiny communication may have an enormous effect, and on the other hand all the resources of national propaganda may go unheeded by the people on whom they are used.

The disproportion between the impinging force and the action produced in the receiving organism is often so spectacular that some physical scientists have questioned whether ordinary causal laws can be applied to behavioral responses like those triggered by communication. Among them was Julius Robert Mayer, one of the discoverers of the law of conservation of energy in physical transformation. He felt that the triggered reaction was an exception to ordinary physical laws and proposed a distinction between "true" causality and another sort "wherein the cause is not equivalent to the effect."[6] Suzanne Langer quoted the philosophically minded German chemist Wilhelm Ostwald as observing "that the action triggered by a stimulus drew its energy from the organism, not from the receiver, and that the physical effect, elaborate and sometimes violent as it might be, indicated the existence of complex and labile structures within the organism in which great energies were chemically bound and could be released by a small catalytic contact."[7] He suggested that there was a special kind of energy that obeyed the unknown laws of this kind of causality.

The idea that something "flows," untransformed, from sender to receiver in human communication is a bit of intellectual baggage that is well forgotten. It is better to think of a message as a catalytic agent with little force of its own except as it can trigger forces in the person who receives it.

Permit us to suggest a homely analogy. There is a man in India who gets up at dawn to bake cakes, which he then sells in the market-place. Of course, he tries to bake the kind of cakes that people have shown they like. He tries to display them attractively. He puts them out where passersby are likely to see them. Then it is up to the patrons. The crowds move past. Some people see the cakes; some do not. Some will be hungry, looking for food; some will not. Some will be looking specifically for cakes, others not. Some have bought good cakes from this baker in the past and will consequently be more likely to buy from him again; some have not had this experience. Some will see the cakes, find their appetites stimulated, and reach into their pockets for coins; they may or may not find any. And if they buy, they may or may not eat the cakes. For example, they may suddenly be invited to lunch and may give the cakes to someone else.

Any analogy falls short. But the acts described in this account do have some resemblance to the two different acts of communication. As the cake must be baked and offered, so must information be processed and offered in the form of signs. As buyers must decide, so must receivers weigh the desirability of buying and the desirability of eating. And whether buyers enjoy the cake, if they do eat it, will depend both on what the baker has put into it and on what they like in cakes.

We will have more to say on this subject. But let us conclude this chapter with a few additional notes about the nature of communication acts. The most obvious quality that distinguishes them is that they are information-processing acts. A fist to the jaw may convey information, but that is not its chief content. On the other hand, a shout of "Fire!" may take as much energy as a roundhouse right, but it does not work like a blow.

Moreover, acts of communication are acts of the whole person. In her monumental work, *Mind: An Essay on Human Feeling,* Suzanne Langer says that this kind of act leads one to deeper and deeper roots, and ultimately to events that belong to chemistry or electrochemistry and involve the whole organism.[8] One communicates with the whole body and draws upon all resources in interpreting the information received.

Finally, there is a symmetry, a certain wholeness, about an act of communication. Dr. Langer has written with her usual insight about this, too: the building of a store of tension that has to be spent, the beginning and the acceleration of meting out that tension, a turning point, and a closing phase or cadence in which the tension is resolved. Even in a simple act of communication, therefore, we have the model of communication as art. Even such a simple sign as a gesture may be given more artistically by a professional actor than by an amateur. A practiced speaker or writer will "turn a phrase," build symmetry and balance into a sentence so as to add a bit of beauty to its raw meaning.

SUMMARY: HOW COMMUNICATION WORKS

Let us sum up. The process of social communication requires at a minimum two people who come together in an information-sharing relationship over a set of informational signs. The purpose of the relationship—information seeking, persuasion, instruction, entertainment, or whatever—determines the roles the participants play. For example, a person who comes for entertainment is willing to "suspend disbelief"; one who anticipates persuasion comes with his or her guard up. But whatever the roles, one participant, drawing on his cognitive needs and resources, and his communication skills, encodes some informational signs and offers them to the other participant. We call this a Type A communication act. If the signs are written, they may be long-lasting; if they are gestures or facial expressions or spoken words, they may be fleeting. In either case, at one point in the process they will be separate from *both* participants.

The second participant, drawing on her own cognitive needs and resources, and her communication skills, decides whether to accept the available signs, and if she does, she processes them according to her own cognitive map. We call this a Type B communication act.

The second participant is likely to encode some informal, largely involuntary signs in the form of facial expressions or other indications of interest or disinterest, belief or disbelief, understanding or lack of understanding, which the first participant can decode as feedback. If the situation calls for it, the second participant may then herself formally encode some signs and carry out a Type A communication act that may evoke a Type B communication act from the other participant. And so forth.

In other words, there is no way that a message can *directly* cause overt behavior. As we have said, it is not like a current that travels on a wire to a certain place where it turns on a light bulb. Some responses are so built into us that the action is almost automatic; for example, we respond very quickly to an automobile horn or a cry of "Fire!" But still there are intervening steps. We must hear it, and we must interpret it: "Is he blowing his horn at me?" "Where is the fire?" The only way an external sign can affect behavior is by changing one's images of the situation. Therefore, if one decides to make any use whatsoever of the message when one processes it against one's own stored images, the result is usually a confirmation of the existing picture, a slight redefinition, or clarification of some point. A complete change is as rare as conversion. But conversion does occur occasionally, and so do abrupt changes in one's perception of a situation. For example, if one is informed that one's house is on fire, that will obviously change one's picture of the situation and lead to a precipitate response.

There is a sad little tale that comes closer than the fire alarm story to illustrating typical communication behavior. A wife became suspicious that her husband was more interested in a detective story he was reading than in the neighborhood news she was trying to tell him. She concluded her newscast abruptly: "And the horse ate up all our children!"

"That's fine, dear," he said, after a moment.

"Henry, did you hear a word I said?" she demanded indignantly.

"No, dear," he said, turning the page.

For Further Consideration

1. Is *thinking* communication?
2. Is *music* communication?
3. When you talk to a person you share communication signs with that person. When you read a book you share communications with the author of that book. How are these two kinds of signs different?
4. Recall three conversations you have had recently. Did you initiate them

or did someone else? So far as you can tell, what was the purpose in initiating them? Was there a goal the conversation was intended to accomplish, or was the conversation "play," in Stephenson's terms? In any case, how would you describe the function of each conversation? (If possible, use the classifications presented in Chapter 2.) Was there any "convergence" of understanding as the conversation went on, and, if so, on what subjects?

References

Most of the collection of readings cited at the beginning of the notes on Chapter 1 contain useful papers on the communication process. D. K. Berlo's *The Process of Communication* (New York: Holt, Rinehart and Winston, 1960) deals directly with the topic. K. Boulding's *The Image: Knowledge in Life and Society* (Ann Arbor: University of Michigan Press, 1956) is well worth reading in connection with this chapter. Useful sources on information theory are: C. E. Shannon and W. Weaver, *The Mathematical Theory of Communication* (Urbana: University of Illinois Press, 1949), and C. Cherry, *On Human Communication* (New York: Wiley, 1957).

1. C. E. Shannon and W. Weaver. *The Mathematical Theory of Communication*. Urbana: University of Illinois Press, 1949.
2. N. Wiener. *Cybernetics*. New York: Wiley, 1948.
3. Weaver, *op. cit.*, p. 103.
4. See Plato, *The Republic*, Book VII.
5. W. Johnson. *People in Quandaries: The Semantics of Personal Adjustment*. New York: Harper & Row, 1946, p. 472.
6. Quoted in S. Langer, *Mind: An Essay on Human Feeling*. Baltimore: Johns Hopkins Press, 1967, p. 284.
7. *Ibid.*
8. See the remarkable discussion of this topic, *ibid.*, pp. 257–306.

4/
THE SIGNS OF
COMMUNICATION

Some years ago Arthur L. Campa recorded a little vignette that came from his long experience with teaching modern languages: the story of a Spanish-American schoolboy named Juan.

Take the case of Juan in a school somewhere in the Southwest. He has a certain amount of "amorproprio" which is mistranslated as "pride," and then because it does not mean the same in English, Juan is said to have "false pride." One day he gets into trouble with Pedro, one of his schoolmates and, there being no word for "compromise" in their vocabulary nor in their culture-content, they resort to physical arguments. The teacher insists that Juan "apologize" to Pedro for what he did. "Go on," she insists, "apologize to him." Again Juan doesn't know what to say, because there is no word in Spanish for it, nor does the apologizing custom exist. The teacher is assuming that just as words are linguistically translated, so are cultural patterns. She continues, "Tell him you're sorry." This he refuses to do because he is a product of a realistic culture, loath to change the realism of the past by the instrumentality of mere words. So he stays after school for being stubborn, disobedient, and generally incorrigible. Juan still doesn't know the meaning of "apology," but if he is intellectually curious he may look up the word in a Velasquez dictionary where he will find it mistranslated linguistically as "apologia." Not knowing this half-dollar word he looks it up in the Academy dictionary where he finds to his amazement the following definition, "Discurso en alabanza de una persona" (an utterance in praise of a person). Now he is mad at the teacher![1]

What is going on behind this sad little comedy? The teacher is trying to "communicate" some information to Juan: what she thinks of his behavior and wants him to do. She has no way of letting him look directly into her thoughts and feelings. All she can do is use certain signs that she hopes will make clear to him what those thoughts and feelings are. "Signs" is a good word because what she shows Juan is just as separate from her thoughts and feelings as a sign beside the road would be. She uses the kinds of signs available to her: English words, doubtless backed up by stern facial expressions and tone of voice. She hopes Juan will "read" in those signs the message she intends him to get.

What has gone wrong? The signs do not mean the same thing to the teacher as to Juan. Perhaps the messages of face and voice are understood more in common than the words, although even in this case the teacher probably feels that her manner indicates righteous indignation or parental disappointment, whereas Juan merely thinks she is being unreasonable. But the word-signs especially are far from being understood in common. Note that there is no more direct connection between the "communicator" and the receiver than if the teacher had handed the boy an orange or a book. The words do *not* resemble a current flowing over a wire from battery to bulb, nor do they flow like a hypodermic injection into the receiver. They are simply signs intended to carry meanings that would be responded to with certain desired behavior. And the meanings the teacher thinks she is sharing are not by any means those derived by the boy.

THE NATURE OF SIGNS

In other words, Juan and his teacher were having trouble with the signs they were using. Therefore, let us try to understand clearly what signs are.

They are the elements of human communication that stand separate and alone between the participants in the communication relationship—the elements that stand for something in the mind of one participant and, if accepted, will come to stand for something in the mind of the other. Some scholars prefer to call them *symbols;* some, *significant symbols.* Whatever they are called, they are the elements in communication that can be decoded into "meaning."

Our dictionaries are repositories of verbal signs. If we look up *signs* in *Webster's Second International,* here is part of what we find:

> Sign (OF *signe,* fr. L. *signum;* prob. akin to L. *secare,* to cut. . . .)
> A conventional symbol or emblem which represents an idea, as a word, letter, or mark. . . .
> A motion, an action, or a gesture by which a thought is expressed, or a command or wish made known. . . .
> A lettered board, or other conspicuous notice, placed on or before a building, room, shop, or office to indicate the business there transacted, or the name of the person or firm conducting it; a publicly displayed token or notice.
> In writing or printing, an ideographic mark, figure, or picture . . . conventionally used to represent a term or conception. . . .
> Something serving to indicate the existence of a thing. . . .

It is worth thinking a moment about how the dictionary arrived at those definitions. The editors were not arbitrary. They were not *creating* meanings. In recent years some Indian scholars have done exactly that in trying to "purify" in Hindu language by expunging words that came from Persian and inventing new words from Sanskrit roots to replace them. But *Webster's* could not get by with that. Its editors are *recording* the meanings that society has agreed upon for particular signs: common meanings. These meanings are not inherent in a sign; they come out of a public consensus on what sign shall be used to represent a particular meaning. The dictionary records something we might call the central tendencies in society's use of a particular sign.

If we read down the page in *Webster's,* we find that there are many special meanings for *sign* used in particular situations or by particular social groups. *Sign* can be used to indicate a heraldic or military device such as a banner. It can mean a constellation or a signal. It can mean a remarkable event: The ancients often thought they saw a "sign" of some deity's pleasure or displeasure. It can mean a portent or an omen. It can refer to a trace or a vestige (for example, a sign of habitation). It can be a sign of the zodiac. It can be a trace in hunting (a sign of the bear). In mathematics it is used to indicate positive or negative quantities (plus or minus sign). In medicine it is used in a rather special way (a sign of a disease). In philology it sometimes indicates an inflectional ending. In theology it sometimes refers to a manifestation of something spiritual or supernatural.

The existence of so many special uses suggests that even "common" meaning, socially agreed-upon meaning, varies considerably with experience and by social group. A student who asks another, "What is the sign of the correlation?" is calling up a quite different meaning from that of an evangelist who says, "God has given us a sign," or for that matter from what we mean when we say that a communicator encodes a message in a set of signs—although in each case the central idea is that the sign represents something.

The central idea in all that we have quoted from the dictionary is *representation:* A sign represents "an idea," "a thought . . . command or wish," a "conception," some otherwise hidden information such as the name of the person occupying an office. A sign stands for something.

The idea of a sign merely representing something is not an easy one. Among primitive people especially, names are often thought of as an inalienable part of whatever they refer to. In such a culture one can therefore treat names like things: Practice magic on a name and it affects the person. Vigotsky, a Russian psychologist, tells the story of a peasant who was listening to two astronomers talking about stars. The peasant said, "I can see that with the help of instruments men could measure the distance from the earth to the remotest stars and find their position and motion. But what puzzles me is: How in the devil did you find out the name of the stars?" To the Trobrianders, as Wendell Johnson has pointed out, the word *ghosts* is not an abstraction for something inside their own heads; it is not merely an inference and therefore testable. It is reality: There *are* ghosts.[2]

But this type of thinking is not restricted to the primitive or the uneducated. Political oratory is full of it. Symbols like the flag, words like *victory* or *national dignity* or *patriotism*, concepts like "good guys" and "bad guys," take on a life of their own that makes it extremely hard in popular usage to distinguish between the symbol and the reality behind it. This was one of the chief lessons the general semanticists taught in the 1940s and 1950s—that words are not things, maps are not territory, names are separate from what one calls them by.

How does a sign come to represent a certain meaning for us? From experience. Beginning very early in life, perception seems to be organized and meaningful. We do not for very long see pinpoints of light, formless shadows, blurring masses of color, moving and stationary masses. Krech and Crutchfield have argued this point vividly.[3] These stimuli blend into recurrent patterns. "Facts" occur but once; as Heraclitus said, a man never puts his foot into the same river twice, because the river he touched before has moved on. It is inefficient, indeed impossible, to store away and retrieve many of these momentary experiences. Therefore, one tends to observe recurrent and related patterns of experience, and very early in life one discovers the utility of having signs to call them by.

We have spoken earlier in this volume about the way signs are learned. A child is rewarded for learning them. Saying "Daddy" or "Mama" is rewarded with love and laughter and fondling and some-times food. And gradually one comprehends the relationship of the sound one has learned to make, to the sensory impressions; "Mama" to the warmth and the perfume, the softness of skin and hair, and the source of food; "Daddy" to the booming voice, the pipe smell, the strong arms, the experience of being lifted high in the air to look around. So the sign becomes a tool to call upon the creatures who can produce these sensory impressions, and a little later when one hears the sign spoken by someone else one feels some of the same sensations as when Daddy or Mama were actually present.

For any individual, then, the meaning of a sign is the set of pictures, emotions, glandular and nervous activities that the sign calls up. These are similar, but not identical, to the responses called up by the referent itself. The response to hearing the name of a girl with whom one is in love is not identical to the response one makes to the girl in person. It is less, both in detail and in strength. It is abstracted from many direct experiences with the girl. It is probably contaminated somewhat by experience with other girls who have the same name as the beloved one. But the responses are still sufficient to serve as a kind of shorthand for the girl herself. One can therefore talk about her when she is not present. One can recognize her name signed to a letter. One can even say her name to oneself under a full moon with sensations somewhat different from those one would expect from repeating the name of another female—for example, Carrie Nation.

But Mary or Natasha or Akiko, or whoever she is, is a particular individual. She exists in one copy only. One can therefore classify her given name, her social security number, or some other individual designation. How does one learn the meaning of a word like *chair*, standing for something that exists in many copies. This meaning, too, must be abstracted from experiences with particular chairs. A little boy is told, "This is a chair." He is told at another time, "Sit down on the chair," although it is a different chair. He sees his father standing behind his mother when she is seating herself at the dinner table, and his mother explains, "See how polite your father is. He pushes in the chair for a lady." And so after a while he has heard the sign often enough to know that it refers to "chairness," the common qualities of the dining room chair, his high chair, the big soft chair in the living room, the reclining chair on the porch, the picnic chair, and others, and whenever he meets the sign *chair* it calls up in him a set of responses he has learned to make to something to sit on a couple of feet above the floor.

Suppose he has lived all his life in a tent or an igloo and has never seen a chair or even a picture of a chair. Then he will not have any meaning to associate with that particular sign until someone shows him a chair or explains to him by means of other signs—pictures, words, demonstrations—what a chair is. As we grow older we learn many signs in this way. Without the ability to learn signs from other signs, we would never be able to make any practical use of words like *purity, infinite,* or *tomorrow*.

Suppose a woman has lived all her life in the Arctic Circle and has never seen any kind of dog except an Arctic husky. And then suppose she is brought together with a woman who has lived all her life in Central America and has never seen any kind of dog except a tiny Chihuahua. If both these individuals have learned English, they will surely have the greatest difficulty in making joint use of the word *dog*. The southerner will find it unbelievable when the northerner talks about a dog pulling a sled over the snow, and the northerner will listen with astonishment if the southerner speaks of holding her dog in her lap.

Yet this kind of misunderstanding or lack of common meaning is not far from what happens whenever two cultures meet. The difficulty experienced by a Wall Street banker and a black ghetto activist in making themselves understood to each other does not arise because they use different signs (at least not a large number of different signs) but rather because the signs mean different things to each.

We have talked about sharing. It is the *sign* that is shared rather than the meaning. Meaning is always individual, built of personal experience, a combination of responses that are doubtless not the same for any two individuals (and that we can't test completely for sameness anyway). The meaning of a sign to any individual is much more than the dictionary common meaning. Meaning is endless. People put all their psychological state into the task of encoding signs. The receivers respond with their total organism. It is therefore impossible to codify or summarize meaning in its entirety. A sign is shorthand for the state of the encoder at the moment with respect to a particular matter or topic. Literally, senders encode themselves, and that is why most communications include meaning far beyond that of the words if one is skillful enough to read the other cues. Similarly, senders decode their sensory impressions of the sign with their total capability. Meaning is their cognitive state at that moment, resulting from experiencing the sign.

Signs, of course, are imperfect vehicles. They are necessarily abstracted from personal experience. No set of signs can ever convey all that a person feels, all that is occurring within. As Wendell Johnson emphasizes in *People in Quandaries,* we can never be sure we "know" how another person feels.[4] We can ask questions. We can observe actions. At one level this is relatively easy. The response to the words "Kiss me" or "Pass the potatoes" or "Send in the coupon today" will tell us quite a bit about whether the basic meaning has been understood. But this is only the tip of the iceberg; the depths of meaning that lie below any simple response to an important question are forever hidden, except as empathy and insight can support good guesses and as very skillful encoding can make the task easier.

In a sense it is two lives that are intersecting when two people share a sign. We bring to that relationship our stored-up experiences, the pictures in our heads, our value judgments and attitudes, the responses we have learned to make to particular sensory stimuli—the personal qualities we call our frame of reference. It is hard to conceive that this would ever be exactly the same for any two human beings. And consequently, meanings of signs will to some extent be different for different people, in different contexts, and even for the same person at different times. Spectacular differences in frames of reference (for example, Arctic experience vs. tropical experience) usually cause us less trouble than the small and delicate individual differences. For example, the woman who knew only huskies and the woman who knew only Chihuahuas would be able to reach an understanding on how to talk about dogs once they realized what the trouble was. Suppose the Chihuahua woman had never seen snow; she and the woman from the Arctic would probably learn how to talk about that, although one would always have a far greater depth of feeling and knowledge about it than the other. It is far from impossible for the banker to understand some of the differences between what "police" means to him and what it means to the activist from the black ghetto. It is possible for an American journalist and a Soviet journalist to comprehend the differences in their response to the concept of press freedom. But it is the tiny discrepancies in experience and evaluation that most often tie up human relationships. These lie deep in experience, are sensitive and hard to explain, and often hold people apart without either of them being quite aware of the reason.

A certain amount of meaning is shared widely in any society. Members of a society must agree on enough details of *denotative* meaning (the kind that identifies something by naming it and can be specified in the dictionary), or else they cannot communicate. Similarly, any society must have a certain degree of agreement on *connotative* meanings (the emotional and value reactions—what are the pejorative words, what are the value concepts, who are the good guys, and so forth), or else its members would find it very uncomfortable to live together.

In his brilliant work on measuring connotative meaning, Charles Osgood has found that within any given culture there are broad areas of agreement on ways of thinking about connotative as well as denotative responses, although there are often wide differences in value judgments.[5] Osgood's approach to this problem was most ingenious. Beginning with a large number of polar scales or "yardsticks" such as *good-bad, strong-weak, new-old,* and so forth, he asked people to judge a great many word-signs against each of these scales. He found that in the United States judgments tend to cluster around three main factors, which he called goodness, potency, and activity. Most connotative meanings seem to be describable (in large part) in terms of how good or how bad, how strong or how weak, how active or how quiet the referent of a given sign is judged to be. Judgments vary for different words and for different individuals, but there is considerable agreement within cultures. Osgood even considered the possibility of a "connotative dictionary," which would consist of average scores for different words on a number of connotative yardsticks. Such a dictionary would probably have to be different for each culture, although Osgood has made studies of connotative meanings in a number of different countries and has found a rather surprising amount of agreement in the connotative factors used.

On the one hand, therefore, a sign triggers an individual response that is made by the whole organism out of its total funded experience and therefore is necessarily unique to each person. In that sense, meaning is clearly individual and can never be expressed or shared in its entirety. On the other hand, we necessarily have to share a certain basis of denotative meaning so that members of a society can talk together, and a certain degree of connotative meaning so that the society can live in peace and comfort.

The practical significance of this is that two people are never talking to each other about exactly the same thing. If they come from different cultures, they may find important differences even in the common, socially shared meanings of signs. Until this is recognized, for example, a journalist from the Soviet Union and one from the United States will have the greatest difficulty trying to discuss concepts like "democracy" and "freedom." And even if the socially shared meanings are held sufficiently in common to avoid serious difficulty with them, still the picture a sign calls up in Mr. A's mind is never quite like the picture it calls up in Ms. B's. If one is unaware of these differences, the results may be quite unexpected!

THE NATURE OF NONVERBAL SIGNS

A sign can be verbal or nonverbal, visual, auditory, tactile, olfactory. It can be speech or writing or print or picture, a gesture or a smile, a hand on the shoulder, a laugh, or a whiff of perfume. Ray Bird-whistell, one of the chief students of gestural communication, which he calls *kinesics*, has estimated that 65 percent of the "social meaning" of a situation in two-person communication is carried nonverbally. How he measures this is not entirely clear, but it is obvious that a very large part of the information derived from any human communication is derived from cues other than words.

However, there are certain restrictive features of nonverbal signs that need to be considered together with figures like those mentioned above. Albert Mehrabian, another scholar who specializes in the study of nonverbal signs, has usefully pointed out that whereas language can communicate about anything, nonverbal communication is limited in range.[6] That is, with nonverbal cues a person can indicate very subtle shades of liking or disliking, feelings about the importance of the subject being communicated, personal reactions and emotions, and the like. Pictorial cues—from line drawing to film and television—can communicate a rich combination of concrete information. Much better than words, they can tell us what something or somebody looks like or acts like, how one actually operates a machine, what one sees from a spaceship or a bathysphere, and the like. But the more abstract the subject, the more difficult it is to present it without words. Why one pushes a certain button rather than another or why a circuit is designed as it is can be explained more efficiently with words than with pictures alone, although an accompanying picture provides an unequaled practical guide for a person who actually intends to push the button or wire the circuit. "Authoritarianism" or "the past tense" can be discussed more efficiently with words than without, although here, as elsewhere, illustrations often contribute. It is true that saintliness is defined by a person's life and beauty by a lovely face or a Greek temple. But few people have had extended contact with a saint's life, especially one who lived some centuries ago, and therefore they tend usually to learn about saintliness in words; and although a picture is incomparably more effective than words in communicating how a Greek temple or a beautiful person looks, still when one abstracts on the idea of beauty, talks about what it is that makes a Greek temple beautiful or how the builders tried to make it beautiful or for what purpose it was used, then the true efficiency of language becomes apparent.

Edward Sapir described nonverbal communication as "an elaborate code that is written nowhere, known by none, and understood by all." That suggests another characteristic of wordless human communication: It is extremely hard to codify or put into a dictionary. This is partly because it is often bound to a situation. A shrug of the shoulders in one situation may not mean precisely what it does in another. Downcast eyes in one situation may mean embarrassment; in another, boredom; in still another, modesty. The same gesture in one culture will not necessarily mean what it means in another. Still another reason why we see no dictionaries of nonverbal communication is that it reflects what we have called the "endlessness" of meaning. It reaches down beyond the level of words into the abyss of feeling and emotion, and therefore does not readily yield itself to description in words.

Some signs are given, some are merely given *off*. Erving Goffman has pointed out that signs deliberately *given* usually convey specific information (for example, pointing to something); signs merely given off—that is, not purposefully made—are usually expressive or indicative, rather than communicative cues.[7] The information they provide, however, often has a great deal to do with the impressions people form of each other. Information of this kind, mostly unintentional, is being *given off* constantly by all of us. Our clothes, our way of walking and speaking, our way of looking, at a person, our homes, our offices, the pictures on our walls—all are telling observers something about what kinds of people we are, what we care about and are interested in.

To a student of human communication, the nonverbal cues that are given off are rather more interesting than those given intentionally. Because each of us behaves as a total personality rather than as a part of our personality, and because the communication act reflects the whole person, much of the information given through nonverbal cues comes from deep down and is hard to suppress. Ekman and Friesen in a 1969 experiment found that judges who were permitted to view feet and leg positions and movements were better able than judges viewing only heads and faces to perceive an effect that the person filmed was trying to conceal—the subjects were in better control of what their faces were saying than what other parts of their bodies were saying. The same experimenters in an earlier study found that they could tell from photographs alone what stage of a psychotherapy interview patients were in at the time they were photographed. Ekman found also that judges could match head or body photographs with verbal transcripts of speech recorded at the precise time when a photograph was taken. Obviously the people in these experiments were talking with their faces and bodies as well as their voices.[8]

Thus, nonverbal signs enter into human communication in a number of different ways. For one, they often carry information without any need whatsoever of words. A painting is a total communication, and in the case of many abstract paintings even a title is as likely to be counterproductive as to be helpful. A red light on the left wing of an airplane needs no accompanying words, nor do shaken fists in angry crowds. In the second place, nonverbal signs may reinforce or expand verbal information. This is what a gesture or a pause before the key word or emphasis in speaking or a "sincere look" does for a speaker and what an accompanying illustration does for a textbook or manual.

Again, the verbal and nonverbal channels may transmit apparently incongruent cues that nevertheless have a congruent meaning. An example is the kind of humor that requires the humorist to speak or write in a serious way while relating hilarious events, or a clown to maintain a doleful face while doing funny things, or a satirist to lead an audience through a serious treatment of a subject until the final punch line reveals that the satirist has been making fun of the subject all the time. When the newscaster Lowell Thomas was on television, he would sometimes wink at his audience as if to say, "Let's not get too serious about this serious news; let's look at the human side of things too." Still another function of nonverbal signs is to contradict the verbal communication. This is what happens, for example, when a confident voice is accompanied by trembling hands or a hostile voice conflicts with friendly words.

Needless to say, the combination of verbal and nonverbal tracks is a classic problem of television and film, and becomes a highly complicated problem especially when one tries to design a film or a broadcast for instruction. What part of the task should the words carry? How many examples or illustrations should be used, and how often should words draw attention to parts of the picture? To what extent must the verbal and nonverbal tracks be carrying the same information at the same time lest there be distraction? These questions are obvious enough, but what may be less obvious is that the same kind of problem exists in print (the relation of the verbal content to the appearance of the page and the illustrations on it) and, in a slightly different way, in radio (the relation of the words to the voice quality, the manner of speaking, and the sound effects, if any).

We have said that it is difficult if not impossible to make a dictionary of nonverbal signs. On the other hand, understanding of some nonverbal "languages" is growing. The language of facial expression is rather hard to separate from its context. In general, a smile, a scowl, or a frown has a universal meaning. But the meaning of a frown may be dislike or disapproval or puzzlement or weariness or boredom. One smile may mean something far different from another smile: The emotion it expresses may be love, happiness, amusement, kindness, graciousness, or many other things. Yet the mobility and expressiveness of the human face is one of the remarkable things about human communication. John Gunther once wrote of President Franklin D. Roosevelt (in *Roosevelt in Retrospect*): "In twenty minutes, Mr. Roosevelt's features had expressed amazement, curiosity, mock alarm, genuine interest, worry, rhetorical playing for suspense, sympathy, decision, playfulness, dignity, and surpassing charm. Yet he *said* almost nothing."[9] There is little doubt that FDR conveyed this information effectively. But the situation and what was being said by whoever was talking clearly were essential parts of the meaning.

Linda Johnson, a student of psychology at the University of Nevada, presented to a number of experimental subjects descriptions of two fictitious persons and then asked the subjects how these men would look.[10] The two descriptions were:

Mr. A. This man is warmhearted and honest. He has a good sense of humor and is intelligent and unbiased in his opinion. He is responsible and self-confident with an air of refinement.

Mr. B. This man is ruthless and brutal. He is extremely hostile, quick-tempered, and overbearing. He is well known for his boorish and vulgar manner and is a domineering and unsympathetic person.

So Mr. A was described very positively; Mr. B, very negatively. How would they be expected to look? The subjects could answer readily the questions Miss Johnson asked and were in close agreement. Here were some of the answers:

	Mr. A (Positive)	Mr. B (Negative)
Would he look directly at you?	Direct gaze	Averted gaze
Would he look mostly upward or downward?	Upward	Downward
Would his eyes be widened or narrowed?	Widened	Narrowed
Would his brow be knitted or smooth?	Smooth	Knitted
Would his nostrils be relaxed or distended?	Relaxed	Distended
Would the corners of his mouth curve upward or downward?	Upward	Downward

What this experiment emphasizes is that people learn expectations of how a "good guy" and a "bad guy" will appear. This is interesting not only because it indicates that nonverbal cues are coming through but also because it suggests how much potential danger lies in such a degree of simplification. Even in fiction a good-looking villain can often mislead the heroine!

Ray Birdwhistell argues that "there is no body motion or gesture that can be regarded as a universal symbol."[11] By itself, perhaps not. Pointing must come close to universality, but the object pointed at will change from situation to situation, and therefore, in effect, additional information must be added to the gesture. When an orchestra conductor raises the right arm, a hush falls over the orchestra and the audience. The gesture might not have the same effect if it were made in a Japanese sumo ring or on the deck of a ship. The meanings of a hitchhiker's thumb, a traffic cop's palm, a V-sign given with two fingers, are quite clear in our culture today; yet we must point out that the traffic cop might not be understood where there were no automobiles or the hitchhiker where everyone walks, and the V-sign does not mean at present what it meant when Winston Churchill used it in the early 1940s. Nevertheless, many observers feel that second only to the face, the hands are the most expressive part of the body. William James was one of the first psychologists to point out that unconscious impulses suppressed from verbal behavior may often be read in the motions, positions, and tensions of the hands.

The Hawaiian hula tells a story through the dancer's hands, and there is a Hawaiian song that says, "Keep your eyes on the hands." This is not the case with the faster, hip-swinging Tahitian dance. A Tahitian girl once remarked, "If you keep your eyes on our hands, you miss the message." But in both of these Polynesian dances there is a message, and it is carried nonverbally.

Allport and Vernon found that for any given individual, the patterns of physical movement in handwriting, walking, and sitting were relatively congruent and expressive of the personality.[12] A famous type designer was once asked how he could distinguish so many printing types so quickly and easily. He said, "I recognize them the same way that I recognize one of my friends when I see him walking along the hilltop. He *is* his walk. I don't have to look at every detail to know it is he. The same way with Garamond. Garamond *is* the type. I can look at the page and see it. Caxton *is* the type. I see the pattern without counting all the details. Caxton type is talking to me." This is what Erving Goffman was saying about human behavior when he wrote, "although an individual may stop talking, he cannot stop communicating through bodily idiom."[13]

Is there a language of eye contact? Simmel said that the mutual glance is "purest reciprocity" and perhaps the kind of communication that humans come closest to engaging in simultaneously and jointly.

"By the same act in which the observer seeks to know the observed, he surrenders himself to be understood," Simmel wrote. "The eye cannot take unless at the same same it gives."[14] Barnlund listed a number of messages communicated by glances: involvement, hostility, suspicion, absence of fear, command, and others.[15] Mehrabian concludes that the more one likes a person, the more time one is likely to spend looking into that person's eyes.

Is there a language of posture? Deutsch said that every person has a characteristic basic posture at rest to which he returns whenever he has deviated from it.[16] Mehrabian says that the more a person leans toward the individual he is addressing, the more positively he feels about that person. If one's posture is very relaxed, this may mean (quoting Mehrabian again) that he dislikes the person he is talking to but is not threatened by him.[17] If one feels threatened, one is likely to be very tense; if one likes the person one is talking to, one is likely to be moderately relaxed. One relaxes most with a low-status person, less with a peer, and least with someone of higher status. Body relaxation is one of the physical communicative behaviors that have been measured fairly accurately. Mehrabian says that extreme relaxation is indicated by a reclining angle greater than 10 degrees. Least relaxation shows in muscular tension in the hands and rigidity of posture. Moderate relaxation is indicated, apparently, by a forward lean of about 20 degrees, a sidewise lean of less than 10 degrees, a curve back, and, for women, an open arm position. There have been a number of such efforts to identify specifically measurable physical or facial characteristics or behaviors that indicate an emotion, attitude, or intention. Fairly detailed codes have been worked out for facial expressions, for example, yet these are somewhat less than specific. One of the more interesting attempts to use nonverbal, visual cues to predict inner states was Maccoby's effort to predict from films of a class whether students were understanding what was being taught them. The predictions were somewhat better than chance and improved when the judges (who were schoolteachers) were given instruction, but the method did not prove very useful.[18]

The language of voice is relatively easy to understand. Actors have proved that they can read the same lines in such a way as to create many different emotional impressions through slight variations in inflection, volume, or timing. Fairbanks and Pronovost, for instance, had actors read the same paragraph so as to convey (what they intended to be) anger, fear, grief, contempt, and indifference. Students listening to the readings on tape were able to identify these emotions readily.[19] Several researchers have tried to produce "content-free" speech by running a tape at such a speed as to make it impossible to understand the words. Even in this situation it was possible in many cases to detect different emotions—for example, love as distinguished from hatred. Other experimenters have instructed actors to emphasize different parts of a paragraph by means of whatever speech tactics they felt were appropriate—pauses, loudness, and so forth. As expected, the emphasized ideas or names were the ones most likely to be remembered by listeners. Therefore, the way one speaks, no less than what one says, communicates significant information.

There is a language of apparel. In a sense, all of us wear uniforms—whether work clothes, play clothes, formal dress, police, military, clerical—and these communicate something about us and our intentions, and sometimes our respect for the person whom we are going to visit or with whom we are going out. Such dress may encourage certain actions and inhibit others in the people who see us. As David Fabun says "The kind of communication that is likely to take place between one man in bathing trunks and another in formal dress is likely to be different than the communication that would take place if both were dressed alike."[20] Roger Brown wrote of "People in Harvard Square" that "If a young man has a beard or a green book bag, he is from Harvard; if he is wearing an outdoor waist-length jacket he is a city boy. Girls in dark, heavy knee-length stockings are from Radcliffe."[21] Wilbert McKeachie found that use of lipstick changed the personality ratings male interviewers gave female job applicants.[22] And for a long time we have known that a young person who wears glasses tends to be judged as more industrious and intelligent than one who does not.

Is there a language of color? Fabun sums up the general conclusion: "Warm" colors—yellow, orange, red—stimulate creativity and make people feel more outgoing, more responsive to others. "Cool" colors, it is thought, tend to "encourage meditation and deliberate thought processes" and may discourage conversation. It has been suggested, says Fabun, that people should do creative thinking in a red room and then proceed to a green one to carry out their ideas![23]

A language of odor? Very little research has been done on communication through odor, although sales of perfume, soaps, deodorants, and after-shave lotions indicate that some people think odors communicate messages. One thing on which both authors and scholars agree is that odors have a profound ability to call back memories out of our past. Food smells remind us of our mother's cooking; flower smells, of springtime long ago, and the country where we grew up, and perhaps a friend we were fond of; train smoke or hot steam still rouses the old thrill of travel. Joost Meerloo wrote a lovely essay, "A World of Smells," about a return to his old home in The Hague:

It comes to me that I am still looking for a special old tree or a fountain, for a landmark where the miracle of something far away first began.

And then, around the corner, a forgotten magic greets my nostrils, the old familiar sea breeze, the wind blowing in from the ocean and filled with salty delights. From that direction once came the storm-wind we used to battle in late autumn, while making our way through the dunes and struggling against the driving rain.

As I walk along I pass my old school and another potpourri of smell memories washes over me . . . the scent of wooden floors intermingled with bathroom odors and children's moist clothes that seem to cling to all schools everywhere.

Further on I find the little harbor with the pungent aromas of various mercantile products—coffee, cheese, and musty wheat flour, as well as the decaying flotsam floating in the water. Here in the park the flower buds open into blossoms and waft abroad their subtlest perfumes. There down a narrow street lives a wine merchant and always when passing I would try to sniff my fill of the intoxicating odors from his shop. The same thing happened when the baker brought his fresh bread out of the oven. It set my salivary juices flowing in great anticipation.[24]

All of us know there is a language of time. When one is invited to a party in the United States, it would ordinarily be impolite to arrive more than, say, half an hour late, and unexpected, if not impolite, to be on time. A business appointment is different. If you are an hour late, you are communicating something rather unpleasant, and you would probably be received in somewhat the same spirit. On the other hand, if you are in Sweden you had better be on time for either a party or an appointment. If you are in Latin America, you will find the time sense vague, and it is not at all a communication of disinterest or dislike to be an hour late. As Fabun says, each of us and each of our cultures has a unique cultural clock, which itself communicates something about us (for example, that we get up early and work hard, that we are punctual or not, and so forth).

And how about the language of space? We know that a slight re-arrangement of furniture may produce significant changes in com-munication flows and in the prejudgments people make of the person to whom the home or office belongs. For example, many physicians and psychiatrists have found that patients are more at ease when there is no desk between doctor and patient. Sommer observed that college students select different seats when they are expecting a casual and cooperative situation than when they expect a competing situa-tion in a class; in the former case, they sit close or choose a corner; in the latter, they sit in the back or choose a place opposite the likely chief competitor.

All people seem to develop a sense of personal space, the distance at which they prefer to interact with others. Across cultures these differences are sometimes spectacular. For example, Latin Americans like to talk close together. Many North Americans like to maintain a considerable distance. Incidents have been reported in which visitors from the "close at hand" culture have jumped over a desk to be able to speak at what seemed to them a proper distance, and hilarious stories have been told of a Latin American backing a North American the entire length of a long corridor, one party to the conversation trying to get closer, the other backing away to maintain what was considered proper distance.[25]

Man-made environment has two communication effects. In the first place, it communicates information about who has made it or who lives there. In the second place, it has an effect on the kind of human interaction that occurs within it. The architect Saarinen once said that he seldom feels indifferent about a room; either it dominates him or he dominates it. The painter Jackson Pollock is reported to have said that when he went into a house designed by Mies van der Rohe he "felt so taut" that he "couldn't say anything."[26] And Barnlund has written about the effects of dramatically different environments for human interaction. For example, he says, "the streets of Calcutta, the avenues of Brasilia, the Left Bank of Paris, the Gardens of Kyoto, the slums of Chicago, the canyons of lower Manhattan" provide different backgrounds for human interaction, and therefore both communication and other behavior are affected.[27]

Thus, a vast amount and variety of information comes to us through nonverbal signs, although they cannot readily be systematized into precise language codes. Now let us turn to verbal signs, where language codes are somewhat more definite.

For Further Consideration

1. When someone says, "What do you mean?" what does he or she mean?
2. Hall (see *The Hidden Dimension*, below) explains some of the problems different people have in deciding how near to one another they should stand when talking, and similar questions of cultural space, in terms of "ownership" of space. That is, in some cases people feel "this is my space, and you should not intrude upon it." Have you had any experiences like that? For example, do you feel that certain space on the sidewalk or the bus belongs to you, and should not be intruded upon?
3. Is there a language of clothes? That is, do we communicate something by how we dress?
4. Ask one or two of your friends to assume facial expressions by which they mean to communicate anger, fear, surprise, pleasure, or puzzlement.

They can do these in any order, but without telling you in advance what emotions they are going to portray. Then try to guess what the emotion is.

You'll find this easier to do if you can see the whole face. But try covering up parts of it, so that you can see, say, only the eyes and the forehead, or the nose and the cheeks, or the mouth and the chin, and then see whether you can guess what they're trying to portray. Are different emotions portrayed better by one part of the face than another?

References

For general reading in this area: R. Brown, *Words and Things* (New York: Free Press, 1958); G. A. Miller, *Language and Communication* (New York: McGraw-Hill, 1951); C. Morris, *Signs, Language, and Behavior* (Englewood Cliffs, N.J.: Prentice-Hall, 1946); C. K. Ogden and I. A. Richards, *The Meaning of Meaning* (New York: Harcourt Brace Jovanovich, 1936); C. E. Osgood, G. J. Suci, and P. H. Tannenbaum, *The Measurement of Meaning* (Urbana: University of Illinois Press, 1957).

Among useful volumes in the burgeoning field of nonverbal communication are R. L. Birdwhistell, *Kinesics and Context* (Philadelphia: University of Pennsylvania Press, 1970); P. Ekman, W. V. Friesen, and P. C. Ellsworth, *Emotion in the Human Face* (Elmsford, N.Y.: Pergamon Press, 1972); E. Goffman, *The Presentation of Self in Everyday Life* (Garden City, N.Y.: Doubleday, 1959) and *Strategic Interaction* (Philadelphia: University of Pennsylvania Press, 1969); E. T. Hall, *The Silent Language* (Garden City, N.Y.: Doubleday, 1959) and *The Hidden Dimension* (same publisher, 1966); R. P. Harrison, *An Introduction to Nonverbal Communication* (Englewood Cliffs, N.J.: Prentice-Hall, 1974); A. Mehrabian, *Nonverbal Communication* (Chicago: Aldine, 1972); J. Ruesch and W. Kees, *Nonverbal Communication: Notes on the Visual Perception of Human Relations* (Berkeley: University of California Press, 1956); T. A. Sebeok, (ed.), *Animal Communication* (Bloomington: University of Indiana Press, 1968).

1. A. L. Campa. "Language Barriers in Intercultural Relations." *Journal of Communication,* 1951, *1,* 41–46.
2. W. Johnson. *People in Quandaries: The Semantics of Personal Adjustment.* New York: Harper & Row, 1946, pp. 137–138.
3. D. Krech and R. S. Crutchfield. *Theory and Problems of Social Psychology.* New York: McGraw-Hill, 1948. For a later version, see D. Krech, R. S. Crutchfield, and E. L. Balachey, *The Individual in Society.* New York: McGraw-Hill, 1962, pp. 20 ff.
4. Johnson, *op. cit.,* p. 109.
5. C. E. Osgood, G. J. Suci, and P. H. Tannenbaum. *The Measurement of Meaning.* Urbana: University of Illinois Press, 1957.
6. A. Mehrabian. "Communication Without Words." *Psychology Today,* 1968, *2,* 53–55.

7. See E. Goffman, T*he Presentation of Self in Everyday Life.* Garden City, N.Y.: Doubleday, 1959, p. 2.

8. P. Ekman, and W. Friesen. "The Repertoire of Nonverbal Behavior: Categories, Origin, Use, and Coding." *Semiotica,* 1969, *1,* 1, 49–98.

9. J. Gunther. *Roosevelt in Retrospect.* New York: Harper & Row, 1950, p. 22.

10. Reported by P. F. Secord, "Facial Features and Inference Processes in Interpersonal Perception." In R. Tagiuri and L. Petrullo, (eds.), *Person Perception and Interpersonal Behavior.* Stanford, Calif.: Stanford University Press, 1958.

11. See R. L. Birdwhistell, *Kinesics and Context.* Philadelphia: University of Pennsylvania Press, 1970.

12. G. W. Allport and P. E. Vernon. *Studies in Expressive Movement.* New York: Macmillan, 1933.

13. E. Goffman. *Behavior in Public Places.* Garden City, N.Y.: Doubleday, 1963, p. 35.

14. G. Simmel "Sociology of the Senses: Visual Interaction." In R. Parl and E. Burgess, (eds.), *Introduction to the Science of Sociology.* Chicago: University of Chicago Press, 1921, p. 358.

15. See D. C. Barnlund, "Introduction—Nonverbal Interaction." In D. C. Barnlund, (ed.), *Interpersonal Communication: Survey and Studies.* Boston: Houghton Mifflin, 1968, pp. 511 ff.

16. F. Deutsch. "Analysis of Bodily Posture." *Psychoanalytic Quarterly,* 1947, *16,* 211.

17. Mehrabian, *op. cit.*

18. N. Maccoby and G. Comstock. *Instructional Television for the In-Service Training of the Colombian Teacher.* Stanford, Calif.: Institute for Communication Research, Stanford University, 1966.

19. G. Fairbanks and W. Pronovost. "An Experimental Study of the Pitch Characteristics of the Voice During the Expression of Emotion." *Speech Monographs,* 1939, *6,* 87–104.

20. D. Fabun. *Communications: The Transfer of Meaning.* New York: Macmillan, 1968, esp. pp. 20 ff.

21. R. Brown. *Social Psychology.* New York: Macmillan, 1966, p. 102.

22. W. McKeachie. "Lipstick as a Determiner of First Impressions of Personality." *Journal of Social Psychology,* 1952, *3,* 241–244.

23. Fabun, *op. cit.*

24. J. A. M. Meerloo. *Unobtrusive Communication: Essays in Psycholinguistics.* Assen, Netherlands: Van Gorcum, 1964, p. 166.

25. R. Sommer. "Further Studies of Small Group Ecology." *Sociometry,* 1965, *28,* 337–348.

26. Quoted by S. Rodman, *Conversations with Artists.* New York: Capricorn Books, 1961, p. 84.

27. Barnlund, *op. cit.,* p. 512.

5/
THE CODES OF COMMUNICATION

It seems remarkable that children can learn so quickly and so early a verbal language. To accomplish this, they have to distinguish the borders between sounds, identify the crucial contrasts between sounds, and then relate such combinations of sounds to environment and group behavior. Ultimately, children must learn to make all these sounds and use them to help satisfy their needs, to learn, and to think. And all this occurs at an age when children are in every other respect infants, dependent on adults.

Psycholinguist John Carroll has commented on this:

> Children progress from diffuse babbling, to the babbling of recognizable consonant and vowel sounds, to the production of words, then two-word sentences, to the construction of simple grammatical sentences by the end of the third year. This is a remarkable feat considering that young children receive little direct language instruction and that linguists have yet to develop a theory of language structure that can generate the almost infinite possible constructions of which natural language is capable, even though children of all language communities learn to comprehend and produce such constructions.[1]

Thus, apparently by a continuing process of social experience and social reinforcement, children accomplished the astonishing feat of learning a language—the first subtle tool of learning they possess—before they master many simpler behavioral skills. This raises several interesting questions. One is whether children bring into the world certain innate ideas of a grammar of language that make it easier for them than for other primates to learn a human language (although perhaps more difficult for them to learn the language of another planet).

This is Noam Chomsky's position.[2] Chomsky, a linguist at MIT, has greatly influenced the field of linguistics in recent years with his theory that children enter the world with certain innate ideas, including a mental representation of a universal grammar, that enable them at a very early age to learn a language and by a series of transformations—Chomsky's is known as a "transformational" grammar—to generate an infinite number of sentences in that language. In other words, language learning is accomplished not solely through association and the rewarding of certain verbal responses but also by certain innate abilities built into the human race through many generations of experience with its languages.

Chomsky has thus entered into the continuing debate over heredity and environment on the side of heredity. As in other parts of that controversy, the decision is likely to be that parts of human language learning depend on genetic inheritance, parts on behavioral experience and rewards. It is not hard for anyone to believe that a child brings into the world certain qualities that make it easier for him or her than for other animals to learn a human language. The question at issue is really *what* is built into him or her: abilities or predispositions, or propositional knowledge such as Chomsky feels would be the inherited basis for mastering a particular language grammar. The jury is still out on this question.

However, Chomsky's theory raises certain other interesting questions. For one thing, if human infants inherit an ability to learn a language that is apparently peculiar to the human race, does that not mean that there was *one* original human population and *one* original language? Hilary Putnam, a philosopher at Harvard, argues this strongly:

Suppose that language-using humans evolved *independently* in two or more places. Then, if Chomsky were right, there should be two or more types of human beings descended from the two or more original populations, and normal children of each type should fail to learn the languages used by the other types. Since we do not observe this . . . we have to conclude (if the Innateness Hypothesis is true) that language-using is an evolutionary "leap" that occurred but *once*. In that case it is overwhelmingly likely that all human languages are descended from a single original language.[3]

Despite the 3000 or so different languages that presently exist in the world, there is a basic similarity among these languages. Joseph Greenberg has pointed out a number of apparent "universals" in language structure throughout the world.[4] Despite the fact that many of us have trouble learning German or Chinese or Swahili as a *second* language, there is nothing in experience to indicate that a German child brought up in England would not learn English as a *first* language quite as easily as could an English child, or an Eskimo child brought up by a Chinese family in China would not learn the language of that country as easily as its brothers and sisters could learn the Eskimo language at *their* home. The inherited ability, whatever it is, seems to apply to all *human* language, though not to the language of dolphins (if there is one) or an artificial language or the supposed language of another planet. And thus Chomsky's thinking leads us back, so to speak, past the Tower of Babel to the Garden of Eden, where, it seems reasonable to assume, all humans spoke the same language.

This line of thinking raises another important question. Human language is a learned human code imposed on experience. Does it not then seem likely that this language code determines how humans process the information they get from experience? This brings us to the Whorf-Sapir hypothesis, advanced by Benjamin L. Whorf and developed further by Edward Sapir.

VERBAL SIGNS AND CODES AND THE WHORF-SAPIR HYPOTHESIS

Whorf and Sapir argued that humans dissect nature along lines laid down by their native languages. Consequently, language serves not only as a channel of learning but as a filter for what is learned. Sapir said,

> Human beings . . . are very much at the mercy of the particular language which has become the medium of expression for their society. It is quite an illusion to imagine that one adjusts to reality essentially without the use of language and that language is merely an incidental means of solving specific problems of communication or reflection. The fact of the matter is that the "real world" is to a large extent unconsciously built up on the language habits of the group. . . . We see and hear and

otherwise experience very largely as we do because the language habits of our community predispose certain choices of interpretation.[5]

It seems only common sense that language should serve to some extent as a lens through which we view the world and a filing system for the meaning we abstract from sensory experience. Whorf gives as an example the Hopi language, which does not distinguish as English does between verbs and nouns. *Man, house, lightning, mountain* are nouns; *run, jump, hit, speak* are verbs. The Hopi people look at things differently: How long do words last? Words like *lightning, wave, flame, puff of smoke,* which are of short duration, cannot be anything but verbs. Nouns are longer-lasting things: *man, mountain, house.* Similarly, Hopi has a noun that covers everything that flies except birds, which are denoted by another noun. The Hopi actually call *airplane, aviator,* and *insect* by the same word and feel no difficulty about it. This Whorf sees as evidence that through their language they organize their world of experience differently from numerous other cultures.

He points out that an Eskimo would find it almost impossible to limit a reference to snow to a single, all-inclusive word. The Eskimo has different words for *falling snow, slushy snow,* and still other kinds and manifestations of *snow.* The Aztecs, on the other hand, represent *cold, ice,* and *snow* by the same word with different terminations. Someone else has pointed out that Arabic has about 6000 words related to "camel," words that for the most part are unknown to cultures where there are few camels and consequently represent different ways of coding human experience with camels.[6]

On the other hand, this concept of language as a determinant of one's knowledge of reality is by no means accepted by all linguists. It has proved a very difficult proposition to research, and much of the scientific evidence one would like to see is not yet in. But scholars like Brown and Lenneberg argue that the fact that English has only one word for *snow,* in contrast to the multiple words for *snow* in Eskimo, does not indicate that English speakers are unable to discriminate between these different manifestations of snow but rather that it is not so important to them as to the Eskimo and that consequently they have not felt the need of many different words for it. Similarly, the Aztecs have much less experience with snow than do either Eskimo- or English-speakers and can get along with still fewer terms. Americans don't see camels very often and hardly need 6000 camel-related words of Arabic.

The question centers around causality. How much does language affect one's processing of information, and how much do one's needs to process information affect one's language? Is there, perhaps, an interaction? An Eskimo needs more words for snow and an Arab more words for camel-related topics in order to process a great amount of information about these two subjects efficiently. If Americans and Aztecs had such needs, might they also create multiple codings? Scientists have created a number of their own words, many at a very high level of abstraction, in order to handle efficiently the kinds of information they must process. Nonscientists entering a scientific meeting may feel that they too are hearing a strange language and that scientists must perceive the world differently from other people. Thus the need of any culture to process information from a given kind of experience must determine to some extent what linguistic forms are developed. And when these forms are in use, is it not possible that they will tend to guide the patterns of abstracting and even what information is coded? For example, will a scientist not tend to code in existing terms when possible rather than creating new ones?

Take, for example, the Hopi treatment of time to which we have already alluded. It is hard to say that this is not related to the relative lack of time pressure on the Hopi culture. But once given a set of categories such as the Hopi culture has developed for its language, would there not be certain difficulties in communicating with another culture about questions in which time was essential? Whorf has written interestingly about what kind of science might be developed out of Hopi categories and how scientists from that background might interact with scientists from a Western culture. "Hopi grammar," he says,

... makes it easy to distinguish between momentary, continued, and repeated occurrences, and to indicate the actual sequence of reported events. Thus the universe can be described without recourse to a concept of dimensional time. How would a physics constructed along these lines work, with no T (time) in its equations? Perfectly, as far as I can see, though of course it would require different ideology and perhaps different mathematics. Of course V (velocity) would have to go too. The Hopi language has no word really equivalent to our *speed* or *rapid*. What translates these terms is usually a word meaning *intense* or *very*, accompanying any verb of motion. Here is a clue to the nature of our new physics. We may have to introduce a new term I, intensity. Every thing and event will have an I, whether we regard the thing or event as moving or as just enduring or being. Perhaps the I of an electric charge will turn out to be its voltage, or potential. We shall use clocks to measure some intensities, or, rather, some *relative* intensities, for the absolute intensity of anything will be meaningless. Our old friend acceleration will still be there but doubtless under a new name. We shall perhaps call it V, meaning not velocity but variation. Perhaps all growths and accumulations will be regarded as V's. We should not have the concept of rate in the temporal sense, since, like velocity, rate introduces a mathematical and linguistic time. Of course we know that all measurements are ratios, but the measurements of intensities made by comparison with the standard intensity of a clock or a planet we do not treat as ratios, any more than we so treat a distance made by comparison with a yardstick.

A scientist from another culture that used time and velocity would have great difficulty in getting us to understand these concepts. We should talk about the intensity of a chemical reaction; he would speak of its velocity or its rate, which words we should at first think were simply words for intensity in his language. Likewise, he at first would think that intensity was simply our own word for velocity. At first we should agree, later we should begin to disagree, and it might dawn upon both sides that different systems of rationalization were being used. He would find it very hard to make us understand what he really meant by velocity of a chemical reaction. We should have no words that would fit. He would try to explain it by likening it to a running horse, to the difference between a good horse and a lazy horse. We should try to show him, with a superior laugh, that his analogy also was a matter of different intensities, aside from which there was little similarity between a horse and a chemical reaction in a beaker. We should point out that a running horse is moving relative to the ground, whereas the material in the beaker is at rest.[7]

It is not necessary at this moment to accept or reject absolutely the Whorf-Sapir hypothesis, certainly not to consider that it is proved or disproved—which it clearly is not, so far as research goes. What is necessary is to recognize the extraordinarily close relation of language to culture. Culture is to language as one's individual personality is to one's communication. Cultural needs to process information determine, over a long period, what form a language takes. When one culture meets another, it often happens that new words, new linguistic forms, are borrowed by one culture from the other along with new ideas and concepts. Individuals grow up in a culture speaking the language of that culture and consequently processing information in the terms and categories and relationships common to that culture. What this means essentially is not so much that our way of seeing reality is being affected by a language as that we are being socialized into a culture. We are growing up as people of that culture, accepting its viewpoints and its customs and its world-view. These are very deep in us. In every communication, therefore, we bring our culture along with us, and it is reflected in and through our language.

It is impossible to discuss language in any very deep way here or to suggest the analyses that have been made of it in recent decades by a group of really first-rate linguistic scholars. Readers who want to sample the literature could well start with the introduction to different linguistic viewpoints in the first chapter of Chomsky's 1968 book.[8] In the next few pages, however, we can at least suggest some of the problems that this flexible, sensitive tool of human communication poses for its users.

SOME PROBLEMS OF LANGUAGE

As Sassure has pointed out, human language really has two components: the one we usually call language, which is the unifying element of all the language behavior that goes on around it, and a second component that Sassure and others have chosen to designate as *speaking*—the particular acts of using language, *actes de parole*.

Language itself, in these terms, is a kind of social norm, a part of the codified culture, a system of agreed-upon signs that can be put into a dictionary and a grammar. Language behavior, on the other hand, is an individual act. It conforms to the practice of the language community and may vary considerably from the dictionary and grammar language. Language, in effect, is a kind of hypothetical construct put together by linguists and grammarians to account for the verbal communication that was going on long before language was systematically analyzed, the kind that all children learn before they learn to write a sentence or talk about sentence structure.

None of us speaks a formal language; we speak the language we have heard, the sounds and patterns in the use of which we have been reinforced. When we learn to write, we come closer to using a formal language (in many cases too formal), but even here we vary from the norm. If enough of us vary, the norm changes, because formal language follows human communication rather than the reverse.

The picture of language behavior that visitors from another planet would doubtless carry away (if they were given a grammar and a dictionary and then permitted to wander around a language community listening and talking) would be of a system of signs corresponding to what we might call in statistical terms a *central tendency*. This central tendency is the formal language. But as our interplanetary visitors moved from place to place, person to person, they would observe great variations around it.

Consider, for example, the varieties of English word-sounds they would listen to in the course of a brief motor tour through the shires of Britain, from London to York to Scotland. Consider how puzzled they might be at some of the contextual variations on verbal meanings. For example, "I love fish" might mean in an aquarium that someone is fond of the finny creatures swimming around in the tanks. In a restaurant, it might mean that someone thinks cooked fish are delicious. When the visitors have mastered that difference, they hear someone called a "poor fish!" and wonder which aspect of fishiness that refers to. They then begin to meet usages like "I'd love to," "Love that tune," "My little love," and "I love you." There is a high probability that they would not translate the last of these phrases into, "I think you are delicious when cooked," but such contextual differences would hardly make communication between cultures and subcultures any easier. Our visiting Martians might need help in translating "Hudnathernex," heard on the New York subway system, into "Hundred and third street next." They might take a little while to grasp the distinction among "What are you doing?" "What *are* you doing?" and "You are doing *what?*" And when they returned home they might write a learned article about the meaning or meanings of "you know," which occurs so often in the speech of today's younger generation. If they began with the formal language, therefore, they would spend much of their time finding their way outward from it.

Strangely enough, one of the greatest strengths of verbal language is also one of its greatest problems. This is its ability to work at so many levels of abstraction. On the one hand, different levels of abstraction make it possible to talk about the same topic (at a different rate) to a child and a Ph.D., to code as much information into a particular sign as one wishes to, and to bounce easily back and forth between reality and the philosophical question of what reality is. Some years ago, S. I. Hayakawa devised what he called a "ladder of abstraction" in order to illustrate the different levels at which human thought and discourse could operate. This is the way, he said, that "Bessie the cow" would be seen at different steps on the ladder:

1. The microscopic and submicroscopic cow known to science
2. The cow as we perceive it
3. Bessie—the name we use to identify the particular object we perceive
4. Cow—a sign we use to stand for the characteristics of "cowness" we abstracted from Bessie and all the other cows we have perceived or learned about
5. Livestock—a still higher abstraction, standing for the characteristics cows have in common with pigs, chickens, sheep, etc.
6. Farm assets—a sign to represent what livestock has in common with other salable items on the farm
7. Asset—what farm assets have in common with other salable items
8. Wealth—a degree of assets, that may include the value of Bessie, but also a great deal more.[9]

The farther one climbs on this ladder, the more the particular characteristics of Bessie are submerged in the total meaning. This is what gives human language its ability to code *different amounts* of information into a single sign. One can work at the most concrete or the most abstract level. One can talk about a particular cow (or a bio-logical part of it). One can code that cow under a sign that lets one retrieve a picture of that particular cow, distinguished from other cows one may know (Helga, Jane, Empress Helena, or whatever *their* codes may be). Or one can go up the ladder and code more and more items and experiences together.

In one aspect this is marvelously efficient because it greatly speeds up information processing. It is a great deal easier and quicker to say or think "farm assets" than to name Bessie the cow, Helga the cow, George the goat, 76 hens and 8 roosters, the tractor, the barn, and perhaps thousands of other things that the abstract term includes. But on the other hand, when you and someone else are standing beside Bessie and talking about her, there is relatively little doubt that both of you will be talking about the same thing, whereas an abstraction like *assets* may be interpreted variously—perhaps differently by the tax collector than by a prospective purchaser, and by little-educated people not understood at all. Thus, at the abstract end of the ladder one can handle information faster, but for fewer people and with greater risk of misunderstanding; at the other end, one can communicate with a wide range of people, but not very economically. Most scientific talk (scientists talking to other scientists) tends to be at a high level of abstraction; most practical, everyday talk tends to be at a low level of abstraction to make it easy for everyone to participate.

Talk about politics and values rapidly climbs into abstractions that make for misunderstanding and the introduction of emotionally loaded words. Wendell Johnson gave an example of how this happens:

> If your radio, your car, or your electric ironer does not function properly you consult a tradesman, a mechanic of some sort, and in the conversation that is carried on by you and the mechanic a language is used that is remarkable for its straightforward effectiveness, its expression of sheer sanity on the part of both of you, and especially on the part of the mechanic. You do not call a spark plug by forty different "respectable" names, and neither of you blushes when talking about the generator. Nor do you consider it a personal insult and become angry when the mechanic tells you that one of your tubes is dead. There is a minimum of identification of the words you use with the facts you are talking about, or of "self" with the realities to be dealt with.
> At any moment, however, all this can change appallingly. . . . The two of you might fall to talking about politics or religion, for example. The mature sanity which both of you had been exhibiting a moment before may well vanish like a startled dove. A kind of sparring attitude is likely to reveal itself in your conversation. And unless one, or

preferably both, of you is very tactful, one, or probably both, of you is going to identify "yourself" with the remarks being made, and the remarks being made with that about which presumably they are being made. . . . You will be fortunate if one, or probably both, of you does not secretly or openly conclude that the other is a "red" or an "atheist."[10]

One secret of effective communication is the ability to keep one's language within the level of abstraction that the audience can handle and to vary the levels of abstraction within it so that the more abstract parts are built on a concrete base and the reader or listener can move easily from a simple and homely image to an abstract proposition or summary and back again if necessary. If you look carefully, you will perhaps be surprised at the high number of simple words and concrete images in the writing even of great poets and novelists, and of some of the greatest philosophers and historians. It is the stuffy writers, the self-conscious writers, unaware of their audience or trying to impress an audience of their peers who search for the uncommon, the multisyllable word, and the highly abstract formulation.

Finding appropriate levels and amounts of abstraction, then, is one of the problems we have in using our language. Another is what we might call the tendency toward "simplistics." When we are faced with complex ideas and highly abstract discourse, we tend to simplify our coding of these by any means possible. One of the devices we use— unfortunately—is what semanticists call the two-valued orientation. We tend to code concepts, ideas, and people as *either this or not-this*— good or bad, friend or enemy, a success or a failure—avoiding fine discriminations or the admission that something can be partly this or partly not-this. We boast of our ability to consider *both* sides of a question, conveniently forgetting that a third side—or even a twenty- fifth side—may very possibly exist and be worth our attention. As Johnson says, viewed against what Karen Horney calls the "neurotic personality of our times," this is not a healthy symptom.[11] It makes for rigidity in person and in policy.

Another kind of simplistics is the creation of symbolic images to code parts of the torrent of information that flows past us. Kenneth Boulding noted in his book *The Image* that the human imagination can bear only a certain degree of complexity; when the complexity becomes intolerable it retreats into simplifying behavior such as symbolic images. A symbolic image, he says,

> . . . is a kind of rough summation or index of a vast complexity of roles and structures. These symbolic images are of great importance in political life, and especially in international relations. We think of the

United States, for instance, as Uncle Sam; of England, as John Bull; or of Russia as a performing bear. These symbolic images are particularly important in the summation and presentation of value images. Value images do not usually consist of a long and detailed list of alternatives in a carefully compiled rank-order. They consist, rather, of a "posture" which in a sense summarizes an extremely complex network of alternatives and situations. In Christianity, for instance, the symbol of the Crucifix or of the Virgin has exercised an enormous evocative power through the centuries because of the way in which these symbols summarize a whole value system, a whole attitude toward life and the universe. Political images do the same thing at a different level. The creators of these symbolic images exercise quite extraordinary power over the imaginations of men and the course of events. Consider, for example, the image of the political party in the United States.

The Republican Party is conceived as an elephant, rather old, rather dignified, a little slow, not perhaps terribly bright, but with a good deal of wisdom, hard working, full of integrity, rather conservative, a little isolated from the world around him, patient, thick-skinned, but capable of occasional inarticulate squeals of rage. The Democratic Party is thought of as a donkey, active, agile, clever, a little unsure of himself, a bit of an upstart, quick, sensitive, a little vulgar, and cheerfully absurd. These images are reiterated by cartoons and have been of great importance in establishing the political climate.

In international relations, the symbolic image of the nation is of extraordinary importance. Indeed, it can be argued that it has developed to the point where it has become seriously pathological in its extreme form. The national symbol becomes the object of a kind of totem-worship. Cartoons and political speeches continually reinforce the image of roles of nations as "real" personalities—lions, bears, and eagles, loving, hating, embracing, rejecting, quarreling, fighting. By these symbols, the web of conflict is visualized not as a shifting, evanescent, unstable network of fine individual threads but as a simple tug-of-war between large opposing elements. This symbolic image is one of the major causes of international warfare and is the principal threat to the survival of our present world.[12]

It goes without saying that most of the leaders who would manipulate public opinion today are themselves expert, or have access to experts, in the creation of simplified images and slogans of the kind Boulding is talking about. And therefore one of the problems of public communication today is to be willing and able to look behind these stereotyped simplifications and measure them against the complexities of one's own experience with reality. Reality is complex. Simplistic language often makes it harder rather than easier to grasp reality. A productive communication relationship must therefore balance between the two extremes. It must be on levels of abstraction where the paricipants can comfortably work and must include enough examples and illustrations to anchor the abstractions.

Ultimately we ourselves are responsible for the kinds of pictures of reality we are able to store away to guide our behavior. We need rather special services from the mass media, the educational system, and other suppliers of our information, but we must *demand* it of them. This requires us to maintain a critical stance and a balanced response. Every writer on semantics remarks on how seldom one meets a person who listens patiently and attentively, and "asks questions as though he were really listening and not as though he were watching for an opening to take over the conversation."[13] How often we suspend our critical faculties in the presence of resounding oratory, fine writing, an impressive television presence! "Some people," says Hayakawa, stop listening "to *what* is being said," and seem to be interested "only in what might be called the gentle inward message that the *sound* of words gives them. Just as cats and dogs like to be stroked, so do some humans like to be verbally stroked at fairly regular intervals. . . . Because listeners of this kind are numerous, intellectual shortcomings are rarely a barrier to a successful career in public life, on the stage or radio, on the lecture platform, or in the ministry."[14] One thing we can do is to discriminate between the different ways that something is *said* to be true. Hayakawa gives these examples:

> Some mushrooms are poisonous (a statement that has been scientifically verified)
> Sally is the sweetest girl in the world (at least that's what someone thinks)
> All men are created equal (this is a directive which we think should be obeyed)
> $(x + y)^2 = x^2 + 2xy + y^2$ (means that this statement is consistent with the system of statements that can be made in algebra)[15]

To which we might add:

> This is the party of the people (means that election time is coming around again, not any particular difference in parties)

To err is human. We cannot expect perfection of ourselves. And yet human frailty is more responsible than deficiencies in language for the imperfect lens we turn on the world around us. Let us conclude with one more example of how some of our human characteristics keep us from using language to perceive a balanced picture of reality. Some years ago a funny-bitter few minutes on BBC's "Brains Trust" program poked fun at the way many people build their pictures of the world around themselves. Bertrand Russell "conjugated" what he called an "irregular verb." It went like this:

> I am firm.
> You are obstinate.
> He is a pig-headed fool.

Later the *New Statesman* and the *Nation* ran a contest for similar "irregular verbs." Here are some entries they received:

> I am sparkling.
> You are unusually talkative.
> He is drunk.

> I am righteously indignant.
> You are annoyed.
> He is making a fuss about nothing.[16]

Let it not be thought, however, that we too are "making a fuss about nothing" in making so much of problems of human language behavior. Language is a beautifully engineered instrument. But even a Ferrari or a Mercedes has to be driven and sometimes tuned up. In fact, the finer the instrument, the greater the invitation to skill. Human language asks the same of its users.

For Further Consideration

1. What seems to you to be the important arguments for and against the idea that all human language had a single origin? Would a single origin for language have made it necessary for humankind also to originate at one place on earth? If language originated in more than one place, would there have been enough contact between tribes living far apart to allow them to share their languages and cultures? If Chomsky is correct about our unique and innate ability to learn a human language, how would this have developed in one species but not in others?
2. It has been said that for two persons who speak different languages to learn to communicate with each other they first must learn each other's culture as well as language. Do you think this is true? To the extent that it is true, what does it tell us about the nature of meaning?
3. We have been talking mostly about verbal language in this chapter and nonverbal communication in the preceding. Is it possible to describe nonverbal communication in the formal terms we use to describe verbal language—words, sentence, parts of speech, vocabulary, etc.? Could one make a dictionary and a grammar for nonverbal communication?
4. One of the reasons for trying to learn to communicate with dolphins is that this might help us to learn to communicate with extraterrestrial beings, if there are such. How might it do so?

References

In addition to the titles suggested for Chapter 4, W. Johnson, *People in Quandaries: The Semantics of Personal Adjustment* (New York: Harper & Row, 1946) and S. I. Hayakawa, *Language in Thought and Action* (New York: Harcourt Brace Jovanovich, 1949) are useful general reading in this area.

There are a number of general books about language. Because of his present importance in the field, N. Chomsky, *Syntactic Structures* (The Hague: Mouton, 1967) is suggested. An excellent and readable book on language from the historical viewpoint is M. Pei, *The Story of Language*, rev. ed. (Philadelphia: Lippincott, 1965).

1. J. B. Carroll. In S. Saporta, *Psycholinguistics*. New York: Holt, Rinehart and Winston, 1956.
2. N. Chomsky. *Syntactic Structures*. The Hague: Mouton, 1967.
3. This is quoted in a popular exposition of Chomsky by J. Ved Mehta in "Easy to Please." *New Yorker*, May 8, 1971, pp. 44 ff.
4. J. Greenberg (ed.). *Universals of Language*. Cambridge, Mass.: MIT Press, 1966. See especially Greenberg's chapter, "Some Universals of Grammar with Particular Reference to the Order of Meaningful Elements."
5. E. Sapir. "The Status of Linguistics as a Science." *Language*, 1929, *5*, 207–214. See also quotations in J. B. Carroll (ed.), *Language, Thought, and Reality*. New York: Wiley, 1956.
6. D. Krech, R. S. Crutchfield, and E. L. Balachey. *The Individual in Society*. New York: McGraw-Hill, 1962, pp. 296 ff. See also B. L. Whorf in J. B. Carroll (ed.), *Language, Thought, and Reality*. New York: Wiley, 1956.
7. B. L. Whorf. "Science and Linguistics." *Technology Review*, April 1940, *62–6*, 247–248.
8. N. Chomsky. *Language and Mind*. Berkeley: University of California Press, 1968.
9. S. I. Hayakawa. *Language in Thought and Action*. New York: Harcourt Brace Jovanovich, 1949, p. 169.
10. W. Johnson. *People in Quandaries: The Semantics of Personal Adjustment*. New York: Harper & Row, 1946, pp. 174–175.
11. *Ibid.*, pp. 9–10.
12. K. Boulding. *The Image: Knowledge in Life and Society*. Ann Arbor: University of Michigan Press, 1956, pp. 109–111.
13. Johnson, *op. cit.*, p. 394.
14. Hayakawa, *op. cit.*, p. 118.
15. *Ibid.*, pp. 290–291.
16. Quoted *ibid.*, p. 96.

6/
THE PATHWAYS OF COMMUNICATION: WHO TALKS TO WHOM

Try sometime to make a list of all the people you would be able to call by name if you saw them. You will find that the list will be a kind of map of your life. Everywhere you have lived or studied or worked you have left a trail of acquaintances. Names will cluster around the places where you have spent the most time, around the relationships that are most important and necessary to you, and the list will thin out with distance and time.

But when you have written down the hundreds of names on your list, you will have only begun to make a map of your communication. There are hundreds or thousands of persons with whom you have communicated but whose names you have forgotten. There are countless persons whom you have met, and in some cases come to know well, through books and other mass media. There are organizations and individuals whom you have met less personally through such forms of communication as STOP signs, advertising, income tax forms, or such culture cues as the way a lawn is mowed or the statues carved above a cathedral door. There are many communications you have overheard, such as a song drifting up from the beach or a quarrel in the next apartment. And finally there is the silent talking all of us do to ourselves, which we sometimes dignify by calling it *thinking* and which uses the same signs one would use in talking with someone else. As a matter of fact, this last communication activity probably fills more time in our experience than any of the others.

This, then, is what the map of any individual's communication looks like:

1. A great deal of internal communication—talking to oneself, thinking things out, remembering, deciding, dreaming
2. Communication with people close to one—family, friends, neighbors
3. Communication within one's work group
4. What might be called "maintenance" communication required by the way one lives and the society one lives in—with tradesmen and service people; with doctor, dentist, lawyer; with barber, filling station operator, taxi driver; with government people such as the tax collectors, the Department of Motor Vehicles, the police and fire departments (fortunately seldom)
5. Communication with casual acquaintances, business and social
6. Communication with (mostly *from*) personalities known chiefly through books and the mass media
7. Finally, a great mass of information from anonymous sources in the media, reference books, and all the miscellaneous cues of the culture through which one moves every day.

Of course the pattern varies with the individual. Some will have more communication with friends and neighbors; some will be reclusive. Some will communicate as a result of wider experience over longer pathways. Some will read the great books; others will simply watch television.

THE WIDE-ANGLE LENS

So much for the individual map. Now, what would we see if we could view human communication with sufficient perspective to see it as a society-wide network of connected individuals and institutions—if we could look at it, for example, as we might a telephone network or a computer system, with lights indicating what circuits are in use?

We would see communication flowing over an almost infinite number of circuits. For any individual most circuits, the most-used ones, lead to other individuals nearby. But there are some very long hookups: postal service, telephone, telegraph, and travel. Throughout the system are placed what in an electronic network we might call amplifiers. These are the mass media organizations—the schools, the libraries, the wire services, and other institutions and organizations—into which many circuits flow and which have the function of filtering out the input and producing a very large output of relatively few messages that go to many receiving points. Each of these institutions has its own internal communication network. On these networks and along the interpersonal chains of communications, we see smaller amplifiers: individuals who serve special functions in passing on communication—teachers, reporters, broadcasters, preachers, public information people, authors, advertising specialists, travelers, gossips, and many others.

Observing this network as a whole, we should be able to identify patterns. There is the casual everyday flow of information—the greetings, the social invitations, the traffic lights, the names read on office doors, the uniforms on policemen, the telephone books and street maps that help make it easy to live in modern society. There is also a long-range flow of news and interpretation that comes often to the wire services and the mass media and lights up for a time the channels of most individuals each day. There are institutions like the schools that also light up a number of information circuits regularly. This pattern of flow corresponds to the basic brain waves that pass through an oscilloscope when an individual is in a state of activity sufficient to maintain the organism rather than meet any special challenges.

But one would also observe, in addition to the even and measured flow of everyday communication, that from time to time circuits light up like a Christmas tree in one part of the network or another, and these may trigger some special activity elsewhere. What is happening in those cases?

A neighbor falls ill. The doctor is called, perhaps an ambulance. Concerned inquiries and offers of help flow to the family. If the case is serious enough, there may be some emergency activity at a hospital or a clinic. Medicine is ordered from a pharmacy. Possibly some of the neighbors are impressed enough to go to their own doctors for a checkup.

A house catches fire. A frantic call goes to the fire department. Spectators gather. There are messages of sympathy and offers of help. A newspaper reporter interviews the fire chief, the owner, the person who first saw the flames. The insurance representative is called in. The incident is discussed in many places. The owner seeks estimates and advice: Should the family rebuild or repair? Where should they live in the meantime?

An election is called. The newspapers speculate about candidates.

The political parties gather, first in leadership groups, then in larger assemblies, to talk about candidates and issues. Candidates offer themselves, speak at meetings and on radio and television. Primary elections and nominating conventions are held so that party members can speak their wishes. Communication boils for a few months around personalities and issues. The candidates visit, speak, are interviewed, get their pictures on posters and in the media, and become well known. Public opinion polls are conducted to try to predict the result. The media report what is happening, what is said, argue the issues back and forth. Doorbells are rung, materials handed out, promises sought. Persuasive materials go through the mail. Housewives organize "coffee hours." People discuss. And then finally the election day arrives and the voters, who have been spoken to so much for so long, now speak for themselves.

Communication flows where it is needed in society. It warns of dangers and tells of opportunities. It assembles the resources of society to meet emergencies. It aids in decision making. It informs, educates, entertains as needed. Some of these needs require little variation in the everyday flow over the network. Some are larger. Some are so large that they nearly take over the network. A San Francisco earthquake requires more from the network than does a single house afire. If an astronaut actually returned from an extraterrestrial mission with an incurable "Andromeda strain"—the premise of a popular motion picture produced in 1970—that information would take over the network in a way that one sick person could not. When gold was discovered in California, that must have commandeered the network to a degree that a sale at the local department store never would. And no one in the United States who was old enough to realize what was happening will ever forget the impact of a brief news bulletin interpolated into the radio broadcast of the New York Philharmonic Orchestra on the afternoon of December 7, 1941, and how the entire network of social communication lit up, jerked Americans away from their Sunday afternoons, their comfortable plans, and their confidence in their national security, took over most of the news, most of the conversation, and most of the private thoughts, and focused attention inexorably on the implications of an event in Pearl Harbor, Hawaii.

SOME PATTERNS OF COMMUNICATION PATHWAYS

So there are at least two patterns of communication flow through society: the kind necessary to maintain the social organism at its ordinary level of functioning and the kind necessary to meet challenges to and serious problems of the organism. What other characteristics of the flow through the network would be noticeable?

For one, we might notice that there are dark places in the network where circuits connecting large masses of people are seldom used. One of these dark places, until recently, was between the United States and China. We might observe a number of points in the network where circuits are little used between groups of people representing different social classes—for example, ghettoes and suburbs, central governments and villagers, rich landowners and tenant farmers.

We should also notice, probably, that most communication tends to flow horizontally in society but vertical communication flows downward more than upward. This is somewhat different in the case of status derived from expertise or authority. Experts are as likely to communicate up as down, depending on where their skills are chiefly needed. People with authority, on the other hand, are likely to communicate downward, and more information will probably go downward from them than upward to them. More information flows from government to any citizen than from any citizen to government. In fact, if we could observe the communication networks of the world in the way that has been suggested, we might be able to distinguish the more democratic from the more authoritarian states by the number of messages that flow upward to government.

An army would furnish an extreme example of hierarchical communication: commands flowing from upper levels downward; the ordinary soldiers, the noncoms, and the commissioned officers all patronizing their own clubs and socializing at their own level; and even within the top group, the general officers somewhat removed from the officers of company or lower field grades. Or consider the communication patterns in an industry. By far the greatest amount of communication takes place among people who work together and share common problems. The workers talk together, the supervisors talk together, the middle-level and top management talk together—all have their own sets of tasks and interests, and a large share of their information channels to people at their own level. When serious problems occur they are reported upward in the hierarchy as far as necessary for the requisite decisions to be made. Sometimes a grievance committee or a strike is required to accomplish this. It is much easier for communication to move down the ladder, for management to pass down orders to the supervisors and supervisors to give orders to the people working for them.

Research literature contains interesting findings about the effects of different communication patterns. Let us take the example of work groups, which are small enough to make it possible to study their communication in detail. H. J. Leavitt has found, and others have confirmed, that groups in which everyone can communicate freely with every other member have higher morale than groups in which there is any restriction on communication.[1] On the other hand, there are several findings that groups where one member is in charge and all communication goes to and from him or her may be somewhat more efficient in solving problems. The kind of problem seems to make a difference.[2]

Studies by J. Thibaut and others revealed that the ability to communicate upward in the hierarchy often substitutes in peoples' minds for their inability to *move* upward.[3] And still other experiments (for example, by Leavitt) showed that the farther members of a group were placed from the center of communication and decision, the less satisfactory they found their tasks. So it does make a difference, often a considerable difference, where the paths of communication reach.

S. C. Dube, a distinguished Indian sociologist, has described the communication pathways that had to be cleared before India could launch out efficiently on its own as an independent nation. It was found, he said, that effective communication had to be established between these segments at least:

1. Between the political sector and the bureaucracy
2. Between the planner and the political decision-maker
3. Between the planner and the research agencies
4. Between the planner and the units of production
5. Between the different departments and agencies of the government
6. Between the different levels of administration
7. Between the general administrator and the technician
8. Between the modernizers and the common people
9. Between aid-giving and aid-receiving countries
10. Between overseas consultants/advisers and their native counterparts.[4]

You may ask whether these channels were not already in existence. The answer is that some of them were, but even in those cases considerable revisions in role patterns and practice had to be accomplished before the channels worked effectively. For example, the bureaucracy (the old civil service of colonial days) and the political sector (made up of the freedom fighters who had led the revolution and then moved into elective and high appointive places in government) had a difficult time learning to work together. The politicians were annoyed by the bureaucrats' emphasis on routine and fixed procedures; the bureaucrats were annoyed by the politicians' impatience and lack of administrative skills. Ultimately both roles had to be modified.

The meaning of this is what we have said before: that when we are studying communication we are studying human behavior. When we study pathways of information, we are studying the relationships of people at different ends of the path. The network we have been talking about is really far different from a telephone circuit board or from anything electronic or mechanical. It is *people* who are relating to one another, influencing one another, sharing information for some common purpose. That is what social communication is.

WHY THESE PATHWAYS?

We thus live in a sea of communication the way we live in a sea of air, and just as naturally. We do not often feel overburdened by the weight of the ocean because we adjust to it; we take what we want from what comes to our attention, make such use of it as we wish to and can, and contribute to the ocean as we feel the need to do. Just as we feel discomfort when the air moves too strongly in a windstorm, so do we sometimes become uncomfortable when communication flows in too great quantities—when there are too many telephone calls, too many documents to read, too many letters to write (though we discover after a while that if we postpone answering letters many of them will never need answering). Just as we feel uncomfortable when the supply of air is thin, so do we when the supply of communication is short—for instance, when someone we love does not write to us or we cannot find out what is really happening in the Middle East. But in this case, too, we usually find a way to fill the gap or adjust to it; the ability of humans to adjust to their environment and society is phenomenal. For most people at most times, therefore, the supply of communication seems adequate in the sense that Mark Twain described the most appropriate length of a man's legs: long enough to reach from the man to the ground.

Now the question is, what determines which pathways will be well worn and which ones little used? Why are certain roads marked on the map with heavy lines and others not so marked?

It is partly a matter of need, partly of convenience and habit and chance. If I want another cup of coffee after dinner, I ask someone for it rather than writing a letter to the newspaper. If I want to hear a symphony, I am more likely to turn on the stereo than the television receiver. If I want to hear the late news while I am driving, I turn on the car radio. I have a neighbor who always reads the morning San Francisco *Chronicle* on the 8 A.M. commuter train and another who takes along the San Francisco *Examiner* from the previous evening because, he says, he cannot stand the *Chronicle*.

Therefore, if we ask whether people select a pathway of communication on the basis of the medium or the message, we must answer that they select both. They select the one that will meet the need most adequately and, other things being equal, most conveniently and quickly.

When the needs are personalized, pathways are pretty well determined. When I asked a certain girl to marry me, I needed an answer from *her*, and the obvious pathway was face-to-face communication under the most favorable conditions possible. When I am ill I need a channel that will bring me information from a doctor, preferably my own doctor, although I suppose I could get some advice from a medical book. But if all I need to know is the name of the capital of Liechtenstein, I have a choice among many channels: atlas, encyclopedia, the *World Almanac,* the library reference desk, the fellow in the next office. In this case, availability is likely to determine which channel I use.

Availability of channels depends on where we grow up, what we can afford, what constraints are placed on us by our culture. For example, if I had grown up in a thatched hut in Africa instead of a clapboard house in the United States, I would certainly have had different pathways of information. There would probably have been no newspapers and no *Book of Knowledge,* but I might have learned to understand talking drums, and instead of my doctor I might have been consulting a witch doctor. If I had grown up in another part of the world, I would probably have been asking that question of a different girl or, very possibly, of her father rather than the girl herself.

Culture and environment thus enter into individual choices of information pathways in several respects. They require, or at least encourage, us to seek certain kinds of information rather than others. Reacting partly to these needs for information, they encourage the growth of institutions and media of communication. And they reinforce patterns of using certain channels and talking to certain people rather than others.

Many years ago I suggested a rule-of-thumb approach to help explain the probability of any given communication being selected by any given individual.[5] It was stated this way:

$$\frac{\text{Promise of reward}}{\text{Effort required}} = \text{Probability of selection}$$

At the time this was formulated, I was probably influenced by George K. Zipf's "Principle of Least Effort,"[6] which helps explain the wording of the bottom term. I could just as easily have said something about availability. But like Zipf, I was impressed by the tendency of human behavior, other things being equal, to flow into a path of minimum effort. But of course other things are not always equal. Consequently, one can raise the probability of selection of a given communication *either* by decreasing the lower term (the expected difficulty) or by increasing the upper term (expected reward). These are individual assessments. The potential reward of asking Ms. X to marry Mr. Y or Mr. Z may be estimated quite differently by these two gentlemen. And an outside observer may estimate either the reward or the difficulty quite otherwise than do the actual participants. For example, I recently suggested to a student who has a problem in a course that he talk it over with his teacher. "Oh, I can't talk to him about that," the student said in obvious distress, although to me it seemed a relatively easy thing to do.

If we consider the fraction of selection in terms of the selection of channels and pathways, I think we can say that the upper term—promise of reward—has chiefly to do with the content and how likely it is to satisfy needs as they are felt at a given time. The lower term, on the other hand, has to do mostly with the availability and ease of using pathways. Habits tend to develop out of experience with these two estimates. For example, one finds satisfactory reading in the morning paper, and soon that journal appears each day at the breakfast table. One finds that the 9 o'clock program on television helps one unwind after a hard day, and one begins to tune to it regularly. Or one finds that a particular author has a pleasant soporific effect, and this author's books begin to appear on the bedside table.

To the test of introspection and nonrigorous observation, the fraction of selection stands up well. Countless audience studies have shown that people select easily available entertainment from their television tube. Even so simple an action as changing channels is often sufficient to keep them tuned to the same station until a program they genuinely dislike (or bedtime) comes along. For this reason, network programmers tend to consider prime time, in particular, as a unit, rather than as a series of unrelated programs.

People also prefer—other things being equal—staying in to going out for equally promising entertainment. Yet when the reward of peer group company is added in, we see teenagers go to the movies or even the public library. Then, when those teenagers marry and grow into adulthood and settle into their own homes, the rewards of going out seem to be reduced, and before long they are watching the TV movies and the TV professional football. When College Board examinations draw near, students are likely to perceive greater reward in their books than in the movies or TV, and they even, occasionally, turn off their radios. By the same token, our choice of interpersonal pathways reflects both our needs and easy availability. Most of such communication goes to and from people nearest at hand, the people one spends most time with.

On the other hand all of us have seen that at *some* times, in *some* situations, some particular kind of information is suddenly so important to us that it is worth almost any kind of effort. Even then we tend to choose the most readily available channel or the one we feel most confident and comfortable about using. But for rewards of sufficient size we are willing to spend years studying to get a Ph.D. or spend $22 billion to go to the moon.

The operation of the fraction of selection is hidden in the black box, and the proposition itself is so general that psychological research on it is not easy. Research has concentrated on one aspect of the proposition: whether people select information that supports their beliefs and values and consequently reduces their sense of cognitive dissonance. Freedman and Sears reviewed the literature on selective exposure[7] and concluded that exposure to communication really is selective and that people tend to expose themselves to information with which they agree. "Republican rallies are mainly attended by Republicans," they point out. "Baptist services are attended mainly by Baptists, the readers of the *New Republic* are mostly liberals and those of the *National Review* mostly conservatives. AMA journals are read primarily by doctors, and APA journals primarily by psychologists. The audiences for most mass communications are disproportionately made up of those with initial sympathy for the viewpoints expressed." They could not find, however, any very convincing proof of a general *psychological* tendency to prefer supportive information. They decided that there must be other reasons—possibly the usefulness of the information (of medical journals to medical practitioners, psychological journals to psychologists, and so forth), friendships, social roles and customs, and others—behind such selective exposure.

Selective exposure is not really in doubt, but its causes are. There must be a variety of causes and combinations of causes, some operative at one time, some at another, but all affecting the judgment we make on the question of reward as opposed to effort.

WHAT GOES INTO THE FRACTION OF SELECTION?

So people walk through life, doing what comes naturally with communication, using their skills and directing their attention where they feel it will be most rewarding, sometimes following along the easiest communication pathways but on other occasions making great efforts to take paths that are not easy to use. Sometimes they communicate merely to pass the time of day; sometimes out of a sense of great urgency or crisis; sometimes in a node where little information flows; sometimes in a great tidal wave through society, as happens, for example, in a period of rapid social change. One's map of communication is a map of life, and the map of communication in the society around us is a better map of that society than most cartographers can draw.

That is the larger picture that emerges of people communicating. As we ask the smaller question, Why does one certain communication circuit tend to light up rather than another? we turn back to the fraction of selection. People make judgments about the promise of reward as against the need of effort, and if we want to think of that in even simpler terms, we can consider why a person selects one form of communication rather than another from all that are available. And then we ask questions like these:

· *How readily available is the communication?* Political pros like to *saturate* a broadcasting station with spot announcements concerning their candidate. Advertisers know that large ads are more likely to be seen than are small ads. Both politicians and advertisers try to rent the billboards where many people pass. And all of us know that we are more likely, of an evening, to pick up the magazine beside our chair than go out for another one, unless that other one contains an article we very much want to read.

· *How much does it stand out?* Do the message signs contrast with the field around them? Are they bigger, louder, more pervasive, different from the colors and patterns surrounding them? All of us have had our attention jerked to a sudden change in our perceived environment: a swift movement in a still forest; a baby's wail in the night; a few seconds of silence in the midst of a noisy party; a falling star against the sky; a spot of orange against the blue of the sea. And if we are parents, we know we must sometimes raise our voices if we want our children to "pay attention" while they are playing.

· *How appealing is the content?* This depends partly on the characteristics of the selector; consequently, a great part of all audience research deals with the question of what people select what kinds of material from the media. For example, we know that the more education people have, the more likely they are to select print over television, public affairs content over westerns or whodunits. We know that men read or view more sports than do women. We know that children's tastes in mass media change considerably as they grow up to adulthood.

Some years ago, working along this line, one of the authors factor-analyzed the news choices of a number of readers and found that they could be described to a great extent in three clusters. One of them was how *near* the news seemed to the readers. Not necessarily physically near, but how likely to affect them or their neighbors. A story of an epidemic of measles would seem nearer to a woman with young children than to an elderly man with no grandchildren. A story about a crime wave in San Francisco would seem nearer to a San Francisco reader than a Bostonian, and nearest of all to a reader in whose neighborhood the crimes were most frequent. There seemed to be a considerable difference among readers, however, in their ability to perceive a story as potentially affecting *them;* for example, a person with higher education or cosmopolitan interests might consider a story of rising tension in the Middle East as near and potentially significant, whereas another reader might pass it by and turn to local politics or the grocery ads.

A second determinant was how *big* the story seemed to the readers —that is, how significant, how exciting, how important. There was a close interaction between bigness and nearness. The election of a mayor in Gary, Indiana, semed bigger to residents of Gary than to residents of Phoenix, Arizona. But among individuals there seemed to be a considerable difference in willingness to read the "big" news of the day. Some, for personality reasons, seemed actually to avoid it or to prefer to take it in the form of headlines or a news summary. Others concentrated on the "big" stories.

In the third place, there was the question of how *serious* or *entertaining* the news appeared to be. In this respect also, there was a considerable difference among people in their preference for public affairs or feature news, which is to say for potentially challenging and disturbing news as against news intended to make them chuckle or say, "I'll be darned!" and settle back comfortably in their chairs.

This kind of study, of course, describes rather than explains. The underlying process must be inferred or otherwise derived.

· *What are individuals looking for?* A person comes to any communication supermarket with a certain shopping list. We call it a "set." A fisherman is set to look for fish rather than wildflowers beside the stream. A student goes to class prepared to look for cues different from those sought in the cafeteria. At any given time an individual may be seeking information on how to pass a test, whether to take an umbrella, what quotation to use in a talk, why a child is sulking.

· *What communication habits have they learned?* Some sources have proved over time to have utility for certain purposes and not for others. A student who has been in class long enough knows pretty well what to pay attention to and how much attention. When commuters settle down into their seats with a familiar newspaper, they have learned to look at certain parts of that paper, probably in a preferred order.

· *What communication skills do they have?* Reading skills, to take one example, are obviously related to preference for the print media. Skill in listening, skill in viewing—things we still know too little about— are related to the use of the electronic media.

These are simple and practical questions. They are asked every day by advertisers and other professional communicators. But what underlies the kind of behavior these questions are designed to iden-tify? For example, what determines people's judgment of what is rewarding and what requires too much effort? What determines how appealing certain content is to them, or what their set is at a given time, or what communication habits or skills they bring with them? Some of this is time-bound of course: One doesn't usually apologize or offer to fight unless something has just happened to bring that about. Some of it is relatively timeless: the habit of acknowledging a greeting, smiling at a pretty woman, or communicating in a way that will help one obtain food when one grows hungry. Much of it depends on what one has been and what one has experienced, the kind of family and community one has grown up in, and the educa-tion one has had.

For Further Consideration

1. Where are the "dark places" in today's world where circuits connecting large masses of people are seldom used? What makes them "dark"?
2. Classrooms are examples of group communication that function in many different ways. Analyze your current classes in terms of the direction, kind, and quantity of communication flow (and remember that there are many forms of communication other than the verbal).
3. Would you organize each of the following groups so that each member communicates freely with all the others, or with a single central indi-vidual through whom all communication flows?
   a. directors of a companywide United Way solicitation
   b. a committee in charge of a campaign to pass (or defeat) a bond issue
   c. the finance committee of a small college, which must decide on the dis-tribution of funds from a large bequest
4. Analyze the front page of a newspaper and identify the reasons that the stories that interest you most do so. Do the same with a general in-terest magazine, such as the *New Yorker*, *Cosmopolitan*, or *Readers Digest*.

   Are the factors that influence your selection of news different from those involved in your choice of nonnews material?

References

For general reading see E. Rogers, *Diffusion of Innovations* (New York: Free Press, 1962); M. DeFleur and O. N. Larsen, *The Flow of Information* (New York: Harper & Row, 1958); and W. Schramm, *Mass Media and National Development* (Stanford, Calif.: Stanford University Press, 1964). Useful material also can be found in D. C. Barnlund (ed.), *Interpersonal Communication: Survey and Studies* (Boston: Houghton Mifflin, 1968), pp. 227 ff.

1. H. J. Leavitt. "Some Effects of Certain Communication Patterns on Group Performances." *Journal of Abnormal and Social Psychology*, 1951, *46*, 35–80.
2. *Ibid.*
3. J. Thibaut. "An Experimental Study of the Cohesiveness of Underprivileged Groups." *Human Relations*, 1950, *3*, 251–278.
4. S. C. Dube. In D. Lerner and W. Schramm (eds.), *Communication and Change in the Developing Countries*. Honolulu: East-West Center Press, 1967, pp. 131–132.
5. W. Schramm. "How Communication Works." In W. Schramm (ed.), *Process and Effects of Mass Communication*. Urbana: University of Illinois Press, 1954, pp. 19 ff.
6. G. K. Zipf. *The Psycho-Biology of Language*. Boston: Houghton Mifflin, 1935.
7. D. O. Sears and J. L. Freedman. "Selective Exposure to Information: A Critical Review." In W. Schramm and D. F. Roberts (eds.), *The Process and Effects of Mass Communication*, rev. ed. Urbana: University of Illinois Press, 1971, pp. 209–234.

7/
THE MEDIA OF COMMUNICATION: MASS AND PERSONAL

The concept of media is not so simple as it has sometimes seemed. For one thing, clearly there were media before there were *mass* media. We certainly have to classify as media such pre-mass media devices as the talking drum, the smoke signal, and even the town crier and the bazaar, because they all extend the human ability to communicate. The town crier is a formal role, and the talking drum might be called a machine, interposed in the communication process much as the newscaster and radio are today.

Paul Deutschmann suggested a way of classifying communication situations (Figure 3) so as to throw light on the relation of channels to pathways.[1]

It is helpful to use his scheme (with our examples added) to indicate how arbitrary the distinction is between the mass and interpersonal channels of communication. "Private" communication is not quite the same when it is face-to-face as it is by telephone or by letter. Private or public face-to-face communication is different alone or on an interview show, in a group of two, a group large enough to fill a living room, a group large enough to fill a hall, an acting crowd, or a

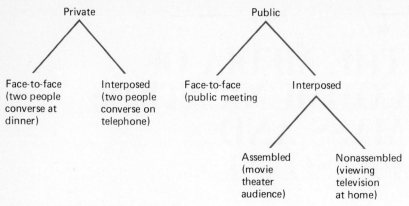

Figure 3   Channels and pathways.

mob. Public communication through a mass medium is different when it is received in a group situation (a movie theater or a Radio Rural Forum) or in a living room and, if in a living room, by one person or several. Indeed, it could be argued that many qualities of an inflammatory face-to-face speech to a mob are less personal, more mass, than a singer crooning through a radio into the ear of a teen-age girl alone in her room.

Thus, although from the viewpoints of production and delivery there are clear distinctions between communication through a mass medium and communication otherwise, from the viewpoint of an audience—whether one person or millions—the distinction is not always that sharp.

When we speak of a mass medium, we usually mean a channel of communication in which a machine (to duplicate and distribute the information signs) and a communicating organization (like the staff of a newspaper or broadcasting station) has been interposed. When we speak of an interpersonal channel, we mean a channel that reaches from person to person without such things interposed. As we have seen, the distinction blurs: For example, on which side of the fence does the telephone fit?

Let us first try to sum up some of the things we think we know about the differences between mass and interpersonal channels, then talk about one of the most famous scholarly hypotheses relating mass media to interpersonal channels (the "two-step flow"), and finally consider McLuhan's much-discussed approach to communication media.

THE NAIVE PSYCHOLOGY OF CHANNELS

It must be confessed that our state of knowledge concerning the effect and effectiveness of these two different kinds of channels is still not far from the level of "naive psychology," by which psychologists mean something for which they do not have much research evidence but still think is worth saying. However, consider some of the fairly obvious differences in the two kinds of channels.

The senses they stimulate

As we have said, each of us communicates as a total person. In face-to-face communication it is possible to stimulate all the senses and for the communication partner to relate to this whole-person communication. When anything is interposed, some restriction is put on the use of the senses. Thus radio and telephone reach only the ear, and print only the eye (although we must not underestimate the tactile pleasure of handling a beautifully made book). Television and sound movies reach both eye and ear. It seems reasonable, therefore, that a face-to-face situation, other things being equal, should make it possible to communicate *more* information and *more complete* information. It seems also that there would be an advantage in being able to communicate at the same time to as many areas as possible, and thus the audiovisual media would have some advantage over the merely audio or the merely visual in communicating a certain amount of information on a given topic.

However, against the apparent advantage of face-to-face whole-person communication one must weigh the advantage of skillful production and programming on the media. Against the advantage of communicating to several senses at once one must weigh that of being able to concentrate attention on *one* sense—for example, on listening to a telephone call (especially if one must listen very hard in order to hear) or on the act of reading (especially if the text is difficult enough to demand close attention). Against the advantage of being able to communicate to both the audio and visual senses, one must weigh the theory of Broadbent, Travers, and others that human perception operates through one channel only.[2] In other words, the path from the sense organs to the brain is a one-lane road, and either audio or visual information can pass over it but not at the same instant. One part of the total message must wait in a short-term memory for its turn, and therefore an individual can by no means expect to process twice as much information from a two-sense communication as from a single-sense one. Furthermore, there is evidence that interference sometimes occurs between the information on a sound track and that on a visual track so that far from being twice as effective, in some cases an audiovisual channel may be *less* effective than a single-sense channel.

Among single-sense channels there is reason to suspect differences also, because good evidence exists that the eye can absorb information more rapidly than the ear, and the sense of smell has a remarkable ability to call up old memories associated with odors.

The opportunity for feedback

In a face-to-face situation, there is maximum opportunity for quick exchange of information. Two-way communication is easy. Consequently, there is continuing opportunity to assess the effect of the signs one puts out, to correct, to explain, to amplify, to answer objections. As the face-to-face group grows larger, the leader can pay careful attention to fewer members, and the talking time must be divided into smaller fractions. When anything is interposed, the feedback is attenuated. Thus, a telephone restricts not the speed but the amount of feedback, because it will not carry—unless it is a picture phone— any of the information that might be communicated visually. Interposing a mass medium restricts both the speed and the amount of feedback, and the distance and impersonality of the media discourage it. When media organizations feel that feedback is very important— as, for example, in advertising or in making an instructional television program like "Sesame Street"—they pretest materials, put audiences in studios, and make arrangements to obtain quick reports from the classroom or the markets.

Control of the pace

In face-to-face communication a person can ask questions, help steer the conversation, and exert some control over its pace. A person reading can set the pace, pause to think over a point, repeat a passage when necessary and desirable to do so. Teachers can do the same thing for a class, though they must average out the feedback cues they receive in order to know how best to meet the class's needs. Listeners to radio, viewers of films or television, however, have no such control. To be sure, they can turn off the receiver, leave the theater, or allow their attention to wander, but they cannot control the pace or cause the flow of information to pause while they think about it. This is one of the reasons why advertising on television has drawn more complaints than advertising in newspapers and why printed texts have proved so effective for individual study.

Traditionally people have believed that control by the sender of the message persuades more effectively, but that receiver control makes for more effective learning. Over the past two decades the devices produced by new technology have tended to help both—for example, satellites provide cheaper and more efficient circulation of centrally controlled information; at the same time, others, such as recording-playback equipment and computerized methods of instruction that provide control of such factors as the speed of instruction, have enlarged the receiving individual's role. The problem is how to combine the cost efficiency of central distribution and control with the efficient fit to personal differences that individual control makes possible.

Message codes

In face-to-face communication a high proportion of all the available information is nonverbal. This is slightly less true of television and sound movies, still less of silent movies and radio, and least of print. Therefore, the silent language of culture, the language of gesture and emphasis and body movement, is more readily codable in some delivery systems than in others. A high proportion of printed communication is coded in alphabets as compared to a very low proportion of television and movies, and almost none of painting, sculpture, music, or dance. Thus, it is possible in printed media to abstract easily; in the audiovisual media, to concretize.

The multiplicative power

Face-to-face communication can be multiplied only with great effort. Even a meeting of a hundred thousand people, such as Nehru sometimes addressed, was not really multiplying face-to-face communication, because information had necessarily to flow mostly in one direction only. Mass media, on the other hand, have an enormous ability to multiply one-way communication and make it available in many places. They can overcome distance and time. The audiovisual media can also overleap the barriers of illiteracy in developing regions. Therefore, the advantages of this multiplicative power must be weighed against the advantages of the kind of feedback provided by face-to-face communication.

A considerable amount of attention has been given in recent years to combinations of the two in an effort to salvage some of the best of each: for example, the Radio Rural Forum, in which groups meet face-to-face to hear and discuss broadcasts made especially for them, and the combination of television teaching with related activities, face-to-face, in the classroom. Attention has also been attracted to the effects of face-to-face communication in very large meetings and the use of interpersonal networks. For example, when huge crowds come together at a sports event or a political rally, the crowd effects are themselves an element of great importance in the communication, and when a message must be spread person to person, the personal networks may sometimes be spectacularly effective, as they were when the news that "Gandhi-ji is dead!" spread by word of mouth over India. On the other hand, a network message may be easily distorted—as several studies of rumor have demonstrated.[3]

The power to preserve a message

Face-to-face communication is gone in a second. So, except when recorded, are the electronic media. It has been difficult, therefore, for a person to relive a motion picture experience or enjoy a television program again, except in memory. Print always has had a great advantage in being able to preserve facts, ideas, or pictures.

That advantage surely will continue, but recent developments in electronic storage and retrieval systems are producing changes. Already it is easier—and cheaper—for telephone company information operators seeking numbers, librarians locating books, and storekeepers checking on inventory, for example, to get answers off a small screen than from a book, a set of cards, or even a computer printout. Families of moderate means now can buy videotape or disc recorders that will store, for use at their convenience, both visual and audio signals from whatever source; they also can buy copies of favorite entertainments, including theater movies and sporting events. It's reasonable to predict that the day when the television networks show hit movies to increase audiences during "sweeps" by rating services is on its way out; the number of viewers who own their own copies increases constantly.

Some people within broadcasting believe that this trend is comparable to the rise of specialized publications, which so radically changed the magazine field, and predict that today's huge television networks will wither away, as did the old *Saturday Evening Post*, *Life*, and *Look*. The enormous potential of cable broadcasting for specialized broadcasting is a major force in the same direction.

That's an intriguing prediction, but the pattern of adoption of new ways of living is not easily divined. It does seem clear, however, that personal control by the receivers of mass communication is going to continue to increase and the forms of centralization to alter.

The power to overcome selectivity

It is easy to change the television channel, hard to tune out face-to-face communication without being rude. It is easier to doze in a large class than in a small discussion group. It is easier to turn off the radio than to make oneself walk out of a movie theater. It is probably easier to avoid reading a news item or an advertisement in a newspaper than to avoid a news item or a commercial on the radio or television, although if the audience can seek out what it wants it may be more receptive. And all of us know that it is easier to command and monopolize attention through face-to-face communication than through media channels—other things being equal. But again, they are *not* equal. If one of your friends is telling you an old story for the third time, face-to-face, your attention is still likely to stray and if your radio is broadcasting a bulletin on the assassination of a President, your attention is very likely to be riveted to it.

The power to meet specialized needs

The mass media have an unequaled power to serve *common* needs of society quickly and efficiently. For example, the weather forecast, the day's chief news bulletins, the Saturday football scores, the announcements of sales and sale prices, a policy address by the President of the United States—all can be circulated much more efficiently by mass channels than person to person. On the other hand, radio, television, films, and newspapers are very inefficient channels for meeting needs that are felt by different people at different times and by only a few people at any given time. What is the capital of Liechtenstein? What is the name of the red-haired girl down the street? How can I change the spark plugs in my car? For answers to questions like these one asks an informed individual or studies a sheet of directions or looks in a handbook. If one finds the information one wants, when one wants it, on television, it will truly be a miracle. For most such specialized information another person is the best source, a bit of print that can be kept around for emergencies is next best, and the electronic media are least effective. The time may come when video cassettes will be so cheap and plentiful that we can afford to keep some information on them rather than in print, but not yet.

Do not think, however, of interpersonal and mediated communication as opposed or mutually exclusive. Actually, as we have tried to point out, the distinctions and boundaries are much less clear than that. Most campaigns aimed at teaching or persuading try to combine media and personal channels so that one will reinforce and supplement the other. Political campaigners use all the media but still arrange door-to-door visits and public meetings. Family planning, agricultural, and health campaigns maintain field staffs but support them with all the media they can afford. And one concept of the supplementary functioning of media and interpersonal communication has been put forward as the "Two-Step Flow" theory, which now warrants our attention.

THE TWO-STEP FLOW THEORY

"Nothing," some researcher once said, "is as practical as a good theory." A good theory gives the researcher an intellectual handle for taking hold of the problem of analysis. The fact that it may eventually be demonstrated to be incomplete, or even incorrect, and its importance in the field diminished does not take away its importance as a starting place. Communication study is in debt to several such theories.

The idea of the two-step flow of communication came out of a study in Erie County, Ohio, of the 1940 U.S. Presidential election, under the direction of Paul Lazarsfeld and some of his colleagues from the Department of Sociology and the Bureau of Applied Social Research at Columbia University.[4] The researchers expected to find that the mass media, at that time chiefly radio and press, had a great influence on the election. However, very few people reported being influenced by the media. In the cases where voting decisions were influenced, it was usually by personal contacts and face-to-face persuasion. To explain these findings, the researchers advanced for the first time the Two-Step Flow hypothesis: "that ideas often flow from radio and print to opinion leaders and from these to the less active sections of the population."

Incomplete and ultimately unsatisfactory as it was, this theory turned out to be a very fruitful one for communication study and research. For one thing, it was hard thereafter to think of "faceless masses" or of audiences consisting of individuals disconnected from one another but connected to the mass channels. Gradually it came to be seen that individuals were connected to one another. Instead of being faceless or passive, they were extremely active. An enormous amount of discussion and persuasion and informing went on within the audience.

Moreover, the Two-Step Flow theory set in motion a number of studies of audience behavior, especially in relation to campaigns and to the media. Robert Merton and some of his colleagues studied opinion leadership in a suburban community, which they called Rovere. Consumer decisions were studied in Decatur, Illinois. The 1948 election campaign was studied in Elmira, New York. The diffusion of information on medicinal drugs among physicians was studied in an eastern city.

The research by the Columbia scholars was supplemented by others. The Presidential elections since 1952 have been researched by the Center for Political Studies, a division of the Survey Research Center at the University of Michigan.[5] Diffusion of news was studied by Deutschmann and Wayne Danielson, and later by Bradley Greenberg.[6] Rural sociologists found that their diffusion model would contribute to the understanding of the two-step flow.[7] Trohldahl and others at Michigan State and Wisconsin looked in more detail at the seeking as well as the giving of advice in electoral campaigns.[8] The spread of information and ideas at the time of the assassination of President Kennedy was the subject of research in several parts of the country. All this research was stimulated or shaped in part by the Two-Step Flow hypothesis. And even though every study pointed out deficiencies in the theory until finally there was not much left of the original conception, today much is known about the flow of information and ideas that was not known before the Two-Step Flow concept was proposed. This is the function of good theoretical hypothesis: It leads toward better theory.

What have we found wrong with the original Two-Step Flow formulation? Simply that it doesn't explain fully enough what actually happens.

In the first place, it neglects the fact that a great amount of information flows directly from the media to users of the media rather than through a middleman. Deutschmann and Danielson, for example, found that most news was so received. Greenberg demonstrated ingeniously (Figure 4) that only the *most* and the *least* widely important news is carried to any extent by word of mouth.[9] Thus, about half the American people learned of the death of President Kennedy by word of mouth rather than from the media, and most local events unimportant enough for newspaper or broadcast coverage are carried from person to person. However, the bulk of the news, which is important enough to cover but not so shocking that it must be passed on at once to others, comes to people mainly through the press and newscasts. In recent political campaigns the bulk of information and persuasion has been piped directly to individuals through the media. This includes press conferences, political addresses, conventions, meetings, and political advertisements. We are by no means saying that personal influence is not exerted in political campaigns, merely that much information and persuasion still comes directly rather than through an "opinion leader" or another kind of intermediary.

In the second place, the concept of a society divided into leaders and followers, or active and passive participants, has not held up. Trohldahl found in Detroit that relatively few voters ever sought any advice at all, whether from "opinion leaders" or anyone else.[10] On the other hand, there is no very convincing evidence that "opinion lead-

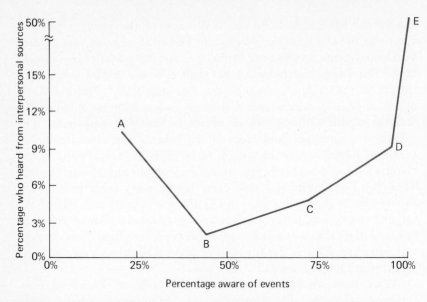

Figure 4 A through E are news items that came to the attention of different percentages of the American public. Word of mouth played an important part in carrying the first news of only the least and the most interesting items. (Source: In B. S. Greenberg and E. B. Parker (eds.), *The Kennedy Assassination and the American Public: Social Communication in Crisis*. Stanford, Calif.: Stanford University Press, 1965, p. 17.)

ers" are typically active forces in social persuasion. Apparently they are just as likely to be passive as to be active and to wait for someone to ask their advice rather than trying to persuade.

The concept of opinion leaders receiving information from the media and passing it on also proved to be too simple. Actually, opinion leaders, when they can be identified, have many sources of information. They go to meetings, try things out, and—most important— talk to other people who serve as *their* sources. In other words, opinion leaders also have opinion leaders.

Therefore, the theory of a *two*-step flow is not a realistic description of what happens. There may be one step, two steps, or many steps. The chain of influence and information may be of considerable length, with the true origin in doubt.

In the third place, rural sociologists have demonstrated that potential adopters of a new idea or innovation are more likely to seek or accept information from the mass media very early in the process, when they are still canvassing what is available, and to seek information from informed and respected people later in the process of adoption, when they have become interested and want to know more about it, especially about other users' experience with it.[11] Again, after they have committed themselves they may try to reduce their dissonance by seeking reinforcement from the media. Thus, the two-step flow more often applies at the stage of information and decision than earlier or later.

Finally, the "opinion leader" concept itself has proved to be far too simple. As Everett Rogers, one of the leading students of diffusion, has justly pointed out, opinion leadership is really a continuous variable.[12] There are all shades and levels of opinion leaders. Some are strong and widely accepted "leaders," others not. From the time of the Decatur study, we have known that advice is usually sought with respect to a particular topic; *generalized* opinion-leadership status is scarce. Furthermore, such leaders appear at all levels of society and at different ages, according to what knowledge they are expected to have. For information about the new movies or the new dances, for example, one would not ordinarily ask an elderly bank president. But the point is that even in their separate specialties people are not neatly divided into leaders and followers. A person who is asked for advice because of special knowledge or expertise may well ask someone else's advice in the same specialty. A person who has sought some special information may pass it on. There are people—gossips, for example, or people who work in places like barber or beauty shops, where they see and talk with many people—who serve to multiply information without having any special expertise. Thus, there are so many levels and forms of information multiplication and influence that to think of a single social role designated "opinion leader" is an unsatisfactory way of trying to understand what is going on.

What is really going on? Perhaps the best way to say it, in the present state of knowledge, is that there is a continuing flow of information and ideas through society. The mass media greatly influence—directly or indirectly—what flows through these channels. Certain individuals also influence it, either by sharing their special knowledge, expertise, or conviction on a certain topic or by being articulate and talkative. As a matter of fact, all people, at some time or other, in some relationship or other, on some subject or other, by seeking or by giving, probably influence the flow. Some influence it more than others. But there are not two classes, the leaders and the led, nor is there in most cases a two-step flow from media to leader to follower. You can think of it as a multistep flow. Better, think of it as a systemic flow with information moving continuously through a social system, following the constraints and the needs of the system, shaped by the roles and sped by the institutions within the system.

THE McLUHAN APPROACH

In a complex field such as human communication, it is not only theories that come along to enlarge and illuminate thoughtful analysis and then gradually slip back into obscurity; so do some human beings. Marshall McLuhan is an example.

During the late 1960s McLuhan was a cult figure among American intellectuals and students. His following began to develop with a book called *The Gutenberg Galaxy: The Making of Typographic Man* (1962). His most popular work came two years later; it was called *Understanding Media: The Extension of Man.* With the publication of the paperback edition, it, and McLuhan, began to turn up constantly in American talk.

One of the contributors to the present volume has for a good many years taught an introductory survey course on the mass media at the University of Michigan. He quickly learned, once the boom started, that students expected McLuhan to be dealt with. For a period of two or three years, casual show-of-hands surveys indicated that almost every student had heard of the man, and sometimes more than half had actually read, or attempted to read, him (many had been assigned *Understanding Media* in high school). Prints of a one-hour television documentary about him, circulated by the university's audiovisual service, had to be booked a year in advance.

His popularity extended far beyond the campus; articles about McLuhan and his ideas appeared in popular magazines and Sunday newspapers, and both his somewhat eccentric personality and his ideas were frequent grist on talk shows. One of Richard Nixon's chief advisers during the Presidential campaign of 1968 was a devotee and influenced some major strategic decisions on the basis of his understanding of McLuhan's principles.[13]

A common result of saturated attention by the mass media is an eventual backlash, when the public, or at least the agendamakers, apparently agree that the subject has been overworked. By the mid-1970s McLuhan was no longer a pop-culture eminence, although his theories still drew notice among communication scholars. That interest also declined, with the exception of some retrospective summaries accompanying his obituaries in early 1981, to the point where references to his ideas generally treated them as oddities, worth two or three paragraphs. As for undergraduates, the same kind of show-of-hands survey in the introductory course in 1980 showed a half-dozen—of about 300—who had heard of him.

Such neglect is more lamentable than any excesses of McLuhan's popularity. He had an important role in the development of communication study (at the superficial level he probably was responsible for making trendy the word "media," once used largely by artists, bacteriologists, and mass communication specialists).

Both his permanent importance and, even more, his wide popularity at one point are made more difficult to explain by the fact that his presentations make his ideas hard to get at. Doubtless because he distrusted the linear, logical presentation typical of printed media (which he held responsible for many of the undesirable trends of the last five centuries), McLuhan chose to write in a disconnected fashion that has been described as resembling Roman candles aimed in all directions. He seldom developed an idea fully and disdained research evidence because he felt that research is biased toward print and incapable of dealing with the new electronic media. His device, as he describes it, is the "probe"—a statement that penetrates the intellectual stereotypes of his audiences and causes them to rethink old positions. These "probes" are often cryptic statements worded so as to shock or puzzle, perhaps deliberately left incomplete or unqualified (as in "The medium is the massage"). Therefore his scholarly stance was somewhat oracular; like the priests of Delphi he produced messages that can be interpreted in different ways but do stimulate thought and in many cases have a considerable impact on the people who consult the oracle.

McLuhan, like his mentor, Harold Innis,[14] was a technological determinist. Like Innis he interpreted the recent history of the West as "the history of a bias of communication and a monopoly of knowledge founded on print."[15] The quotation is actually from a paper by James Carey; because of McLuhan's style of writing, it is sometimes more satisfactory to quote his interpreters.

By the "bias of communication" (which is the title of one of Innis's books) is meant the dominance of print. Both Innis and McLuhan regard this as an undesirable development. The swift growth of printed communication since the fifteenth century, Innis argues, has killed the oral tradition, replaced the temporal organization of Western society with a spatial organization, transformed religion, privatized a large portion of people's communication activities, brought about a relativity of values, shifted the locus of authority from church to state, and encouraged rampant nationalism. These are interesting and challenging insights, although most scholars would not credit so much effect exclusively to the development of print technology. Other technologies had some effect, too—fast transportation, new power sources, machinery, electronics, and with these the Revival of Learning, the growth of democracy, the rise of a middle class, the division of labor, and the stirring of a new social idealism. Granted that print had something to do with all of these, they had something to do with print, too. However, the replacement of the oral society clearly has made fundamental changes in our whole orientation to our environment; it has transferred power from those who can remember the past and the holy writ to those who know about faraway places and different ways of doing things, and it has made possible the formation and sometimes the collision of large social groups under central leadership. The changes from an oral to a media society are visible today in dozens of developing countries.

So far, these ideas are Innis's, accepted by McLuhan. McLuhan's approach to them, however, was psychological rather than institutional. It was in fact reminiscent of the Whorf-Sapir hypothesis, although McLuhan was interested in how media rather than languages influence people's view of the world and the way they think. His central idea (to quote Carey again) is that "media of communication . . . are vast social metaphors that not only transmit information but tell us what kind of world exists; that not only excite and delight our senses but, by altering the ratio of sensory equipment that we use, actually change our character." McLuhan was not the first to say that "the things on which words were written down count more than the words themselves," but his way of saying it is the one most often quoted: The medium is the massage, a phrase that became the title of his book, written with Quentin Fiore, published in 1967.

Perhaps the most interesting of McLuhan's additions to Innis is his analysis of how print has its supposed effect. He contends that communication through print imposes a "particular logic on the organization of visual experience." It breaks down reality into discrete units, logically and causally related, perceived linearly across a page, abstracted from the wholeness and disorder and multisensory quality of life. Above all, it causes an imbalance in our relation to environment by emphasizing the kind of information received through the eye rather than the kind received in personal communication from all of the senses. Because reading and writing are essentially private activities and deal with abstracted experience, they "detribalize" people, take them out of a highly knit oral culture and put them into a private situation far from the reality with which their communication deals. And of course the development of print tends to standardize the vernacular, improve distant communication, and therefore replace the village with the city and the city-state with the nation-state.

McLuhan was, therefore, attacking not only the linearity but also the abstraction of printed language, which, as we have said, is both its greatest strength and the source of many of our problems with it. In place of the ability to abstract, he was concerned with the ability to imagine. This is behind his other most-quoted concept, the distinction between "hot" and "cool" media.

A "hot" medium at one time seems to be one that does not maintain a sensory balance; at another, one that comes with the meaning relatively prefabricated and requiring as little imaginative effort as possible to leap from signs to a picture of reality. A "cool" medium, on the other hand, is one that has sensory balance and requires considerable imagination. McLuhan himself was not entirely consistent in classifying the media but considered print and radio to be "hot" media, using one sense each and (according to McLuhan) requiring relatively little imagination, whereas sound films to a certain degree and television above all are "cool media," which, McLuhan said, demand a maximum degree of imaginative effort on the part of their viewers. Strangely enough, for his conclusions concerning imagination McLuhan did not rely chiefly on the need to organize and abstract on the great amount of concrete experience furnished by television, but rather on a perceptual argument: that the television screen presents a large number of small dots of light, which the sensory and central nervous systems must organize into pictures of reality.

It is almost futile to check McLuhan's ideas against research evidence because he seldom states them in testable form and because he and his chief followers have been scornful of scientific research, arguing that it is biased in the direction of print, linearity, and logic, and unable to deal with the concepts of electronic communication. A more fruitful activity is to take those insights of McLuhan's that seem promising and follow them out in one's own thinking until one comes to a point at which testable and usable propositions can be formed. And it hardly needs saying that the effects of an age of print, of the transition from oral to media culture, and of the acts of imagination required in communication are well worth conceptualizing and studying—indeed on a much broader basis than that on which McLuhan has examined them.

However, one cannot leave McLuhan entirely in one world and all scientific scholarship in another. Perhaps the oracular quality of his writing and speaking is responsible for some of the extreme nature of his statements, but these have been picked up by amateurs with the same rigidity. Therefore, it is well to point out that whereas McLuhan's emphasis on the effect of the medium itself was salutary, still researchers have found a much larger portion of the variation in the effects of a communication within the message than within the medium. The message is the message, and the medium is the medium, and one affects the other but not to the exclusion of either. For example, could anyone argue that the effect of the news of President

Kennedy's death was determined chiefly by whether it came via television, radio, print, or word of mouth? Or that the different effects of the Kennedy news and a domestic serial can be attributed chiefly to the fact that someone received the news by print and the serial by television?

Similarly, there is no evidence that the perception and combination of the points of light on a television screen are responsible for any essential difference in effect. If this were so, we should expect the perception of halftones in a newspaper to have the same effect and the perception of type from the dots of a halftone to have an essentially different effect from that of print reproduced by offset or letterpress. Indeed, the whole question of imagination required by a given form of communication is in need of post-McLuhan rethinking, a need for which we must give McLuhan full credit. May it not be that the act of imagination necessary to translate print into a picture of reality could be greater than that required of a television viewer? Or that the absence of a sound track on silent films may actually be an invitation to imagination greater than that in sound films?

On the other hand, McLuhan's emphasis on the effect of the medium itself is useful, and his suggestions of the effect of a balance or imbalance of sensory channels and of linear print on the logic of thinking are worth further study.

CONCLUSION

These approaches seem to throw brief bright flashes, rather than a clear light, on the media of communication. Understanding the differences among forms of communication is obviously not a simple matter. It is easier to examine the mass media as institutions and organizations, which we shall do in the next chapter, and ultimately more useful to think of channels and pathways in terms of a continuing flow of information through society. Some of the flow is short range—person to person. Some of it is long range, carried by a wire or a postal service or a mass medium. Some of it reaches a single individual, some an assembled group, some a number of widely dispersed individuals or groups. Each of these ways of circulating information has its own strengths and weaknesses, its own advantages and disadvantages for any particular purpose at a given time. At various points in the system, there are people or working groups, with or without communicating machines, that multiply and distribute and put their own stamps on the flow of information.

But there is a danger in thinking of these acts of information sharing as single acts. In the wide-angle lens they are related. The flow of information does not often stop with any receiver. In one form or another it is likely to move on. And the sum of all these short and long, wide and narrow, personal and mediated relationships is the continuing surge of information that keeps society alive.

For Further Consideration

1. Most communication scholars agree that face-to-face communication is the most effective—it conveys more information, particularly of the non-verbal sort, than any other form.

   Television, among all media, most closely approximates face-to-face communication. There are significant differences, however. What are they, and what effects do they have?
2. Although several specialized uses are possible, for most people the video-tape recorder now on the market is chiefly useful for recording and storing televised material from the networks. When prices of this equipment come down to the current price of a color television set, do you believe that almost everybody will buy one? Why, or why not?
3. Systematic research aside, what are your personal feelings about the Two-Step Flow theory, based upon your own observation? In the formation of political opinions, for example? Judgments of the quality of films, books, and television programs? In which situations are you an opinion leader and in which a follower?
4. *Is* the medium the message, in your opinion—that is, is the fact that the media are involved in a particular situation of more significance than the *content* they are trying to convey?

References

For general reading: two early studies, H. Cantril and G. W. Allport, *The Psychology of Radio* (New York: Harper & Row, 1935, and P. F. Lazarsfeld, *Radio and the Printed Page* (New York: Duell, Sloan, and Pearce, 1940). See also W. Schramm, *Men, Messages, and Media* (New York: Harper & Row, 1973); E. Katz and P. F. Lazarsfeld, *Personal Influence: The Part Played by People in the Flow of Mass Communications* (New York: Free Press, 1955); and M. McLuhan, *Understanding Media: The Extensions of Man* (New York: McGraw-Hill, 1966).

1. P. J. Deutschmann. "The Sign-Situation Classification of Human Communication." *Journal of Communication*, 1967, 7, 2, 63–73.
2. D. E. Broadbent. *Perception and Communication*. Elmsford, N.Y.: Pergamon Press, 1958. R. M. W. Travers et al. *Research and Theory Related to Audiovisual Information Transmission*. Salt Lake City: Bureau of Educational Research, University of Utah, 1966.
3. G. W. Allport and L. J. Postman. "The Basic Psychology of Rumor." *Transactions of the New York Academy of Sciences*, II, 1945, 8, 61–81.

L. Festinger and J. Thibaut. "Interpersonal Communication in Small Groups." *Journal of Abnormal and Social Psychology*, 1951, *46*, 92–99.

4. P. F. Lazarsfeld, B. Berelson, and H. Gaudet. *The People's Choice*. New York: Duell, Sloan, and Pearce, 1944.

5. A. Campbell, P. E. Converse, W. E. Miller, and D. E. Stokes. *The American Voter*. New York: Wiley, 1960.

6. P. J. Deutschmann and W. Danielson. "Diffusion of Knowledge of the Major News Story." *Journalism Quarterly*, 1960, *37*, 345–355. B. S. Greenberg. "Person-to-Person Communication in the Diffusion of News Events." *Journalism Quarterly*, 1964, *41*, 489–494. Also, B. S. Greenberg and E. B. Parker, (eds.), *The Kennedy Assassination and the American Public: Social Communication in Crisis*. Stanford, Calif.: Stanford University Press, 1965, ch. 1.

7. E. M. Rogers and F. F. Shoemaker. *Communication of Innovations: A Cross-Cultural Approach*. New York: Free Press, 1971.

8. V. C. Trohldahl. "A Field Test of a Modified 'Two-Step Flow of Communication' Model." *Public Opinion Quarterly*, 1966–1967, *30*, 4, 609–623.

9. B. S. Greenberg. "Person-to-Person Communication in the Diffusion of News Events," *op. cit.*, 489–494.

10. Trohldahl, *op. cit.*

11. See summary in Rogers and Shoemaker, *op. cit.*

12. See also E. M. Rogers, "Interpersonal Communication and Mass Media." In I. Pool et al., (eds.), *Handbook of Communication*. Skokie, Ill.: Rand McNally, 1973.

13. See J. McGinniss, *The Selling of the President, 1968*. New York: Trident Press, 1969.

14. H. Innis. *The Bias of Communication*. Toronto, Canada: University of Toronto Press, 1961. Also, *Empire and Communication*. Oxford, England: Oxford University Press, 1950.

15. J. W. Carey. "Harold Adams Innis and Marshall McLuhan." *Antioch Review*, 1967, *27*, 1, 5–39.

8/
THE DIMENSIONS
OF MASS MEDIA

One afternoon in the late 1940s, in a sunny village of southern France, I heard a drum being beaten vigorously, not to say enthusiastically. In fact, someone was beating the stuffing out of the drum. People began hurrying out of houses, shops, even the church. I followed them to a tall young man, a block or two away, who was indeed beating his drum as though he wanted the world to know. When enough of us had gathered, he began to speak in a wonderfully resonant and carrying voice. He had three or four things to tell us. There was to be a meeting in a nearby town to greet General de Gaulle. There had been a fire. The National Assembly had taken an action of local importance about taxes. And a farmer had a bull for sale.

It took me a minute to realize that I was listening to a town crier. In the era of *Figaro* and *Le Monde*, communication patterns had suddenly rolled back a thousand years, and I was hearing news as people had heard it when the earliest medieval cathedrals were just being built. And—*la plus ça change, la plus que même*—it was in the form of a newscast with a commercial!

I would call the town crier one of the authentic communication media. And that brings us back to the question raised in Chapter 1: How old are the media?

It we think of media as machines interposed in the communication process to multiply and extend the delivery of information, the first mass medium was printing from movable metal type, and the great age of media development has been the period from the Industrial Revolution to the present.

However, if we think of a communication medium simply as a social institution designed to speed and extend the exchange of information, the "mass" media were latecomers to this group.

The town crier was by no means the first of the communication institutions. The school is so ancient that no one knows when a tribe first thought of gathering a group of children to be taught by a knowledgeable elder rather than by their own mothers and fathers. The church, ever since its ancient origin, has been conveying information directly and indirectly to masses of people. Libraries are at least as ancient as the clay tablets of Babylon and the stones and papyri of Alexandria. Bazaars, markets, fairs have for many thousands of years brought people together to exchange news and ideas and pleasantries. When markets or public events or circuses have not been readily available, people have developed their own ways of assembling to exchange information. Even today, in many villages of Asia the clothes-washing hour is as much a time for social communication as it is a work period. In Africa the *palaver* has long made it possible for tribal people to talk over their problems with the chief. The forums of the Mediterranean world were gathering places where people could meet, information was passed, new laws were promulgated, and decisions were taken in public view. In many parts of the world, traveling players, puppet shows, dance troupes, and ballad singers went—and still go— from community to community, entertaining and carrying information. In the Middle East the coffeehouse has long been a center for discourse as well as relaxation. And in addition to all these places where people could come to talk and be talked to and informed, there is a long tradition of "silent media": statues communicating the greatness of the gods of the ancient world, buildings and monuments communicating the achievements of a kingdom or a ruler, memorials like the Taj Mahal and the pyramids, and remarkable conceptions like the cathedral, which not only brought together a community and communicated a way of life but also taught the history of a people and what they could expect in a life to come.

These face-to-face media, like their print and electronic successors, existed to facilitate social communication. They were institutionalized around that function and organized with rules, goal expectations, professional roles, and support. Like modern media, even the most serious of them included a considerable admixture of entertainment. And the fact that most of them are still in use today is testimony to their effectiveness.

When the machine-interposed media came in, they made changes in many of the face-to-face media. The printed book made it possible in some countries to extend education to nearly all children. The newspaper added a new function to the coffeehouse. The mail-order catalog made possible a different type of bazaar, and advertising made large stores a continuous marketplace. Films and television formalized the traveling players.

Thus the modern mass media are not really something new in the world, except with respect to how far and how fast they can disperse information. They are simply the latest of a long series of efforts to gather and exchange information more efficiently. And even in content they are not so new and different. As they have to some extent remodeled the face-to-face media, so have the face-to-face media taken over the newer ones. The forum is in the press; the town crier and the ballad singer on radio; the circus, the dance troupe, and the players on television; the palaver in the broadcast press conference or interview show.

The personal channels are still active and effective side by side with the media. In Asia community development programs rely more than anyone would expect on puppet shows and traveling players. The Chinese opera has been revised to carry a political message. When Gandhi was killed, when Indian and Chinese troops fought on the roof of the world, it was word of mouth that carried the news to most of the Indian people. But that is a developing country, you say. In the United States, where there are five radios for every household, where daily newspapers and television receivers are available in almost every home, could such a situation exist? But what happened when President Kennedy was assassinated? As we noted in the preceding chapter, almost exactly half the people heard the news first by word of mouth. And how does one explain the enormous gatherings of young people in America in recent years—the rock festival at Woodstock, for example, and the political demonstrations that have drawn a hundred thousand people or more? Granted that they were stimulated and abetted by the mass media, still they were clearly a throwback to the old patterns of mass communication before machines were interposed.

THE STRUCTURE AND FUNCTION OF THE MASS MEDIA

There are several texts that describe in detail each of the mass media and deal with these institutions in their societal setting.[1] There is no need to do that here. At the same time, so much of communication study has grown out of analysis of the media, and so much remains to be done, that we must refer constantly to the media in talking about the whole process of human communication (there has been almost no study, for example, of the way living in a culture saturated with the output of the mass media affects face-to-face communication and such things as the interpretation of nonverbal messages). At this point we need to remind ourselves of some dimensions and characteristics of the media that shape the process of, to use a once-popular phrase, "people speaking to people."

This diagram (Figure 5) sets out their standard structure and function.

And this diagram (Figure 6) shows for one particular set of media, the broadcasting industry, the supporting services that develop:

The same kinds of related services cluster around the print and film media also. In fact, the structures of all of the media in the United States are much the same: (1) an organizational unit with creative, production, technical, sales, and management components; (2) in most cases privately owned; (3) with a minimum of government regulation; (4) aided by a variety of related services; (5) operating as gatekeeper, processor, and amplifier of information to (6) produce informational and entertainment products for (7) large audiences.[2]

The dimensions of the industries organized in such clusters in the United States alone are impressive (figures from 1977–1978):

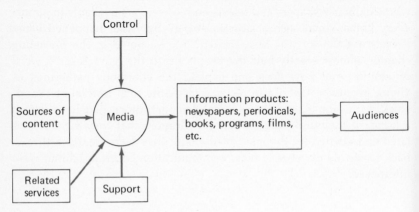

Figure 5　The basic structure of media.

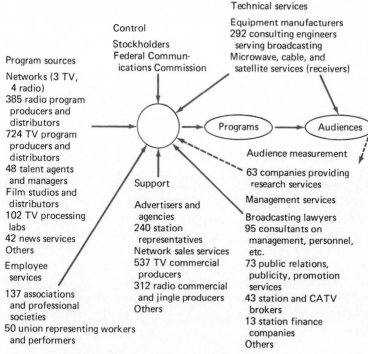

Figure 6   The dimensions of supporting services.

996 television stations (727 commercial: 516 VHF, 211 UHF; 269 noncommercial: 111 VHF, 158 UHF)

8173 radio stations (4497 AM, including 25 noncommercial; 3676 FM, including 839 noncommercial)

4001 cable television systems

1762 daily newspapers (346 published in the morning, 1435 in the evening, 650 on Sunday)

About 9000 weekly newspapers

About 9000 magazines

About 1250 book publishers (of which 50 companies issue 75 percent of the books)

About 2250 film-making organizations, including about 1000 making films for television (1976)

About 13,000 "four-wall" motion picture theaters and 3800 drive-ins (again, the figure is from 1976; since that time the number of four-wall theaters has grown enormously, through the subdivision of established theaters into multiple units and the rise of shopping center theaters)

Dollar figures are correspondingly large. As early as 1976 total receipts for the film industry were around $2.5 billion. In more recent years, the magazine industry has grossed around $2.3 billion from advertising alone; data on its circulation revenue are not available, but probably would double that figure. Recent grosses for the book-publishing industry have been over $5 billion annually. In broadcasting, television takes in more than $7 billion a year; radio, about $2 billion. Newspapers recently have grossed around $10 billion a year from advertising alone. In other words, the mass media are something like a $30-billion-a-year industry.

About half of the world's radio receivers and one-third of all the world's television receivers are in the United States. More than half the world's consumption of newsprint takes place in the United States. The enormous amount of newsprint used here, however, reflects the size and number of American papers rather than the number of copies sold. Among the nations of the world, the United States stands well down the list in number of copies of daily newspapers per thousand people (with 287, as against Sweden's 572, Japan's 526, and the United Kingdom's 400; such countries as New Zealand, Australia, Denmark, Switzerland and West Germany are ahead of the United States as well).

SUPPORT OF THE MEDIA

In the United States system the pattern of media support is private enterprise with a minimum of government intervention. Some broadcasting stations are owned by state universities or school systems. Both state and federal agencies carry on a certain amount of publishing, and the U.S. Government Printing Office might be considered the largest publishing house in the country. But the government does nothing or practically nothing with general-interest material or news. This is chiefly the province of private ownership and enterprise.

This pattern of support and ownership is by no means typical of support throughout the world. About 69 percent of the world's radio broadcasting systems are operated either by government or a public corporation created by government, and more than 15 percent of the remaining systems are partly government, partly private. In television, almost 60 percent of the systems are operated by a government agency or a public corporation, and 16 percent are partly government, partly private. Only 13 percent of the radio systems and 21 percent of the television systems are wholly privately owned, and these are mostly in the Americas. There is a somewhat larger proportion of private ownership in the world press than in broadcasting, but in the socialist countries the press is thoroughly integrated into the political system, as it is in many of the less developed countries.

Another variation on the American system is represented by such countries as France and Italy, where publications frequently are kept alive by covert subsidization. Since the early 1970s, for example, not a single Italian daily newspaper has made a profit and most have undergone continuing massive yearly losses. Yet the country has had a total of around 80 dailies throughout the period. The subsidies that keep them going come in a variety of forms.

Political parties openly own a few and pay their deficits; some have been owned by huge industrial organizations, most of which have to be kept alive, in turn, by government support; government directly contributes aid in forms ranging from tax relief to cash handouts.

Newspapers in other Western countries benefit to some extent from the same kind of help, generally covert. They do not bear, in most cases, an identifiable stamp of conscious political manipulation. The chief difference between them and the press of the United States rests in the fact that their existence is dissociated from their ability to attract readers; they are not creatures of the market economy.

The nature of support differs among the privately owned American media. Television and radio, of course, receive their money wholly from the sale of advertising. On the other hand, books are financed entirely by the sale of copies; and films (except those that appear on television), predominantly by the sale of admissions to theaters, although a small fraction of the exhibitor's income comes from theater advertising. Newspapers and magazines, on the other hand, depend both on subscriptions and on advertising, with advertising the senior partner. Between 60 and 75 percent of the cost of a newspaper or a magazine is likely to come from advertising; the subscription price that we pay typically covers less than one-third of the total cost of producing and delivering the journal or periodical to us.

One end of this spectrum might be called *indirect* support and, with a mixed area in between, the other *direct* public support. Although there are no tickets to buy and no subscriptions to pay for most television, still the average American home contributes over $300 a year indirectly to the cost of advertising.[3] In countries where broadcasting is a part of government or under a public corporation, users pay through general taxes or a tax on receiving sets.

These differences in patterns of support help us understand two parallel currents that seem to be flowing in our mass media. On the one hand there is a strong trend toward reducing competitive ownership in large city newspapers and toward the formation of both newspaper and broadcasting chains owned by the same individuals or companies. In 1910, when there were 1200 cities in the United States with daily newspapers, 57 percent of those had competing managements; today, when 1536 cities have dailies, only 2.3 percent of them (a total of 35 cities in the whole country) have competing managements. And fewer than a dozen cities have competing papers issued at the same hour of the day—that is, two morning or two evening papers under different managements.

The figures on newspaper chains tell the same story. In 1910, when newspaper titans like Heart and Scripps were active, only 3 percent of the dailies in the country were owned by chains; today, the figure is about 63 percent. The largest four chains in the country (Knight-Ridder, Gannett, Newhouse, Tribune Co.) have 22 percent of the country's total circulation.

Between 1939 and 1969 the percentage of AM radio stations owned by chains increased from 14 percent to 31 percent. Although the FCC forbids any owner to have more than seven television stations, of which only five can be VHF, still the number of individuals and corporations owning three or more stations increased from 34 to 119 between 1956 and 1976. In the top 50 markets of the country, where 75 percent of the American people live, the three major networks—NBC, CBS, ABC—have over 90 percent of the measured cumulative audience, which means that three programming organizations furnish well over 75 percent of all the television viewed in America.

So, on the one hand, there is a powerful trend toward concentration of ownership and less competition. On the other hand, there is what looks like an opposite trend. Some of the largest magazines in the country have gone out of business in the past 30 years, but smaller and specialized magazines are flourishing. Despite the concentration in television and AM radio, there has been a very large growth in small radio stations (largely FM) and a considerable growth in UHF television. Moreover, as large city newspapers have diminished in number, suburban newspapers have increased in both number and affluence, and there has been a modest but significant development of what were once called "underground" newspapers in the form of antiestablishment weeklies.

In part, the change in broadcast ownership trends is an artifact of the FCC requirement that all television sets receive UHF signals. UHF has therefore looked to some people like a potentially good long-term investment, although it has not proved very profitable over the short term. Furthermore, the growth in the number of FM receivers and the possibility of establishing FM radio stations with low capital cost and very low program cost, inasmuch as they could broadcast mostly recorded music, have made it more tempting to enter that field. But that is only part of it.

The tradition of American media has been a highly competitive one, as might be expected of private ownership. This competition has been partly in ideas and service but even more, of late, for audience and the resultant income. It is hardly conceivable that American commercial networks would establish something like the BBC's Third Programme, which was designed deliberately to appeal to highly educated listeners and a highly rarefied atmosphere of taste—and consequently reaches a very small audience. In a system like ours the rewards have come with large audiences because that is where the advertising goes.

In the printed media the bulk of the cost comes in making the physical product. The larger the circulation, the greater is the proportion of the cost that goes into printing and delivery. For example, as Ben Bagdikian points out in his *The Information Machines,* a small paper that grosses $4 million a year will spend half of it on printing and circulation, a paper with a $14 million gross will spend $8 million on the posteditorial functions, and a paper with a $60 million annual gross will spend $40 million of it for paper, production, and distribution.[4] In any case, the subscriber usually pays no more than half of the paper's manufacturing costs alone.

The costs of printing and newsprint have been rising rapidly. This means that there is some point at which bigness ceases to be more profitable than smallness. Advertising charges for large magazines can only be raised so far, lest advertisers turn to competitive media like television. Therefore, a very large general magazine comes to a point of growth at which income no longer rises with circulation. Subscribers pay perhaps 25 percent of the cost of the copy they buy. If advertising does not pay the rest of it, the periodical is in trouble. This is why it has proved more profitable in recent years to operate magazines at a middle level of circulation rather than a very high level.

What does this mean for newspapers? If two newspapers in a large market can merge, the total advertising income of both can be concentrated in one at higher rates. If two newspapers with separate managements can combine their printing and distribution departments, they can handle these at lower unit costs, and there may also be some advantage in offering advertisers a combined rate for using the two papers. Consequently, there have been a number of mergers in recent years.

What does it mean for broadcasting? In the case of broadcasting stations, there is little cost increase with increasing audience. Once the basic expenses of studio and transmitter have been met, the operation is no more expensive for an audience of a million people than for one of 20,000. The chief cost variable is programming. In the case of even a medium-sized station, about a third of the budget goes to programming and only about 10 or 15 percent to technical operation. (The remainder is sales and management.) It is the ability of programs to attract audiences that makes the difference in the attractiveness of the station to advertisers. The primary requisite of commercial broadcasting, therefore, is programs that attract large general audiences. This is why high-cost entertainment programs from the three networks are so important in determining how the viewing audience is distributed among stations.

In the long view, however, not all of these developments can be explained in economic terms. The magazines that are comparatively most profitable now are specialized ones serving particular interests and needs rather than general tastes. There has been a great trend toward specialization in radio—news stations, talk stations, music stations of different kinds, even "underground" and "overground" rock music stations. There has been a reaction against the pattern of the successful metropolitan newspaper, which now consists typically of general news plus a great many entertaining features. The attraction of serving local interests, as in the suburban communities, has been rediscovered. Some publishers have gone back 150 years and resurrected the pattern of underground special interest newspaper. In television, attractive alternatives to the large general interest network programs have been discovered by some independent stations, presenting movies, reruns, sports, and syndicated nonnetwork programs. A number of these have done well. And the noncommercial "public" stations, supported by community organizations and offering a local and high-taste alternative to commercial programming, have noticeably increased their audiences.

Theoretically, then, it would seem that there are both economic and taste correctives limiting the tendency of a private enterprise system to concentrate ownership in one place and as much of the audience as possible on a single set of general programs that please most and offend none. For magazines, at least, there seems to be a point of growth beyond which few enterprises can operate profitably. For both broadcasting and print there seems to be a limit to the attractiveness of bland, self-imitating, general audience programming and content. Beyond this, the way forward seems to be to pay attention to special audience interests and needs.

THE EXTENSIONS OF MEDIA:
THE KNOWLEDGE INDUSTRY

Early in this chapter it was pointed out that much of the consideration of communication has to begin with the mass media (and most
of the remainder of this book is concerned with them). Nevertheless,
it would be a sorry mistake to regard the dimensions set out thus
far as the limits of what the concept of "media" implies. Indeed, one
thing the machine-interposed media, particularly the electronic media,
have done is to help create an enormous knowledge industry in the
world that had no parallel before their time. Fritz Machlup, a Princeton
economist, summed up this development in admirable fashion in
1962, in a volume he titled *The Knowledge Industry*. At the time of
this writing, he is revising and elaborating this work in a series of
volumes. The figures that follow are updated from other sources, but
Machlup's analytical categories from the first volume still stand.[5]

The knowledge industry is organized along these lines:

Multipliers of messages: the mass media—newspapers, magazines,
books, films, radio, television

Carriers of messages: telephone, telegraph, postal services, satellite systems, and so forth

Providers of information for individual needs: libraries, abstract
services, computer services, data banks, and the like

Manufacturers and maintainers: printing organizations, makers of
electronic and printing equipment, technicians to install and
service the machines interposed in the media, and so forth

Special services contributing to content: news agencies, studios to
make programs, writers, performers, artists, designers of educational materials, makers of computer programs, and so forth

Economic support agencies: advertising agencies and departments,
distribution and sales agencies, and others

Administrative support agencies: legal counsel and guidance, publicity and public relations, financial and accounting services,
administrative consultants, and the like

Personnel support: unions and trade associations, organizations for
in-service and pre-service training of personnel, talent agencies,
and so forth

Data-gathering services: general research and development, field
and audience research, intelligence-gathering services, opinion
research, censuses and other major suppliers of statistics, and so
forth

Education: schools and colleges, universities, home-study opportunities, special schools for industry, for the military, for government, and so forth

It goes without saying that these activities represent a substantial part of our gross national expenditure. Hard figures require not only detailed analysis but elaborate explanation and definition. Even a quick scan, however, of data for 1978–1979 indicates that the United States is spending over $300 billion, perhaps as much as $350 billion, or somewhere in the neighborhood of 20 percent of the gross national product in the "knowledge" area.

About a decade ago, Bagdikian calculated that the average U.S. household spent $688 a year for communication services—telephone, newspapers, radio, television, tapes and discs, books, and postal service. A rough projection of the same categories for 1980 shows that figure to have risen to over $1300. Such a figure does not include some other elements of the knowledge industry, including, most importantly, education.

The average American household spent $1987 on education in 1978. That figure has risen dramatically since the first edition of this book in 1973, when the cost per family for education was around $1000; the gross national figure has gone from $75.3 billion in 1971 to $151 billion for 1978, about 8 percent of the gross national product for that year.

In addition to that, public libraries alone (excluding private and special libraries) cost $770 million in 1977. It also is important to take into consideration such categories as (the figures are in millions of dollars):

Postal service (1978) $18,000
Telephone   " $41,953
Telegraph   " $ 555; $397 for overseas cables
Research and development (1976)
     $35,581
Printing and publishing (1978)
     $42,838 (includes printing of newspapers, books, and periodicals; the bill for business forms alone was $2,328)
Paper mills, excluding building paper (1978)
     $ 6,385
Office and computing machinery (1978)
     $15,700

Photographic equipment and supplies (1978)
$ 5,600
Advertising (all kinds, estimated for 1978)
$43,000

The number of skilled workers involved in the knowledge industry can be suggested by the fact that there are over three million teachers in schools and colleges, about 650,000 postal employees, about 823,000 telephone employees, and over 400,000 newspaper employees. (It is interesting to observe that the number of both telephone and postal employees has gone down over the past decade, for the most part reflecting the development of new technology.) Add to these the numbers engaged in printing, in the manufacture and maintenance of all kinds of communication equipment, in the broadcast and film media, in publishing other than daily newspapers, in libraries and research and advertising, and it is apparent that the knowledge industry employs a substantial part of the American labor force and that these employees include a very large proportion of the nation's highly trained workers.

The main thrust of the figures we have given is not merely that the knowledge industry is a very large one intimately connected to all other industry, but rather how intimately it touches the life of every home.

The average family in America:

has one young person in school or college
has one television receiver (the actual figure is nearly 1.5 receivers per average home)
has several radios
receives a daily newspaper
receives one or two magazines
has a small shelf of books
makes seven telephone calls a day and calls long distance every other day
indirectly supports over $500 worth of advertising per year
is the recipient of whatever comes out of about $100 per year spent on basic research and an additional amount, very hard to estimate, on developmental research

Of course, not many homes are likely to fit this description exactly. Many homes have no children in schools; many others have several schoolchildren. Some homes receive several newspapers, and a few receive none. Similarly, one household may actually be spending thousands of dollars on communication activities and services (particularly when the children are in college), while another is spending only a few hundred. But the knowledge industry is in the life pattern of modern society alongside food, housing, automobiles, and the other services that are omnipresent in our everyday lives.

For Further Consideration

This rather brief chapter serves mainly to present some facts and figures, but the following are interesting questions:

1. Why should the the Japanese, the English, and the Swedes read many more newspapers than U.S. citizens? (A condition that has been true, incidentally, since the first collections of comparative data, long before television.)
2. In the 1960s the idea of taking almost all authority away from the FCC—including even assigning frequencies for transmission—was put forward. In one form or another, the same idea has been put forward in several bills introduced in Congress. The fundamental idea is to make broadcasting, as much as newspaper operation, completely responsive to marketplace considerations.
   What seem to you to be the pros and cons of this idea?

References

1. Among these, E. Emery, P. Ault, and W. Agee, *Introduction to Mass Communication* (New York: Harper & Row, 1979); P. Sandman, D. Rubin, and D. Sachsman, *Mass Media* (Englewood Cliffs, N.J.: Prentice-Hall, 1972); and D. Pember, *Mass Media in America* (Chicago: Science Research Associates, 1977).
2. I. Pool et al., (eds.). *Handbook of Communication.* Skokie, Ill.: Rand McNally, 1973.
3. B. H. Bagdikian estimated $306 in *The Information Machines: Their Impact on Men and the Media.* New York: Harper & Row, 1971, pp. 207 ff.
4. Ibid., p. 174.
5. F. Machlup. *The Production and Distribution of Knowledge in the United States.* Princeton, N.J.: Princeton University Press, 1962. The new series is entitled *Knowledge: Its Creation, Distribution, and Economic Significance,* and Volume One, *Knowledge and Knowledge Production,* was published in late 1980 by the Princeton University Press.

9/
SENDERS, RECEIVERS, AND THE PROCESS OF CHOOSING

Our primary concern with the mass media in this book is with their role in the whole process of human communication, which is another way of saying their role in society. This chapter takes a look at the process through which media professionals choose the material that is to be printed or broadcast or filmed and offered to the audience; the makeup of the audiences that choose what is offered; and *what* they choose.

It might be noted in beginning that media audiences in the United States, with rare exceptions, are self-selected; they have freedom to choose. Those who start a new magazine set out the first issue in hope there will be enough people out there who like it to make it pay; the network programmers schedule the first installments of a new situation comedy and wait for the brutal, but casual, judgment that will cost them millions if it goes the wrong way; the book publisher decides that even if more than 400 new cookbooks are published in the United States each year, there is an audience for one more. It is almost impossible to compel people to read or watch or listen. Given the fact that mass media operate in a market economy, the self-selected character of audiences is of enormous importance.

For their part, the professionals who produce the mass media are substantially free from outside authority that might dictate what they must produce (there are, of course, powerful influences in traditional practices, commercial considerations, the need for structural efficiency, and other factors). Essentially the relationship between producer and consumer in the American system is a voluntary and complex one.

SELECTING THE NEWS

The way the media are organized tells us a great deal about how they must necessarily operate and the problems they have. Their function is to make information widely, speedily, readily available. In systems, they are chiefly filters and amplifiers. They select from all the information available to them in society the items they wish to circulate. They process and amplify these for a very large audience.

The act of selection is probably the most important part of their operation. Instead of referring to them as filters, let us use the term *gatekeeper*, which Kurt Lewin contributed to social psychology. The mass media are among the chief gatekeepers of the flow of information through society.

Gatekeepers are placed throughout the information network. They include the reporter, deciding what facts to put down about a court trial or an accident or a political demonstration; the editor, deciding what to print and what to discard from the wire news; the author, deciding what kinds of people and events to write about and what view of life to present; the publisher's editor, deciding what authors to publish and what to cut out of their manuscripts; the television or film producer, deciding where to point the camera; the film editor, deciding what to edit out and leave on the cutting-room floor; the librarian, deciding what books to purchase; the teacher, deciding what textbooks or teaching films to use; the briefing officer, deciding what facts to tell superiors; and even the husband at the dinner table, deciding what to tell his wife about the day's events at the office.

How this function affects the product can be illustrated from any medium, but perhaps nowhere as spectacularly as in the case of news. In the first place, the drop-off between sender and ultimate receiver may be prodigious. A typical newspaper that receives both the Associated Press's "slow" service—about 72,000 words in the 12-hour news cycle—and its high-speed service—which carries 864,000 words in the same period—may have almost a million words to choose from —and what originally went on the wire may have been only a fraction of what was considered significant at the point of origin.

The study of how a gatekeeper works—how a decision is made, what to pass on, what to change, and what to refuse passage—is therefore one of the truly significant topics in communication research. David Manning White made a very interesting study of a newspaper gatekeeper 30 years ago in Illinois—a wire editor who frankly admitted his prejudices and hoped that because he recognized them he could still decide as objectively as possible.[1] The Lang study of the MacArthur parade in Chicago showed how much more exciting television made the event appear than it seemed to people who were present.[2] The studies of what happens to rumors as they pass from person to person and the investigation by Tannenbaum and Gerbner as to why journals use the material they do on mental health and illness have been gatekeeper studies. Research of this kind is valuable in two ways: By showing how the gatekeeping is done, it gives the audience a better idea of how to evaluate what comes through the gate; in addition, it challenges a gatekeeper to evaluate the reasons for selecting and rejecting.[3]

The speed with which the mass media operate is one of the factors that make their gatekeeping so difficult. Book publishers have several months, if necessary, to decide on a manuscript, and then they have additional months in which to edit and improve it if they decide to publish. A news editor on a daily newspaper has an entirely different problem.

Several years ago, well before the advent of high-speed wires, Ben Bagdikian reported an observation study of one news editor on a suburban evening paper.[4] Between 6 A.M. and 1 P.M. this gatekeeper processed 110,000 words of news, including 5,000 words of local news that took special attention. He decided to use about 20,000 words. He inspected 96 wirephotos and selected 16. He went through a number of press releases, approving or discarding. He made and remade the dummies of the news pages. He was responsive to updates and rewrites. He talked to reporters and others. All this was done in the seven hours of the editing day. Perhaps the figure on which to focus our attention is the 110,000 words of copy that passed over this editor's desk in the course of the day. This is the size of a slightly larger than average book.

Move one step farther along the scale of speed, and consider what happens in a television studio where a news event is being reported. A gatekeeper, the program director, sits with eyes focused on three or four monitors. Two of them may have different camera angles on the scene being broadcast; a third may have a feed from another location; a fourth may hold a visual intended to explain something that is going on or expected to go on. This gatekeeper has to point at one of the monitors or flip a switch to determine what the viewer is going to see on the screen in the next second. The gatekeeper doesn't have a year or a few hours; the decision must be made in a split second. There isn't time to think it over or research it or ask advice. As Walter Cronkite said in his book *Challengers of Change,* this is truly a new form of editing and a new skill in the world of news.[5]

What gets past the gatekeeper must then be handed over to a different group of people to be amplified and distributed. In the case of a newspaper, it goes to the printers and the circulation department. In radio or television, it goes to the studio and transmitter engineers.

This is one of the peculiar characteristics of the media. The creative and production people, the writers and editors and skilled studio technicians, are responsible for the product on the basis of which audiences buy or do not buy, tune in or tune out. But their work on the product is completed as soon as it leaves their hands. Thereafter it must be turned over to technical and business people. The technical people are responsible for the quality of the picture that reaches the picture tubes or the appearance of the copy that comes to the reading tables of the media audience. The sales people are responsible for the advertising, subscriptions, and copy sales that keep the medium in business. One division of the business staff is responsible for delivering copies of the printed media. And management is responsible for keeping these complex and very different components of the medium working together.

The mass media—in a bigger, more professional way and with incomparably more audience—do exactly what individuals do in the network of social communication. They too decide what information to select, how to process it, what to pass on. The medium is, in effect, a communal sensory apparatus, central nervous system, and communicating musculatures. This is what makes the operation of a newspaper or a broadcasting station seem to anyone who views it closely a "slight miracle." Management, backed by role prescriptions, training, and tradition, has the task of coordinating the work of hundreds of individuals so that they function like one communicating person.

Because each component of the organization is really serving as part of this single communicating person, each has an influence on the product. The part played by the content staff—writers, editors, performers, producers, and so forth—is, of course, basic. But some of the decisions on what the medium will carry are essentially technical ones: Is it "television"—meaning, is there a significant visual component? Will the scene photograph well? Can the sound be made good enough? In the print media, how much copy can be set in time for the edition? Will there be time or machines to reset a story to include new developments? How many stories should be on an attractive front page? Can we get a camera to the scene of the news?

There are other decisions that depend largely on salespeople. One of the most important for a newspaper is, How many columns of news will the day's advertising justify? For television or radio, Can enough local advertising be sold to pay for a particular program that comes without network support? What kinds of programs will attract advertising, and what kinds will not? If a public service program draws a small audience and the audience of the following commercial program is correspondingly reduced, will the advertising sponsors cancel out?

Management obviously has an influence on the product too. The publisher or station manager represents the owner. The organization works for the owner, who has the right to say what kind of medium it should be. Most management stays close to editorial policy but has little to do directly with the content of news or local programs or features. Even so, the viewpoints and preferences of management are often communicated subtly and silently to writers, editors, and producers. An illuminating study of the newspaper was Warren Breed's "Social Control in the News Room," which grew out of a long period of participant observation and demonstrated quite conclusively that the news staff learned readily what management wanted simply by noting what behavior was rewarded, although this was never overtly stated.[6]

The "slight miracle" is the welding of all of these viewpoints and activities and sometimes divergent and conflicting interests, all of these individual communicators and their networks of communication within the organization, into a single efficiently operating unit that submerges individual personalities in an organizational personality.

THE AUDIENCES OF MASS COMMUNICATION

On a typical winter evening, about one hundred million Americans are likely to be watching television (a modest increase in numbers over the past decade reflects the growth in population; the percentage of the populace watching has remained steady). On any weekday, over 61 million copies of daily newspapers will be read by 92 million people. The approximately 75 percent of American adults who read newspapers regularly spend an average of 35 minutes a day on them; the approximately 40 percent of Americans who read magazines regularly spend an average of 33 minutes per day on them; the one-third of Americans who read books regularly spend an average of 47 minutes a day on them. The television receiver in an average American home (if there *is* an average home) is turned on more than six hours a day during the winter months, and all the media together absorb more than five hours per day of an average American's time (if there *is* an average American)—more than is allocated to anything else except work and sleep.

It is no news that mass media audiences are very large in the

United States, and indeed in most other countries where media are widely available. Of greater interest to us is the pattern we can discern in this impressive amount of media use.

PATTERNS THROUGH LIFE

American children born in the 1970s or 1980s will become acquainted, even in their first year, with the activity on the picture tube whether or not they understand what is going on. They may find that television is occasionally their surrogate baby-sitter. They will hear the radio. They will have stories read to them and will be shown printed pictures. After a while they will find these pictures themselves and probably ask for the television to be turned on. The electronic media will dominate their experience until they learn to read. At that time there will be an enormous expansion of interests and ability to understand new concepts, and the wonders of print will begin to compete with the marvels of the picture tube.

The amount of exposure to media in the early years is startling to anyone who has not recently observed children. Yet it was already the prevailing pattern in the early years of television, as Table 4 shows.

Nielsen figures show an increase in average hours of viewing per week by children 2 to 11 years of age, from 19.2 hours in 1967 to 21.9 in 1976; and from 9.7 hours to 24.8 hours during the same nine years by teen-agers 12 to 17 years old.[7] So far as the age of beginning television viewing and the amount of viewing during early years are concerned, John Murray and Susan Kippax have pointed out that there are wide differences in results from various countries, but that

Table 4 CUMULATIVE PERCENTAGE OF CHILDREN WHO HAVE BEGUN TO USE GIVEN MEDIA BY A GIVEN AGE (SAN FRANCISCO, 1958, N = 754)

Age	TV	Radio	Maga-zines	Comic Books	Movies	BOOKS Read to Them	They Read	NEWSPAPERS Read to Them	They Read
2	14	11	3	1	0	38	0	0	0
3	37	20	11	6	8	58	0	0	0
4	65	27	20	17	21	72	2	4	0
5	82	40	33	35	39	74	9	9	0
6	91	47	41	50	60	75	40	12	9
7	94	53	53	61	70	75	73	12	44
8	95	62	59	68	76	75	86	12	59

SOURCE: W. Schramm, J. Lyle, and E. B. Parker. *Television in the Lives of Our Children.* Stanford, Calif.: Stanford University Press, 1961, p. 218.

they seem to be tied to the hours of available broadcast more than to anything else.[8] Donald Roberts refers to wide variations among studies, the "elusiveness" of the concept of the average child viewer, and comments that the data from Schramm, Lyle, and Parker, quoted above, "have generally stood the test of time."[9]

In the first eight or ten years of life, family patterns of media use have most influence on the time children spend and the content they seek in the media. In the next ten years, their media behavior reflects the development of their reading skill, the broadening of their knowledge and interests, the influence of school and peer groups, the demands and uncertainties of teen-age role as they search for their own identity and their place in life, and the maturing of their tastes and needs toward adulthood. At first their media choices are mostly for entertainment: comics, entertainment programs on television, popular music. As they experiment with teen-age roles, they find it socially attractive to go out for entertainment and information to movies and the public library. Beginning in the early teens, they bring schoolwork to do at home. They often study to the background of rock music on their transistor radios but have less time for television. As their interests broaden, their tastes broaden also. They read fewer comics, more about hobbies or careers. They begin to read some public affairs news in the newspaper. Some children even discover the editorials. As the younger children turn toward slapstick and fantasy, the teen-agers consult advice columns.

Here is another table (Table 5) that shows the general pattern:

Table 5 AVERAGE TELEVISION
VIEWING BY AGE

Age	Hours per Day
2	.3
4	2.2
6	2.3
8	2.5
10	3.5
12	3.9
14	3.8
16	3.6
18	3.1
20	2.9

SOURCE: A composite of five studies drawn by D. F. Roberts in G. Comstock et al., *Television and Human Behavior.* New York: Columbia University Press, 1978, p. 178.

In the second ten years of life there appears to be a maturing of tastes, a reflection of new social roles, and a reduction in time given to mass media after the middle teens, when the demands of school and social life compete seriously with the media for time.

In the adult years television, newspapers, and radio are almost universal media. Television receivers are in about 95 percent of American homes; radios, in about 98 percent (as well as in 75 million automobiles and 10 million public places). Newspapers come into about 85 percent of all homes. Moreover, the use of television and newspapers (no directly comparable figures are now available for radio) rises or remains fairly stable at a high level during adulthood. Newspaper reading falls off slightly from a peak in the 40s, possibly because of vision changes, whereas television is actually used more in the years after 55. One of the remarkable findings of audience research is the amount of use given the mass media by people in their older years, when the media may be serving to combat loneliness and alienation from the central activities of society. Nielsen data of 1976 showed correlated increases in viewing time and age from age 12 onward. Women over 50 at that point were viewing an average of five hours per day, up a fraction of an hour from 1967; men over 50 were viewing about 4.6 hours per day.

Newspaper reading showed the same general trend, with about 79 percent of the 50-plus population, but with a sharp drop-off above age 65. Teen-agers and young adults, however, have been increasing television usage while abandoning newspapers; television viewing increased two to four hours a week in both groups, while the percentage of readers went down a full ten points between 1961 and 1973.

Newspapers, television, and radio, as we have said, can be considered universal media. They reach into almost all homes, have cumulative reading audiences of over 100 million a week, and show spectacular records for individual audiences.

For example, according to Nielsen figures, 20 individual programs between 1960 and 1977 drew more than 40 percent of the total viewing homes (the largest, the last installment of "Roots," broadcast in January 1977, drew 51.1 percent). Most of these audiences, in other words, numbered between 50 million and 75 million viewers. Routine prime-time viewing involves audiences of 25 million to 35 million.

What about magazines and movies? According to the Magazine Publishers Association, 90 percent of the U.S. population are magazine readers. Statistics on movie attendance over the years have been spotty because the tendency of the industry has been to be secretive, but figures released for 1980 indicated that audiences were down to less than 20 million per week, less than one-third of what they were

Table 6   U.S. TV-VIEWING AUDIENCES

	Men (percent)	Women (percent)	Teenagers (percent)	Children (percent)
Mon–Fri				
10 a.m.–1 p.m.	8	26	9	8
1 p.m.–5 p.m.	15	25	30	45
All nights				
1:30 p.m.–11 p.m.	47	54	42	53

SOURCE: Adapted from Nielsen data as presented in C. J. Sterling and T. R. Haight. *The Mass Media: Aspen Institute Guide to Communication Industry Trends.* New York: Praeger, 1978, p. 375.

when the industry was at its pretelevision peak. Even so, a more accurate measurement should perhaps count the audiences of movie reruns on television, where most film viewing now takes place.

What information do we have about media use by time of day? The early hours of the day belong to radio; the later ones, to television. Nielsen reports that the use of television doubles, at least, at night, and that the daytime audience is largely women and children, although even in the evening hours women make up a larger part of the audience than do men, as Table 6 shows.

PATTERNS OF TASTE

We can get an idea of television tastes from the following figures compiled by Nielsen for 1976. The rather surprising thing about them is how little variation there is by type. The greatest variation, of course, is between the commercial networks and public television. The audiences for the latter are much smaller; cumulative audience figures for a one week period reached only 31.4 percent of television homes. Nevertheless, the public television audience is increasing; the same measurement in 1966 showed only 13 percent. The gain probably represents the growing popularity of such prime-time series as "Monty Python" and "Upstairs, Downstairs."

The commercial networks still command the mass audience, however. In Table 7 we have prime-time Nielsen figures for commercial programs for fall, 1976.

The remarkable similarity of these figures is carried on in specific breakdowns for age and sex: women, by a slight margin, are the heaviest viewers, but the audience composition from one category to another is remarkably alike. Such apparent lack of discrimination may say something very significant about the seriousness and intensity with which the average viewer watches; the only important decision, perhaps, is whether or not to turn the set on. Once it's on, the specific

Table 7 NIELSEN AUDIENCE RATINGS FOR DIFFERENT KINDS OF PRIME-TIME NETWORK PROGRAMS (FALL, 1976)

Type	Average Rating (percent)
General drama	19.0
Suspense & mystery	18.5
Situation comedy	20.1
Variety	14.9
Feature films	21.5

program is likely to be watched whatever it is, at least to the point where it creates genuine distaste.

Nevertheless, changing tastes are worthy of much more study than they have received. One of the most significant trends in the currently available evidence is the pattern of change in taste through life. As people grow older and begin to value knowledge and wisdom more and physical accomplishment less, they turn more toward serious public affairs content in the media. This can be illustrated, for example, by Steiner's 1963 study of the television audience (Table 8).

Schramm and White found a steady increase in the amount of public affairs news, as compared with features, read in newspapers throughout six ten-year groupings beginning with the teens. The same study found that the reading of editorials increased steadily through age 60, while the reading of comics declined, sports reading fell after the 20s, and reading of crime and disaster news decreased after the 30s. Handel found somewhat similar changes in tastes in his early study of the movie audience (Table 9).

This seems to be a very general trend. The question is, What lies behind it? In order to answer the question, we must consider what effect education has on media behavior.

Table 8 PROPORTION OF INFORMATION PROGRAMS COMPARED TO ENTERTAINMENT PROGRAMS SELECTED BY DIFFERENT AGE GROUPS (1960 NATIONAL SURVEY, TOTAL, $N = 2427$)

Age	Percentage Information vs. Entertainment	Ave. Number Information Programs per Viewer per Week
Under 25	20	5.2
25–34	33	8.9
35–44	31	8.8
45–54	35	11.2
55–64	44	16.4
65 and over	48	22.4

SOURCE: G. Steiner. *The People Look at Television.* New York: Knopf, 1963, p. 178.

EDUCATION AND MEDIA USE

Most scholars find that education correlates more closely than any other variable with patterns of information intake, and age and education together account for a high proportion of the variance in media habits. For example, the choice of "serious" media content increases with both age and education. This can be illustrated by another of Steiner's tables (Table 10).

Although these data are now 20 years old, later research confirms their accuracy so far as general direction and proportion are concerned. George Comstock and his fellow authors in 1979 found that little was

Table 9 CHANGING LIKES AND DISLIKES FOR DIFFERENT TYPES OF MOTION PICTURE STORIES, BY AGE AND PERCENT (1942 SURVEY IN 45 CITIES AND TOWNS, N = 2000)

Age	Slapstick	Mystery, Horror	History, Biography	Serious Drama
12–16				
Like	4.0	8.5	3.8	5.1
Dislike	4.4	7.6	8.7	6.4
17–29				
Like	2.4	5.4	5.8	10.3
Dislike	10.8	8.3	7.3	3.9
30–44				
Like	2.9	4.5	6.3	10.8
Dislike	11.0	10.4	4.5	2.9
45 and over				
Like	1.1	5.3	7.1	12.2
Dislike	12.6	11.3	3.7	5.3

SOURCE: L. A. Handel. *Hollywood Looks at Its Audience.* Urbana: University of Illinois Press, 1950, p. 125.

Table 10 PERCENTAGES OF DIFFERENT KINDS OF TELEVISION PROGRAMS CHOSEN BY PERSONS OF DIFFERENT AGE AND EDUCATION (1960 NATIONAL SURVEY, N = 2428)

Age	HIGH SCHOOL OR LESS			
	Light Entertainment	Heavy Entertainment	News	Information and Public Affairs
Under 35	76	3	22	2
35–54	66	3	27	4
55 and over	56	3	34	7
	COLLEGE OR BEYOND			
Under 35	53	9	33	5
35–54	59	7	28	6
55 and over	38	2	47	13

SOURCE: G. Steiner. *The People Look at Television.* New York: Knopf, 1963, p. 177.

changed in the relationships between selection of media material and educational level; the only alteration of any significance was an increase in television viewing by the educated during the 1970s, with the gradual effect of eroding the differences.[10]

This table shows a fairly strong positive relationship of both age and education to the choice of television news and public affairs material, and a negative relationship to the choice of entertainment. Lazarsfeld and Kendall found a strong relationship between education and the reading of books and magazines but a weaker one between age and reading.[11] Link and Hopf, in a study made when radio was still dominant and television was just beginning to come in, found that time of use and percentage of readers making use of print both increased with education, but radio and movies were used less by college-educated people than by those with less education.[12] Lazarsfeld and Kendall also found that radio listening decreased with education. Handel found that movie attendance definitely fell off (in the heyday of theater movies) among older people in highly educated groups.[13] Steiner, too, discovered that the more education people had, the fewer television programs they were likely to see a week.

But the amount of leisure time available to different people must be taken into account. More highly educated people are likely to go out to meetings and concerts, have more memberships and civic responsibilities, and have more money to seek entertainment outside their homes. And they become busier as they grow older. Consequently, they have less time for the media. This argument is made cogently by Samuelson, Carter, and Ruggles. By statistically manipulating the media-use reports of a sample of San Francisco adult males so as to allow for the amount of available leisure, they were able to obtain small but positive correlations between education and the use of radio and television, and strong and positive correlations between education and the use of printed media (somewhat weaker for newspapers than for books and magazines).[14] It is reasonable, therefore, to suppose that within the limits of free time, human appetite for *all* mass media rises with education.

To say only this, however, is to miss the point that when highly educated people have to decide how to distribute their available time, they are more likely to reduce the time allocated to the electronic media than that allocated to print. This must reflect the priorities they put on kinds of content. Recall also Steiner's finding that appetite for public affairs and news on television rises with education and age, but appetite for entertainment does not, and Schramm and White's conclusion that the more highly educated one is, the more likely one is to read public affairs news, editorials, serious columns, and letters to the editor. Public television, which offers very little entertainment and emphasizes public affairs and "educational" programs, has an audience strongly skewed to viewers with college and postcollege education.

Now, what must be going on in the growth of human personality to explain patterns like these? Let us begin with the idea of the "life space." Kurt Lewin used this concept to represent the stored and funded experience of individuals—the ideas and concepts they had run up against, the meaningful contacts they had had with their environment, all of which had been processed in some way and the usable residue stored as a basis for the "pictures in their heads" and guides for their social behavior.

All of our experience contributes to filling our life space. Therefore, other things being equal, the older we are, the more our life space should contain. But the intensive period of filling it in, the most systematic experience we have in organizing it, is during our school years. The school years make another contribution that is significant in terms of our media behavior: They develop our reading skill. Someday the curricula may make a parallel contribution to using the audiovisual media, but not now. At present the basic skill, basic to the other basic skills taught in school, is reading. And our reading skill continues to improve as we continue our education because we read more and more difficult subject matter.

Enlarging our life space, whether in or out of school, expands our range of interests and needs for information. It does not especially expand the need for entertainment. Indeed, entertainment, fantasy, 'escape,' may well seem to compete with the serious business of seeking current information. Therefore, with greater age and education there is a tendency, as we have seen, to select increasing amounts of informative material. More interests and a broader distribution of interests within our life space are calling for information and understanding (Figure 7).

When time pinches, highly educated people tend to seek their information in the printed media, where they can often find it more easily and quickly. *They* are in charge of the selection and the pace when they use print. And their highly developed skill of reading leads them to print. This, rather than rejection of the audiovisual media for entertainment, seems to explain the considerable preference of more highly educated people (relative to less educated people) for print over electronic media.

The strong and steady use of the newspaper throughout the life cycle can be explained in terms of its success in meeting the need for current information. The heavy use of television throughout life can

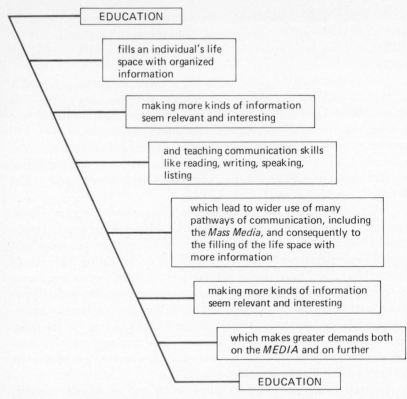

Figure 7 Relation of education, mass media, and information-seeking in the life of an individual.

be better explained in terms of its power to furnish entertainment, and only secondarily by its informational services. The increased use of books and magazines with education can be explained in terms of the demands of the life space. The decreasing use of books, magazines, and movies during adult life must be explained by other variables such as the principle of least effort, which makes it increasingly easier for adults to enjoy the media close at hand than to go out, to use what is in the living room (radio and television) and what comes in every day (the newspaper) rather than making special purchases or going out to borrow. In addition, the changing pattern of roles throughout life—the new responsibilities that fall on the shoulders of the teen-ager, the young mother, the young person trying to make a career, the couple putting down roots in a new social setting, and finally the retired person—all these must enter into the patterns of media choice.

This model, despite all the things we have put into it, leaves out personality and individual differences, which obviously have much to do with what and how much use people make of a given medium or a given kind of content. But if we begin with the human life space, the contribution to it made by education and other experience, and the relationship of media content to the kinds of information and interests represented in one's life space, we are in a position to understand a great deal of what audience research discovers.

A great deal more remains, however; we will look at the audience–media relationship again, this time in the context of the effects of communication, in Chapter 12.

For Further Consideration

1. Should the news selector consciously "play god"—i.e., select stories with their possible effect in mind?
2. Think of some important developments that never "made the agenda." Why didn't they?
3. It is frequently observed that college students watch less television than either younger or older people. Analyze your own use of TV. Do you watch less as a student? To what extent is this a matter of lack of time only? To what extent a matter of finding other, more stimulating interests? Are there shows you still make a considerable effort to see regularly? Do you consult program listings more carefully?
4. Which of the following seems to you to have the best prospect of solid audience retention over the next several decades?

   Specialized magazines
   Network television
   Morning newspapers

   Make the case for your judgment.

References

For general reading: on news selection, H. Gans, *Deciding What's News* (New York: Pantheon Books, 1979), and B. Roshko, *Newsmaking* (Chicago: University of Chicago Press, 1975). These concentrate on the process within newsrooms. There are a number of good treatments of audiences; the most comprehensive, perhaps, is G. Steiner, *The People Look at Television* (New York: Knopf, 1963). There are extensive examinations also in G. Comstock et al., *Television and Human Behavior* (New York: Columbia University Press, 1978) and C. Sterling and T. Haight, *The Mass Media,* cited earlier. The best sources of recent audience data are the yearbooks of the media and the various audience measurement services.

1. D. M. White. "The 'Gate Keeper': A Case Study in the Selection of News." *Journalism Quarterly,* 1950, *27,* 383–390.

2. G. E. Lang and K. Lang. "The Unique Perspective of Television: A Pilot Study." *American Sociological Review*, 1953, *18*, 3–12.
3. G. Gerbner and P. H. Tannenbaum. "Mass Media Censorship and the Portrayal of Mental Illness: Some Effects of Industrywide Controls in Motion Pictures and Television." *Studies of Innovation and of Communication to the Public*. Stanford, Calif.: Institute for Communication Research, 1962, pp. 203–226.
4. B. H. Bagdikian. *The Information Machines: Their Impact on Men and the Media*. New York: Harper & Row, 1971, pp. 61 ff.
5. W. Cronkite. *The Challenges of Change*. Washington, D.C.: Public Affairs Press, 1971, pp. 61 ff.
6. W. Breed. "Social Control in the Newsroom." Reprinted from *Social Forces* (May 1955). In W. Schramm, (ed.), *Mass Communication*. Urbana: University of Illinois Press, 1960, pp. 178–194.
7. A. C. Nielsen Company. "National Audience Demographic Report." Quoted in G. Comstock et al., *Television and Human Behavior*. New York: Columbia University Press, 1978.
8. J. Murray and S. Kippax. "From the Early Window to the Late Night Show: International Trends in the Study of Television's Impact on Children and Adults." In L. Berkowitz, (ed.), *Advances in Experimental Social Psychology*. New York: Academic Press, 1979.
9. In Comstock et al., *op. cit.*, p. 177.
10. *Ibid.*, pp. 149–150.
11. P. F. Lazarsfeld and P. Kendall. *Radio Listening in America*. Englewood Cliffs, N.J.: Prentice-Hall, 1948.
12. H. C. Link and H. A. Hopf. *People and Books*. New York: Rohm Industry Committee, Book Manufacturers' Institute, 1946.
13. L. A. Handel. *Hollywood Looks at Its Audience*. Urbana: University of Illinois Press, 1950.
14. M. E. Samuelson, R. F. Carter, and L. Ruggles. *Education, Available Time, and Mass Media Use*. Seattle: University of Washington, School of Communication, 1963.

10/
SOCIAL CONTROL AND MASS COMMUNICATION

Concentration of ownership and proliferation of general-audience entertainment in a system like ours raises questions of control and national policy. Every nation promises its people freedom of expression, yet each one controls its mass media to greater or less extent as, indeed, it controls all its social institutions.

The First Amendment to the United States Constitution specifies that "Congress shall make no law . . . abridging the freedom of speech, or of the press," and the Fourteenth Amendment forbids any state to "make or enforce any law which shall abridge the privileges or immunities of citizens of the United States." Article 125 of the Constitution of the Soviet Union states that "the citizens of the USSR are guaranteed by law (a) freedom of speech; (b) freedom of the press." Article 12 of the Spanish Charter of July 13, 1945 proclaimed that "all Spaniards may freely express their ideas."[1]

It is evident that different societies are defining freedom differently. The United States is concerned with political freedom, freedom from the hand of government. The Soviet Union is concerned with freedom *from* certain economic and social class controls, and freedom *within* a set body of doctrine. When Soviet leaders say that the United States media are not free, they are thinking of the fact that they are owned by capitalists. When United States leaders say that the Soviet media are not free, they are thinking of the fact that they operate under the Minister of Culture and under the constant surveillance of party and government bodies. The United States would say that its media are free to compete for audience and for profit without government interference; the Soviet Union would say that its media are free to serve the people under the guidance of representatives of the people, free from a capitalistic bias.

It may be helpful to sketch briefly some of the history of controls on mass media. When printing came into existence in Western Europe, it was under authoritarian governments that were already concerned about revolutionary tendencies and justifiably worried about how much further printed matter might rouse the people. When printing moved out of the shops of a few specialists and began to produce tracts and news sheets, governments took pains to control the new medium. They gave licenses to publish only to people they considered politically "safe." In the seventeenth century they established precensorship—approval of books and periodicals in the areas of politics and religion before publication, and later postcensorship—fines and jail terms for publications that they considered treason or "seditious libel" (a term meaning a lower level of dissent).

These controls were not a new idea. They grew out of a long tradition of authoritarian thought. Plato thought the state was safe only under the guidance of its wise men. Hobbes considered the power to maintain order to be sovereign and not subject to individual objection. Hegel said that "the State, being an end in itself, is provided with the maximum of rights over and against the individual citizen, whose highest duty it is to be a member of the State." This line of thinking led to a policy of "caretaking" on the part of the government, which excused the restriction of individual freedom on the ground that it was done for the greater good of the whole state.

But revolutions took place anyway, and the policies of the new governments were built on the philosophy of the Enlightenment, including belief in the innate rights of man and confidence that man, given a fair chance, can rationally distinguish truth from error. John Milton and John Stuart Mill gave voice to these doctrines in words we still quote. Milton said, "Let her [Truth] and Falsehood grapple: whoever knew Truth put to the worse in a free and open encounter?"[2] Mill wrote in his treatise *On Liberty*, "If all mankind minus one, were of one opinion, and only one person were of the contrary opinion, mankind would be no more justified in silencing that one person, than he, if he had the power, would be justified in silencing mankind."[3]

This was the intellectual atmosphere in which American mass media came into being.

Out of these doctrines grew a private enterprise press, relatively free from government control in order to keep watch on and criticize the government, and supposed to operate in a "free marketplace of ideas" from which readers could select what they felt to be right and true.

By the late nineteenth and early twentieth centuries, this unlimited libertarianism had been modified in practice. Psychology cast doubt on the ability of "rational man" to sort out truth from error, given the ability of one side to say more and say it better. Concentration of ownership in the media raised the question of whether a truly free "marketplace of ideas" existed and whether all viewpoints, popular or unpopular, would be represented. Film and broadcast media, because they were supposed to have a heavy influence on morals and beliefs, and because channels had to be allocated to avoid interference, invited a higher degree of control by official bodies. Consequently, in the twentieth century the media were asked to assume more responsibility for their own performance than merely to present their own ideas and observations freely, and government undertook, even in the most libertarian societies, more acts of control.

Since 1917 a new type of mass media system has developed in some of the socialist countries that is not at all like the libertarian system of the nineteenth-century West and not quite like the old authoritarianism. This new authoritarianism appeared first in the Soviet Union, grounded in the thinking of Hegel, Marx, Lenin, and others and beginning with the proposition that private ownership is incompatible with freedom of the press. "Only when the resources necessary for the control of the press are *public* property do the people enjoy effective freedom of the press," said a Soviet delegate to the United Nations Economic and Social Council. What is the press to be free to do? "Not to trade in news," said a Soviet spokesman, "but to educate the great mass of the workers and to organize them, under the sole guidance of the party, to achieve clearly definable aims." Out of this thinking grew a mass media system integrated fully into the government and the party, a planned and systematic press that discusses the controversial events of the world with a unanimity of opinion and interpretation that would be startling to a Western reader.

Beside the transformed libertarian systems of Western Europe and North America, and the communized systems of Eastern Europe and China, lineal descendants of the authoritarian systems of the sixteenth and seventeenth centuries still exist in many of the emerging and somewhat unstable nations.

In fact, there is much greater variation among systems than we have suggested with these three patterns. Terrou and Solal say that all media systems today can be classified as either "subordinate" or "nonsubordinate" to government. This is doubtless true, but it fails to describe the more subtle and distinctive differences within each group.[4]

This is especially true of the differences in broadcasting systems. At one end of the spectrum would be the many countries where broadcasting is actually a part of the government and its content is closely watched or the socialist countries in which it is integrated into the political machinery and under careful surveillance of the party. At the other end would be a country like Sweden, where television functions as a private company under the direction of a board of eleven members, of whom the chairman and five others are appointed by the government, or a country like the United States, where stations are privately owned and the government is most wary about interfering with their handling of content.

Between these limits are many different patterns. For example:

British Broadcasting Corporation (BBC)—a nonprofit corporate body set up by a royal charter, with a board of governors appointed by the sovereign, and granted almost complete freedom with its programs

NHK (Japan)—a "public juridical person" (corporation) free in large part from government control but regulated by a government agency

German broadcasting—under chartered corporations in the several provinces, which are neither governmental agencies nor private companies but are intended to be as free as possible from government controls

French broadcasting—long a state monopoly tightly controlled by government, especially in the De Gaulle era, the single agency was divided into seven different organizations in 1974, and political control has lessened somewhat; the major officers, however, still are appointed by the president

Italian broadcasting (RAI)—a government monopoly under the supervision of a mixed private-government corporation; court decisions a decade ago opened the door to private broadcasting, which has grown enormously and thus far is completely unregulated.

In any broadcast system one normally can expect control, at least to the extent of allocating frequencies, and laws to protect audiences against libelous or obscene material, owners of material against violation of copyright, and governments against seditious broadcasts. With the exception of frequency allocation, newspapers are subject to these same controls whatever the system. All systems, that is to say, must regulate and control their media to some extent.

However, beyond these basic controls the different systems go about communications in very different ways. We have mentioned the almost complete integration of the Soviet type of system into the operation of party and government, and the layers of controls that are placed on the media in authoritarian countries. In countries with libertarian traditions the government is most loath to step in, but it does. The United Kingdom is an example. British media have been as "free" as any on earth, and British news is known worldwide for its credibility and absence of government control. Yet all British broadcasting has been under a public corporation until recent years, when private enterprise television, supported by advertising, has been permitted to come in beside the BBC. The press has been called to account for its performance by an occasional Royal Commission, whose wisdom and balanced decisions have provided a model for all media councils and investigations. There is no precensorship of the press, but under the Official Secrets Act journalists occasionally have received heavy fines and jail sentences for stories deemed damaging to national security.

In the United States, governmental agencies have picked their way among the problems of controlling the media as though they were walking on eggs. The easiest problems have been those related to the "free marketplace" philosophy of the Founding Fathers. As the amount of competitive ownership and management in the cities decreased almost to zero, the Department of Justice became concerned about the number of mergers. More through indirect pressure and the threat of antitrust action than through actual court actions, it has brought about a number of changes. In broadcasting, the FCC has refused some transfers of broadcasting licenses to newspapers in the same city on the principle that this would unduly limit the free marketplace. It has expressed general distrust of cross-media ownership and, as noted, has placed limits on the number of stations any individual or corporation may own.

But the really troublesome problem is what controls, if any, to exert over content. Newspapers in the United States have been free from such controls except under the laws of libel, sedition, and copyright. Films have not been subject to national censorship, although there are some state and city censorship boards. It has proved almost impossible to get a court to decide that a film or book is legally obscene. Broadcasting content is the most sensitive area. Here the FCC has moved very slowly—too slowly for most of its critics. The commission has established a "fairness" doctrine under which any person or organization that has been attacked on the air has the right of reply on the air. This is generally honored, and when a station has refused to do so (for example, in the *Red Lion* case,[5] when a station in Pennsylvania would not grant a journalist the right to reply to an attack by the Rev. Billie James Hargis), the courts have been ready to step in and enforce the right of reply. The only real questions about this doctrine have been what constitutes an attack and who has the right to reply. For example, when the President of the United States broadcasts, inasmuch as he is a political as well as an official figure, does the opposition party or a senator whose position he is opposing have the right to free reply on the networks? When a network, with all its skill and resources, attacks an individual, how can that person assemble the resources to reply effectively to the attack?

The crunch comes because of the way in which frequency allocations are given out by the FCC. If there is but a single application for a frequency, the commission has to determine only that the applicant is financially, technically, and legally qualified ("legally" in this case means chiefly citizenship). However, if there is more than one qualified applicant, the commission must take into account what kind of public service the applicant promises. "Public service," insofar as it differentiates applications, means chiefly the amount of local programming, the amount of news, and coverage of public problems. When one applicant is chosen, a license is given for three years, at the end of which an application for renewal must be filed.

This is where the commission and the broadcasters have not seen eye to eye. The broadcasters have made a large capital investment in their stations, but the value of their property depends on the frequency on which the station operates. For example, a VHF channel in a city like Los Angeles may be worth $75 million as against a capital investment of $3 million to $7 million. Therefore, the frequency has seemed to the broadcasters to be a property right of great value that should not be taken from them any more than the land should be pulled out from under their stations.

As long as there have been no competitive applications at the time of renewal, this has caused no difficulty, and in truth most renewals have been granted fairly automatically. But in recent years there have been an increasing number of new applicants for existing allocations at renewal time, and many of these have been community groups concerned about the way their station is or is not serving the "public interest, convenience, and necessity," as the Federal Communications Act says it should. So the commission has been handed a very hot potato. The original allocation was made, in most cases, on the basis of a promise by an applicant to provide certain public services in programming. At the time of renewal, especially if there is a competing applicant, should not the commission examine the record of the successful applicant to see whether the promise has been kept? This, however, would require it to become concerned with the programming of the station and, to that extent, to "control" programming.

The commission has been sharply divided on this question ever since the famous Blue Book of 1948 *Public Service Responsibilities of Broadcast Licensees*[6] raised the possibility of reviewing a station's performance at time of renewal. Needless to say, the commercial broadcasters have bitterly fought any such review by the FCC on the ground that it represents government control of content, in conflict with the First Amendment. The commission itself had moved only twice (although it handles 2500 renewal applications a year) to take away a station's license because of its performance, each time in response to prodding of the courts, until in 1970 it vacated the license of a Boston commercial station and turned the frequency over to a competing group. To say that American station owners were aghast is to put it mildly.

The significance of this question, which we have had to present so briefly but is discussed at much greater length in readily available sources, is simply how to ensure responsible public service in the mass media. We talk mostly about "freedom" of the media. Soviet theorists talk mostly about the "responsibility" of their media. But in our system we too want responsible performance in covering the events of the world, appealing to different levels of taste and interest, providing fair access to competing opinions, and the like. With our traditional aversion to any government control of content—so that the news media can be free to report to the people on the performance of their government—we have placed our bets on *voluntary* "responsible" performance by the media. For this reason we have encouraged professional training, professional associations, and inter- and intramedia criticism of the sort represented by the *Columbia Journalism Review* and similar publications. Television and film criticism now appears in most newspapers, and a steadily increasing number of books and articles in general magazines analyze media performance. For the most part, we have counted on responsible news coverage in the press and responsible program service in broadcasting.

The Commission on Freedom of the Press, chaired by Robert Maynard Hutchins, said in its 1947 report (which was given a disapproving cold shoulder by the media) that if media owners and operators did not perform responsibly something would have to be done about it.[7] This commission called for the formation of a council or board to review and criticize media performance. But behind all this was clearly the threat that the government would have to do something about performance.

Even the Hutchins commission was loath to suggest that the government have anything to do with media content. And yet, what if it is determined that the media are *not* acting responsibly in some way or failing to serve the public interest? What if it is suspected that the people are *not* being given a "real choice" in taste, that opposing viewpoints do *not* have adequate access to media visibility, that the people are *not* being provided in every respect with an adequate coverage of events? This is the problem with which the American mass media system always has wrestled. When the administration of Richard Nixon began a series of attempts, keynoted by Vice-President Spiro Agnew's attack on television, to discredit and diminish the role of the media in American society, the media became frightened because of the specter of government control.

This has not happened, and even the bitterest critics of the media are not anxious for it to happen. But the debate that has centered on the question of responsibility and control illustrates how a social system founded on the ideas of Milton and Mill, and the politics of Jefferson and Adams, struggles with the problems of mass communication.

Marxist and Maoist critics would say that the argument is beside the point, that the real controls on American media come from their ownership by rich people and large corporations. And it is impossible to argue that the ideas of this social and economic class have not dominated the editorial pages of the nation and to some extent (see the study by Breed previously mentioned) news coverage. Yet the same Republican party that has been supported editorially for two decades by 60 to 80 percent of all newspapers has continually complained that news correspondents have been overwhelmingly opposed to that party's policies and candidates.

Another viewpoint, more often expressed by broadcasters than others, is that the public itself, through audience ratings and circulation figures, and resulting advertising support, controls the media and in general gets what it wants. Carried to its logical conclusion, this implies that audience size is a test of public service and seems to encourage a system in which all programs reach the largest possible number of people rather than serving different needs and tastes, and in which all newspapers maximize circulation by feature and entertainment materials rather than serious coverage of public affairs. Working along this line, network broadcasters frequently cancel programs that are only one rating point behind their competition, but this has been done for the advertiser rather than for the public. When newspapers engage in a circulation war, the weapons are usually feature materials rather than news or analysis, and this too is aimed at taking over a market and collecting advertising income rather than any very enlightened view of public service. Critics ask, therefore, whether the attempt to serve maximum audiences is motivated by economic interest or the public interest and whether a public vote of the kind expressed by circulation or small differences in audience ratings is very significant if there is no real choice available—if there is only one newspaper or only one kind of programming.

Therefore, economic controls on American mass media are far more potent than government controls. But the system as a whole is struggling with a definition of what constitutes responsible performance in the media and how to attain it—recognizing, on the one hand, that free media must be economically secure, and on the other, that the basic goal is to maintain the free marketplace of ideas on which the system is built.

The basic principle is that the controls any society places on its communication institutions grow out of the society and represent its beliefs and values. The Soviet system integrates them into its entire political system so that they are controlled like any other political institution. The noncommunist authoritarian system controls through government restriction and supervision and often by government ownership, assuming a "caretaker" point of view. The social system in the United States exercises a bare minimum of political and government control, and through private ownership permits a great deal of economic control. How questions of public control come to be decided in this or any other country will obviously have much to do with the future of the mass media.

THE CONTROL PROBLEM IN PRACTICAL TERMS

In Los Angeles a housemaid found a seven-year-old boy sprinkling ground glass into the family's food in order to find out (so he said) whether it would work as well as it did on television.[8] In 1971 television showed a crime program built around the placing in a passenger airplane of a bomb that would be triggered by air pressure when the plane descended to a certain altitude; within a month, more than half a million dollars was extorted from Qantas Airlines in Australia by the same threat, and soon after that the trick was tried also in the United States.

This is the kind of effect of the mass media that most bothers parents and law enforcement officers: the moral effect, especially the kind of effect that leads to asocial behavior. True, we have worried about our children and about crime in our society since time immemorial. The mass media have merely provided a new reason for worrying.

Not parents alone but also child specialists, psychiatrists, and social and psychological researchers of many kinds share this concern. The chief question is whether television is teaching undesirable social behavior and in particular whether violence on the air leads to violence in human life. The argument has been heated, with representatives of the broadcasters arrayed against specialists and concerned laypeople.

There has been a great deal of research on the problem. Research on children, of course, is limited by different ethics from those applied to laboratory animals or inert materials. We cannot experiment on children in ways that have been used to study causality elsewhere; we cannot, for example, try different ways of bringing about overaggressiveness, delinquency, or crime in order to identify the truly active and dangerous combinations of causes. Therefore, it has been much harder to demonstrate direct causal effects in the extremely complex relationship of children to television than, say, to find out the effects of heat on a metal or the result of infecting a laboratory animal with a certain virus. Nevertheless, a great deal has been found out.

The most important finding is the enormous amount children learn from the mass media—especially from television, which absorbs so much of their time. They learn facts, they learn attitudes, they learn how people act and what is expected of them in many social situations. They model no small part of their behavior on what they see on the tube. They learn both directly and indirectly. Indeed, they pick up a startling amount of incidental information from media content that is intended to entertain rather than inform. For many children entertainment media (especially television) provide a kind of social map. They learn what the distant world is like, who and what is worth looking at, what kind of behavior is valued. And this map is extremely vivid because children give themselves to entertainment media. The media attract them, excite them, arouse them.[9]

Many laboratory studies have demonstrated that children can learn violent behavior from television or films and be made more aggressive by viewing violence.[10] To be sure, this has been demonstrated in the laboratory, where the relation of television to behavior can be kept free of other influences; the doubt concerning such laboratory findings, of course, is whether they would work in real life. And it is evident that the relationship between viewing and behavior in society is nowhere near as simple and direct as in the laboratory. Social restraints, social norms against violent behavior, are so strong that they will inhibit most tendencies toward violence. The research conclusion is that violent television is likely to have a "contributory effect" on real-life violence. As Leonard Berkowitz, one of the chief students of human aggression, summed it up, viewing television violence "heightens the probability" that someone in real life will commit a violent act.[11]

We have lived with that uneasy conclusion for decades. Expressions of concern and demands on the media to present less violent entertainment have risen and fallen like the tracings of an electrocardiagram. At the end of the 1960s, an attempt to derive clearer directives from research was mounted by the office of the Surgeon General of the United States. Acting on the instruction of Congress, it supported 23 related research studies at a cost of more than a million dollars to try to answer once and for all, so far as research can answer it, the question of whether TV violence is harmful to children.

The results of these studies were published in five volumes.[12] The battle about interpretation of the evidence began, however, even before the research. The television industry was permitted to blackball from the supervisory commission seven scholars whose attitudes toward television violence the industry regarded as negative. On the other hand, two employees and three former employees or frequent consultants of the networks were appointed to the commission. The report of the commission itself was so full of qualifications that it hardly provided a clear directive, and early and incautious newspaper reports actually presented it as concluding that television violence is not harmful. But the results of the 23 studies, as contrasted with sections of the commission report, were convincing enough that the Surgeon General went before the Senate Commerce Subcommittee, which had sponsored the investigation, and said:

> My professional response today [March 21, 1972] is that the broadcasters should be put on notice. The overwhelming consensus and the unanimous scientific advisory committee's report indicates that televised violence, indeed, does have an adverse effect on certain members of our society. . . .
>
> It is clear to me that a causal relationship between televised violence and anti-social behavior is sufficient to warrant appropriate and immediate remedial action. The data in social phenomena such as television and violence and/or aggressive behavior will never be clear enough for all social scientists to agree on the formulation of a succinct statement of causality. But there comes a time when the data are sufficient to justify action. That time has come.[13]

Senator Pastore, chairman of the subcommittee, reflecting on the meaning of the Surgeon General's statement that televised violence has an adverse effect on "some members of our society," noted that if only one child a year were led into "unfeeling violent attitudes" and if that child affected only one other, in 20 years there would be 1,048,575 violence-prone people in our midst.[14]

There have been no comparably organized and financed research projects since the Surgeon General's report, although there have been literally thousands of additional studies. None has produced clear answers; however, by now the massive amount of evidence has tended to support the more unsettling findings of the Surgeon General's project.

Now, what do we do about a problem like this?

In a more authoritarian system it would be less of a problem. In the Soviet Union the mass media have been used, in all good conscience, to help produce a "new Soviet man," the kind of citizen considered desirable. In China all the forces and elements of public communication have similarly been focused on teaching the attitudes, values, aspirations, and behaviors the nation's leaders have considered desirable. In both countries, incidentally, the amount of violence on television has been greatly restricted.

But in our system things do not work that way. We expect our government to keep its hands off the media and our media to act responsibly without being forced into it. Consequently, we have besought our media industries to police themselves, and we have advised parents to keep their children away from violent programs or to provide a corrective to media violence by means of alternative experiences.

One can but sympathize with parents who read advice like that, because it asks them to add further to child-rearing burdens that are already beyond their powers to cope with. They are already faced with the problems of drugs, rebellion in sex mores and politics, and a spreading distrust of the older generation. And individual parents do not feel that they should be blamed for the example of a whole society. The daily news has been full of violence in the Middle East, in the cities, and in movements that often aim at the highest moral objectives. How, then, can one expect parents to convince their children that violence is not an acceptable way of life? Yet what they can do they must do. And a family in which respect and affection are a way of life, in which the two generations talk together and sometimes play together, provides a certain amount of insurance against undesirable character effects, whether from the media or other sources.

But the media, particularly commercial television, are in a position to do something directly about the problem. Will they do so? Is it not possible for the skilled and creative people in the mass media to make programs that will attract children without attracting them to violence? Is it not possible to treat violence not as a shooting gallery experience but as it looks in real life, ugly and resulting in suffering and sorrow? If we want children to learn alternatives to violence, we must present models whom the child admires and identifies with, behaving in nonviolent ways. The gripping scene in the classic "To Kill a Mockingbird" in which Atticus walked away from a fight despite the fact that he had already proved himself the best shot in town, despite the fact that a "no-goodnik" had spat in his face, despite the fact that his son Jem was watching, hoping his father would thrash the other man—the fact that he could walk away from that situation and still keep the respect of his son and of the audience is the kind of dramatic alternative to violence we need. A few more like it, rather than simplistic violent solutions, would make a difference.

Similarly, if we do not want to have film or television violence imitated, we can avoid putting it in a situation or setting where children are likely to find themselves. We can avoid directing it toward a target for which children might later easily find a counterpart, avoid using tools on which children might easily get their hands in an aggressive moment.

These are things it would seem we have a right to expect of the media on which children spend more time during their first 16 years of life than they spend in school or on any other activity except sleeping. Is it tolerable that anything less should be acceptable? Apparently it *is* tolerable. We are unwilling to interfere with the content of our media, set up watchdogs over them, or prescribe what they shall present because of our dislike of censorship and our overriding concern that we not weaken a free marketplace of political ideas.

This is one example of the control problem as it looks in real life. It will continue to be worth watching. Government has made no frontal moves toward more control; the FCC still abjures any role in steering programming, although various actions—for example, elaborate examination in 1979–1980 of the amount and content of advertising during Saturday morning broadcasts—have made clear that body's deep interest in the effects of what's broadcast. The networks have made triumphant announcements from time to time of the decline of violent episodes in prime time, although that may be more closely related to trends in taste than to control of content; a season in which situation comedies are the fashion obviously is going to have fewer killings than one in which police shows are dominant. The government, the public, and the media industries all have a role in the decisions that lie ahead; how those decisions are made will be significant to the continuation of a free system.

SOME OTHER FACES OF SOCIAL CONTROL

Attempting to reduce the deleterious effects of television on children provides the most dramatic confrontation of the problem of social control, but there are other manifestations. For example, the media influence the way institutions and institutionalized relationships operate. For many years there has been a small but highly audible group of American communication specialists, the best known of whom is Herbert Schiller, whose members believe that U.S. mass media have been the instruments of a "cultural imperialism" that has stunted and deformed the development of emerging countries. There are leaders throughout the world who feel that a media system with relatively unlimited freedom will inevitably increase international tensions; this idea, in various rhetorical adaptations, has been pressed since the beginnings of the United Nations and UNESCO, and the facile explanation that this is only a ploy of the Soviets is not enough to explain it away. The idea of preventing newspapers from interfering in "the peaceful relations among states" goes back to European press laws of the early nineteenth century. There also have been, of course, since the beginning of modern mass communication, various critics who have contended that the media have corrupted taste and all but extinguished what is sometimes called "high culture."

There are other such issues in which the powerful and influential seem to feel, publicly or privately, that the media should be forced to assume more responsibility for their impact. One more example: Since the early 1970s there has been a growing group of Americans, including some journalists, who are concerned about the possibility that current styles of political reporting may be undermining the way the democratic system works in the United States. The trouble began, many feel, after the Watergate affair, when reporters started to focus attention on the personality and personal character of political figures. Most of the long-time conventions under which such activities as excessive tippling and womanizing had never been reported were abandoned; such things began to be news. The story of the relationship between a member of the House and his secretary occupied front pages for days, until his resignation was forced. Books and articles about the philandering of John Kennedy (perhaps the last great hero in American politics) appeared, generally in the form of confessions by self-identified partners. Nelson Rockefeller died of a heart attack; the first account of what happened, issued by an official spokesman, contained some gaps, and the media, with the *New York Times* leading the charge, went after the story until they were satisfied they had the truth (which was hardly sordid, although considerably less elevated than the first version). Idol-breaking became the style.

In the late summer of 1979, with a Presidential campaign beginning to take shape, such disparate commentators as Nicholas Von Hoffman, Joseph Kraft, and Richard Reeves were expressing their concern that the reporting of the personal flaws of politicians had reached the state where no candidate would be seen by the public as fit to be President.

Accompanying the rise of such journalism was a sharp decline in voter interest and participation. It would be naive to see cause and effect in these parallel phenomena; many other factors clearly were involved. Nevertheless, citizens who began to feel cynical about their country's leadership found more fuel for their belief in the media than ever before.

Not only elected officials received such treatment, it should be added. Robert Woodward, a popular hero of the Watergate affair, and Scott Armstrong published a gossipy "inside" book about the Supreme Court called *The Brethren*. It was based to a considerable extent upon interviews with unidentified law clerks, some of whom came forward after it was published and accused the writers of misleading them and distorting their conversations. Anthony Lewis, once Supreme Court reporter for the *New York Times*, wrote an angry column calling for an end to such journalism and deploring the lack of conscience in reporting in mean and trivial terms a fundamental American institution that is greater than the sum of its parts. But "Sixty Minutes," a highly rated television program based on investigative journalism, gave the book lengthy and favorable attention; so did much of the press, and *The Brethren* became a best-seller.

Public opinion surveys indicate cynicism about the democratic process and those who run for office. Does acceptable social control include anything more forceful than exhorting journalists and editors and program planners to show more faith in the system? Today certainly it does not; to political leadership it still is an unmentionable idea. In the privacy of their own minds, however, it is certain that many have not found it unthinkable, and the history of social control of mass communication still has a long way to go.

For Further Consideration

1. Why should print journalism in most countries be much more free of social control than broadcasting?
2. Provide an answer, with examples, to Milton's question ". . . whoever knew Truth put to the worse in a free and open encounter?"
3. What might be the advantages, from the point of view of society in general, of a government-owned and license-supported broadcasting system?
4. In the past few years broadcasters in the United States have been questioning the need for the "fairness" doctrine mentioned in this chapter. What arguments could you make in their behalf?

References

For background, see "Communication: Control and Public Policy," in *International Encyclopedia of the Social Sciences.* Also, F. Siebert, T. Peterson, and W. Schramm, *Four Theories of the Press* (Urbana: University of Illinois Press, 1963) and W. L. Rivers and W. Schramm, *Responsibility in Mass Communication,* 2d ed. (New York: Harper & Row, 1969).

On television and children, see H. Himmelweit, A. N. Oppenheim, and P. Vince, *Television and the Child* (London: Oxford, 1958); W. Schramm, J. Lyle, and E. B. Parker, *Television in the Lives of Our Children* (Stanford, Calif.: Stanford University Press, 1961); two Japanese studies that have been summed up in a volume by T. Furu, *Functions of Television for Children* (Tokyo: Sophia University, 1971); and G. Maletzke, *Jugend und Television* (Hamburg, Darmstadt: Schroedel, 1964). A major contribution to the research on children and television is G. Comstock et al., *Television and Human Behavior* (New York: Columbia University Press, 1978). This sums up much of the relevant material in the five-volume report of the Surgeon General's Scientific Advisory Committee, *Television and Growing Up: The Impact of Televised Violence* (Washington, D.C.: U.S. Government Printing Office, 1972). For a useful bibliography with entries up to about 1972, see G. Comstock, *Television and Human Behavior: The Key Studies* (Santa Monica, Calif.: The Rand Corporation, 1975).

The literature on the freedom and responsibility of the media, especially recently on "cultural imperialism" in relation to developing countries, is very extensive. A balanced treatment of the problem is Anthony Smith, *The Geopolitics of Information: How Western Culture Dominates the World* (London: Faber and Faber, 1979). A much discussed approach to the problem is to be found in the report of the MacBride Commission, *Many Voices—One World* (Paris: UNESCO, 1980). Other treatments of the Third World relationship include Herbert Schiller, *Communication and Cultural Domination* (White Plains, N.Y.: International Arts and Sciences Press, 1976), and Jose J. Vilamil, (ed.), *Transnational Capitalism and National Development* (Atlantic Highlands, N.J.: Humanities Press, 1980). More general treatments include W. L. Rivers and W. Schramm, *Responsibility in Mass Communication* (New York: Harper & Row, 1969); Jacques Ellul, *Propaganda: The Function of Man's Attitudes* (New York: Random House, 1973).

1. F. Terrou and L. Solal. *Legislation for Press, Film, and Radio.* Paris: UNESCO, 1951. Also, F. Siebert, T. Peterson, and W. Schramm. *Four Theories of the Press.* Urbana: University of Illinois Press, 1963.
2. J. Milton. *Areopagitica,* 1918 edition, p. 58.
3. J. S. Mill. *On Liberty,* 1947 edition, p. 16.
4. Terrou and Solal, *op. cit.*
5. *Red Lion Broadcasting Co.* v. *FCC,* 381 F2d 908, D.C., 1968; affirmed 395 U.S. 367, 1969.

6. Federal Communications Commission. *Public Service Responsibilities of Broadcast Licensees.* Washington, D.C.: FCC, 1946.

7. Commission on Freedom of the Press. *Toward a Free and Responsible Press.* Chicago: University of Chicago Press, 1947.

8. See for summary G. Comstock et al., especially ch. 5. *Television and Human Behavior.* New York: Columbia University Press, 1978. W. Schramm. *Motion Pictures and Real Life Violence: What the Research Says.* Stanford, Calif.: Institute for Communication Research, Stanford University, 1968, pp. 6 ff. Quotations are from W. H. Haines, "Juvenile Delinquency and Television." *Journal of Social Therapy*, 1955, *1*, 69–78. And from R. S. Banay, "Testimony Before the Committee to Investigate Juvenile Delinquency." Committee on the Judiciary, U.S. Senate, 84th Congress, S. Res., April 1955, 62. Washington, D.C.: U.S. Government Printing Office.

9. For instance, Comstock, *op. cit.*, especially ch. 8. G. A. Hale, L. K. Miller, and H. W. Stevenson. "Incidental Learning of Film Content: A Development Study." *Child Development*, 1968, *39*, 1, 69–78. Also, E. E. Maccoby. "Role-Taking in Childhood and Its Consequences for Social Learning." *Child Development*, 1959, *30*, 239–252. C. A. Ruckmick and W. S. Dysinger. *The Emotional Responses of Children to the Motion Picture Situation.* New York: Macmillan, 1933. A. E. Siegel. "The Influence of Violence in the Mass Media on Children's Expectations." *Child Development*, 1958, *29*, 35–56. And R. C. Peterson and L. L. Thurstone. *Motion Pictures and the Social Attitudes of Children.* New York: Macmillan, 1933.

10. For summary, see notes 8 and 9. Also, among others, A. Bandura and R. H. Walters, *Social Learning and Personality Development.* New York: Holt, Rinehart and Winston, 1963. Among many published experiments the reader may be especially interested in A. Bandura, D. Ross, and S. Ross, "Transmission of Aggression Through Imitations of Aggressive Models." *Journal of Abnormal and Social Psychology*, 1961, *63*, 3, 578–582. Same authors, "Imitation of Film-Mediated Aggressive Models." *Journal of Abnormal and Social Psychology*, 1963, *66*, 1, 3–11. D. P. Hartman. *The Influence of Symbolically Modeled Instrumental Aggressive and Pain Cues on the Disinhibition of Aggressive Behavior.* Doctoral Dissertation, Stanford University, May 1965. A. E. Siegel. "Film-Mediated Fantasy Aggression and Strength of Aggressive Drive." *Child Development*, 1956, *27*, 365–378. F. E. Emery and D. Martin. *Psychological Effects of the Western Film—A Study of Television Viewing.* Melbourne: Department of Audio-visual Aids, University of Melbourne, Australia, 1957. And K. Heinrich. *Filmerleben, filmwerkung, filmerzeihung—einfluss des film und die aggresivitat bei jugendlichen experimentelle untersuchungen und ihre lernpsychologischen konsequenzen.* Hannover, Darmstadt: H. Schroedel, 1961.

11. Berkowitz's viewpoint is expressed in L. Berkowitz, *Aggression: A Social Psychological Analysis.* New York: McGraw-Hill, 1962. Among his many experiments and interpretative articles are the following two.

L. Berkowitz. "Violence in the Mass Media." *Paris-Stanford Studies in Communication*. Stanford and Paris: Institute for Communication Research and Institut Français de Presse, University of Paris, 1962, pp. 107–137. L. Berkowitz and E. Rawlings. "Effects of Film Violence on Inhibitions Against Subsequent Aggression." *Journal of Abnormal and Social Psychology*, 1963, 66, 405–412.

12. Surgeon General's Scientific Advisory Committee. *Television and Growing Up: The Impact of Televised Violence*. Washington, D.C.: U.S. Government Printing Office, 1972.

13. "Proceedings of the U.S. Senate Commerce Subcommittee, March 21, 1972." Washington, D.C.: U.S. Government Printing Office, 1972.

14. *Ibid.* Quoted in syndicated article by Norman Mark, *Honolulu Star-Bulletin*, April 1, 1972.

11/
HOW COMMUNICATION HAS AN EFFECT, I

Albert Einstein is said to have been asked by a student, "What finding helped you most when you were developing the theory of relativity?" Einstein replied without a moment's hesitation, "Finding how to think about the problem."

The same story is told about Sir Isaac Newton and several other scientists. We have no proof that any of these conversations actually took place, but we are prepared to believe that they did, and, if so, that the answer was the same one Einstein gave because this is the way scientists work and science progresses.

Scientists usually work toward models of the process or structure they are studying. Thus we have models of the structure of the universe and of the atom, models of the process by which the genetic pattern is passed from one building block of life to another, models of the economic system, and we are beginning to have models of the communication process. By *model* we mean simply a useful way to think about a process or structure, a very clear description that lets us look at the essential parts without obscuring them under detail. Some models are mathematical, but a model does not have to have equations, or even diagrams; the important requirement is that it provide an insight into the relationships that determine why something works as it does or how it is put together. As we try to understand communication and its effects we have more and more need of guides of this kind to help us interpret what we already know about it and relate new knowledge to what we have learned before. That is why we are beginning this discussion of communication effect by looking at some of the most useful models presently available.

As we search for more useful ways to think about communication effects, it is instructive to review how natural scientists, who have had far longer experience in model-making than we have, groped toward understanding their world. For a number of centuries the best way to think about the universe seemed to be in terms of four basic elements—earth, air, fire, and water. That was useful until the concept of atoms and molecules came into being. The scientists developed a detailed chart of atomic weights and learned a great deal about what atoms were combined into what molecules. Chemistry and physics were built on that model. Then the subatomic universe opened up, and it became possible to think beyond the atom to protons, electrons, and neutrons. Now we are looking even beyond that model to a still more microscopic universe filled by mysterious particles called by such exotic names as mesons, bosons, leptons, baryons, and hadrons. The key to this new model is the "quark," a particle named whimsically after a puzzling line in James Joyce's novel *Finnegan's Wake*—"Three quarks for Muster Mark." The quark is now thought to be the smallest and most elementary of all particles. No one has ever seen it, it may not even exist separately from other particles, and if it does it will doubtless prove to be less than a billionth of an inch in size. If it is discovered, then we shall have a new way to think about the structure of the universe.

Why has this quest been undertaken at all? Why are particle physicists building enormous machines to search for a particle that none of them has ever seen and may never be able to see? Chiefly, to understand. To find a better way to think about the problems they are dealing with. And because they know that a better model will be of use practically as well as theoretically. "I know that a glass of water has enough energy in it to run the country," said Dr. Leon Leberman, director of the laboratory in northern Illinois named after Enrico Fermi. "I don't know how to get it out. I also know that without understanding it, I'll never get it out."

Any scientist will tell you that there is really no *right* model of process or structure, in the sense that it describes every detail and will be changeless despite new discoveries. There is a *best* model, or a *most useful* model, for any given time and for a given set of facts and observations. There are few models that cover as much territory as the search for the basic structure of matter or the building blocks of human genetics. Rather, the sharpest generalizations tend to deal with limited parts of a field, such as the making of proteins or the energy sources in our sun or the nature of black holes.

Natural science is far ahead of social science in understanding and modeling its universe. Scientific method in social science is hardly a century old; we are still working with some of the insights Aristotle developed, from analysis rather than experiment, 2300 years ago. We have no reason to think that social and psychological questions are any more readily subject to scientific investigation than are questions in natural science—in fact, we suspect that the opposite may be true.

Furthermore, communication is only one part of a very large and complex social universe. It is an essential part because it enters into almost every aspect of human behavior in society. Thus it compares to studies of society about as studies of human genetics compare to studies of the material universe. We know that knowledge of matter has broadened and deepened as knowledge of subatomic physics and chemistry have grown. But in social science there has been no such burst of discovery as we have seen in natural science during the past several centuries and no such sharing and collaboration in the production of knowledge as has occurred, for example, among nuclear physicists, biochemists, crystallographers, and biologists, which resulted in the creation of an entirely new concentration of knowledge and model-making now called molecular biology and led to the dramatic leaps in understanding represented by DNA, RNA, and the making of proteins in living structures.

We must therefore not expect to find any single comprehensive model of communication effect comparable to some of the more general models of natural science. Nor can we reasonably expect to find one model we can say is *right*. All are subject to change as we learn more. We must recognize that we are in a primitive stage of the very difficult and complex scientific area we call communication and that we must expect to have to examine *models* rather than *a model* because there have been so many varying approaches to communication. But there is no reason why we should not examine some of the most promising models, taking from each of them what seems to be most useful in helping us think about communication and helping us move toward the essential understanding of it we all seek. This is what we plan to do in the following pages, looking not at all the available communication models, because there are far too many for that purpose, but sampling among those that have proved most useful to researchers and students.

1/A Discarded Model—The Silver Bullet

If we had asked in the 1920s for a model of communication effect, we should probably have heard that the mass media, used by a skillful propagandist, can work on people like bullets on a target. The situation is like a shooting gallery: All that is needed is to hit the target, and the target falls down. So far as we know, this belief has never been espoused by any scholar of the first rank, and is now universally discredited, but it was once widely believed and illustrates how far communication theory has moved in a few decades.

The so-called Silver Bullet theory was a journalistic invention (in the bad sense of that good word) rather than a scholarly theory. It grew out of public fear, in some cases near hysteria, that was nurtured by German propaganda during World War I and immensely increased by the propaganda of Naziism. In 1920 a new tool for propagandists had come into wide use—radio broadcasting. A number of frightened people and a few sensational writers wondered if a situation had not arisen in which the skillful propagandists of Hitler and Goebbels could shoot their carefully made Silver Bullets of propaganda through the new radio gun into people who would be powerless to resist them. It was like a shooting gallery: All that would be needed would be to hit the target; the bullets were irresistible. So the story went.

How widespread this belief was, we cannot be sure, but it was apparently common in the general public for a decade or so. In any event, it did not last very long. Enough research was on the books by the end of the 1930s to demonstrate that belief in an irresistible Silver Bullet was groundless, and the funeral sermon for Silver Bullets was finally preached in 1964 by Raymond Bauer in an article entitled "The Obstinate Audience,"[1] which demonstrated what had already been concluded several decades earlier: that people were not like targets in a shooting gallery; they did not fall down when hit by the Silver Bullets of propaganda. They could reject the bullets, or resist them, or reinterpret them, or use them for their own purposes. The audience was "obstinate"; it refused to fall over. And communication messages were not like bullets anyway; they were not shot into receivers, but rather placed out where receivers could do what they wanted to with them. The receivers were not merely targets, but equal partners in the process. Although some messages could persuade some people, there was nothing automatic about the process. The Silver Bullet was laid to rest in peace and replaced by theories that took much more account of the human qualities of communication and ascribed far less power to the physical properties of the process.

2/The Limited Effects Model

In the Bureau of Applied Social Research at Columbia, scholars began to study the mass media in terms of their limited ability to bring about change amidst the other forces and the resistances of society.

Best known of the research organizations working mostly on mass communication has been the Columbia Bureau of Applied Social Research, which for 25 years was headed by Paul Lazarsfeld. From this organization have come two lines of thought about communication effects that have been widely influential. One of these we call, for want of a better name, the "theory of Limited Effects," meaning that the effects of mass media are sharply limited by the very nature of the media and their place in society. (The other is the approach to understanding media through trying to understand for what purposes audiences employ the media and the gratifications they derive from such uses.)

The Columbia group came to hold the concept of Limited Effects from three kinds of experience. The first was their reaction (shared by many other scholars) against the unreasoning fear of propaganda and what they called "an almost magical belief" held by many Americans in the enormous power of the media. Lazarsfeld and Merton poked fun at these folk beliefs, beginning their paper on "Mass Communication, Popular Taste, and Organized Social Action" (which still stands as one of the best essays ever written on mass media) by chuckling over the statement of an American lecturer that the "power of radio can be compared only with the power of the atomic bomb."[2] They quoted William Empson, a British philosopher and critic, to explain why Americans have entertained such beliefs. Empson wrote:

[The Americans] believe in machinery more passionately than we do; and modern propaganda is a scientific machine; so it seems to them obvious that a mere reasoning man cannot stand up against it. All that produces a curiously girlish attitude toward anyone who might be doing propaganda. "Don't let that man come near. Don't let him tempt me, because if he does I'm sure to fall."[3]

Lazarsfeld and his colleagues saw little to justify such a respect for the power of the media. As sociologists they recognized the power of personal influence, group and class membership, and social organization in determining how individuals think and act. As researchers they found in their data nothing to indicate any overwhelming effect of exposure to the media. Their studies of Presidential elections in 1940 and 1944, published in book form under the titles *The People's Choice* and *Voting*,[4] concluded that only about 5 percent of the people changed their voting intention as a result of an election campaign. What people learned from their friends, their union and business organization memberships, their political party history, the political tradition in which they had grown up, were far better predictors of how they would vote than was their exposure to electioneering through the media.

As skeptics concerning "media magic," as sociologists who were aware of other powerful influences in society, and as researchers who had studied media influence themselves, the Columbia group came to the conclusion that the social effect of the mass media, far from being "magic" or "irresistible," was sharply limited, and they expressed this viewpoint in three much read publications: the paper "Mass Communication, Popular Taste, and Organized Social Action," already mentioned; a book by Klapper entitled *The Effects of Mass Communication*; and a book by Katz and Lazarsfeld, *Personal Influence*.[5]

These made the limitations on mass media effects quite clear but never claimed that the media had no effect. The question to ask, therefore, is what did Lazarsfeld and his colleagues conclude that the media *could* do?

In the essay referred to, Lazarsfeld and Merton cite three powerful social effects the mass media can exert:

1. Mass media can confer status. Favorable attention in the mass media raises and legitimizes the status of persons, organizations, policies. One has "arrived" when singled out by the media. One is worth paying attention to. And citing the "men of distinction" advertisements for Calvert whiskey, the authors point out a circular process of status conferral that seems to operate: "If you really matter, you will be at the focus of mass attention, and if you *are* at the focus of mass attention, then surely you must really matter."[6]

2. Mass media can enforce social norms—to an extent. Malinowski observed about the Trobriand Islanders that no organized social action was taken about deviation from social norms unless there was *public* announcement of the deviation. Publicity can close the gap between "private attitudes" and "public morality." The

media can reaffirm social norms by exposing deviations from norms to public view. As Boss Tweed is said to have remarked about Thomas Nast's sharp political cartoons, "I don't care a straw for your newspaper articles: My constituents don't know how to read, but they can't help seeing them damned pictures!"

3. Mass media can act as social narcotics. The Columbia sociologists feel that the enormous flood of information tends to narcotize rather than energize the average reader or listener. Media absorb time that might better be used for social action. *Knowing* something about problems tends to be confused with *doing* something about them. Thus, although the media have clearly raised the level of information, they may have contributed to superficiality of knowledge and lack of participation. In this respect, Lazarsfeld and Merton say, mass media may be "among the most respectable and efficient of social narcotics. They may be so fully effective as to keep the addict from recognizing his own malady."[7]

Furthermore, they express some doubts about the contribution of mass communication to public taste. It had been hoped that media like radio would raise the level of taste, but rather they seem to be cheapening it. For generations men have fought for more leisure, Lazarsfeld and Merton said, but now that they have it, "they spend it with the Columbia Broadcasting System rather than with Columbia University." The enormous audiences of media have provided a new way by which power groups in society can exert indirect social control over thought and action by advertising and public relations, by sponsoring programs the power groups want presented, and the like. As Lazarsfeld and Merton analyzed these effects, they concluded that the general tendency was not to bring about change but rather to encourage the status quo. Political campaigns tend to reinforce voters to vote as they would vote anyway. Public relations campaigns tend to avoid "rocking the boat," keeping important change from occurring that would threaten existing power groups. Opinions heard on the media tend to "cancel each other out." And in one of their severest criticisms of the media they say,

> To the extent that the media of communication have had an influence upon their audiences it has stemmed not only from what is said, but more significantly from what is *not* said. For these media not only continue to affirm the status quo but, in the same measure, they fail to raise essential questions about the structure of society.[8]

It *is* possible, under certain conditions, they say, for media to have important social effects. They suggest three such conditions: (1) when one viewpoint monopolizes the media, as when an entire country rallies behind its leader in a war; (2) when the efforts of the media are combined toward "canalizing" change—making a small and specific, rather than a broad, general change; and (3) when face-to-face communication is organized to supplement media exposure.

Katz and Lazarsfeld took up a number of cases in which personal relationships and personal communication had been used to reinforce the media.[9] Among these were the influence of local campaign organizations, the use of field staffs and discussion groups in the diffusion of innovations, and the like. They also discussed what had come to be known as the Two-Step Flow hypothesis, which we have already discussed.

Klapper summed up most fully the conclusions of the bureau researchers. He said:

1. Mass communication *ordinarily* does not serve as a necessary and sufficient cause of audience effects, but rather functions among and through a nexus of mediating factors and influences.
2. These mediating factors are such that they typically render mass communication a contributory agent, but not the sole cause, in a process of reinforcing the existing conditions. (Regardless of the condition in question—be it the vote intention of audience members, their tendency toward or away from delinquent behavior, or their general orientation toward life and its problems—and regardless of whether the effect in question be social or individual, the media are more likely to reinforce than to change.)
3. On such occasions as mass communication does function in the service of change, one of two conditions is likely to exist. Either:
   a. The mediating factors will be found to be inoperative and the effect of the media will be found to be direct; *or*
   b. The mediating factors which normally favor reinforcement will be found to be themselves impelling toward change.
4. There are certain residual situations in which mass communication seems to produce direct effects, or directly and of itself to serve certain psychophysical functions.
5. The efficacy of mass communication, either as a contributory agent or as an agent of direct effect, is affected by various aspects of the media and communications themselves or of the communication situation (including, for example, aspects of textual organization, the nature of the source and medium, the existing climate of public opinion, and the like).[10]

Klapper submits these generalizations with a word of caution lest they be interpreted as implying the impotency of mass communication.

It must be remembered that though mass communication seems usually to be a *contributory* cause of effects, it is often a major or necessary cause and in some instances a sufficient cause. The fact that its effect is often mediated, or that it often works among other influences, must not blind us to the fact that mass communication possesses qualities which distinguish it from other influences, and that by virtue of these qualities, it is likely to have characteristic effects.[11]

Outside the laboratory it is rarely possible to separate mass communication from the other influences that bear on every individual. These are what Klapper refers to as "mediating factors"—the receiver's predispositions; the selective exposure, selective perception, and selective retention that supposedly support those predispositions; the groups to which audience members belong and the group norms to which they hold; personal influence and personal communication that supplement or counteract persuasion by mass communication; and (in words reminiscent of Lazarsfeld and Merton) the nature of commercial mass media in a free enterprise system, which makes it more likely that they will operate to reinforce and maintain existing social and political beliefs rather than to change them.[12] It is hard to separate these out; complex behavior always has complex roots. It is hard also to assess the long-term cumulative effect of exposure to mass media— for example, the effect of seeing many hours of violence that is absorbed but not imitated until some event in some situation for some people triggers off a resulting action. Therefore, many of the most potent effects of mass communication may remain hidden except as they are seen to reinforce existing ideas already held or as they operate in an area where not much is known or ideas are not strongly held. Only occasionally, as Klapper and his colleagues say, can a spectacular direct effect be seen. Anyone who was alive on Halloween 1938 will remember when a radio broadcast by Orson Welles and a CBS theater group, intended to be no more frightening than a Halloween mask or a carved pumpkin face, sent people running for the hills. They broadcast a radio version of H. G. Wells's story *The War of the Worlds*, in which Martians were described as invading the United States. In that case, conditions were right for media effect. People, who had been listening breathlessly for alarming news of the coming war in Europe, mistook the broadcast for news. Some of them checked further and found it was fiction, not fact. Others did not wait to check. They got into their cars and drove as far and as fast as possible away from New Jersey, where the imaginary Martians were said to be landing.[13]

3/The Uses and Gratifications Model

One of the most popular recent approaches has been to examine the mass media in terms of the uses people make of them and the needs for which they provide gratification.

Almost as soon as it was founded, the bureau at Columbia became deeply interested in the uses people make of the mass media with which they spend so much time. The daytime serials, for example, draw millions of women to the radio every day. Herta Herzog interviewed 100 of these listeners at length, and obtained shorter interviews with 2500 others. Her results, published in a now historic paper entitled, "What We Really Know about Daytime Serial Listeners," were surprising.[14] The radio plays were digging deeply into the emotions of their audiences. A large portion of the women in the audience seemed to enjoy the serials chiefly as a means of emotional release— a "chance to cry." They also enjoyed the chance to express some of their aggressions vicariously. They said it "made them feel better to know that other people have troubles too." They experienced the sorrows of serial characters as partial compensation for their own troubles.

A second large group of listeners used the serials as an opportunity for "wishful thinking." They "drown their troubles" in listening to the soap operas and in some cases use the happier situations in the plays to compensate for failures in their own lives. Thus, says Herzog, "a woman whose daughter has run away from home to marry and whose husband 'stays away five nights a week' lists [two serials] as her favorites, each portraying a happy family life and a successful wife and mother."

The third, and perhaps least suspected, form of gratification obtained from daytime serials was their use as a source of advice. Women told the interviewer they liked the stories because they "explained things." "If you listen to these programs and something turns up in your own life, you would know what to do about it" was a typical comment.

It is obvious, and was obvious even in the early years of the bureau, that the effects of mass media must be determined in part by what audiences use them for. If for escape from reality, one effect; if for interpretation of reality, another. If to fill time, one effect; if for deep emotional or intellectual involvement, another. Ever since those early studies, it has been next to impossible to study questions like the effect of television on children, or the effect of political reporting in the newspaper without trying to find out first just how and for what purpose the persons being studied used those media.*

A second study of this type that made a deep impression was Bernard Berelson's "What Missing the Newspaper Means."[15] A long newspaper strike in New York had left people without a daily newspaper. Berelson conducted a number of interviews with those people, trying to find out how their behavior was different without newspapers and for what uses and gratifications they chiefly missed newspapers. In some ways his results were as surprising as Herzog's. Relatively few people said they missed the newspaper for what most of us have considered its primary use—as a device to convey the distant environment. The kind of news most often said to be missed, especially by older people, was the obituaries; without them, people could not tell if one of their friends or acquaintances had died. The chief gratification the readers said they missed was not related to any particular kind or topic of news. Without the newspaper, people said, they felt oddly "detached from the world"; as though they weren't "with it"; as though the curtains were down and they couldn't look out, even though they didn't usually look out very often anyway. The newspaper had become a habit, something to do every morning about breakfast time or something to be read on the train while riding down to work. Without it, they had to find a new way to fill the time. And in this respect also they felt rather lost, and detached from the sort of life to which they had become accustomed.

These two are only examples of the kinds of studies that have continued to appear, and lately at an increasing rate, since the 1940s. Obviously, it is a very large job to try to survey the uses different kinds of people make of different kinds of material in different media and the gratifications they derive from those uses. Not only is the task large, it is difficult. It is extremely difficult for an interviewer to get someone to understand himself or herself well enough, overcome inhibitions sufficiently, and assemble the necessary vocabulary to explain the use he or she makes of mass media. This helps to explain why this

---

* Aristotle anticipated this approach by more than 2300 years, just as he anticipated some aspects of the persuasion models. In his *Poetics*, he described the effect of Greek tragedy and the chief reward to its audiences in terms of the audiences' opportunity to purge themselves of base and ignoble thoughts by vicariously experiencing the emotional stress, the punishment, and the violence on the stage. His word for this process is "catharsis." S. Feshbach used this same idea recently in a series of psychological experiments designed to find out whether children might get rid of, rather than stimulate, their own tendencies to violence by watching violence on television.

kind of research is still at an exploratory level, trying to survey the field and the alternatives rather than to put together a theory. Blumler and Katz, in a collection of studies published in 1974, made no attempt either to publish a summary list of studies or to suggest a theory, although they did list five ways in which social needs might generate media-related needs and uses:

1. The social situation produces tensions and conflicts, leading to their easement via mass media consumption.
2. The social situation creates an awareness of problems that demand attention, information about which may be sought in the media.
3. The social situation offers impoverished real-life opportunities to satisfy certain needs, which are then directed to the mass media for complementary, supplementary, or substitute servicing.
4. The social situation gives rise to certain values, the affirmation and reinforcement of which is facilitated by the consumption of congruent media materials.
5. The social situation provides a field of expectations of familiarity with certain media materials, which must then be monitored in order to sustain membership of valued social groupings.[16]

This is still far from a theory, but it illustrates some of the direction that theory-making might take.

The point is that this is still a live field of research, of high interest to scholars trying to understand the effects of the mass media. Theoretical generalizations of importance are likely to emerge from it. One encouraging feature is that this approach to effects study combines another element that has now become almost a requisite of thinking about communication effects—the idea of an active receiver in the communication relationship. More and more, students of effects have come around to the idea expressed in the first American book on television and children, published in 1961:

> In a sense the term "effect" is misleading because it suggests that television "does something" to children. . . . Nothing can be further from the fact. It is the children who are most active in this relationship. It is they who use television rather than television that uses them.[17]

4/The Adoption-Diffusion Model

The increasing uses of communication to support development and innovation has stimulated efforts to systematize a process for such uses.

We have already noted that one of the three conditions which Lazarsfeld and Merton in their historic essay predicted that mass communication might have "important social effects" is when "face-to-face communication is organized to supplement media exposure."

Since the 1940s the chief field tests of this prediction have been provided by studies of agricultural innovation, chiefly in the heartland of the United States and Canada, and by social and economic development programs in agriculture, family planning, health, and related topics, in Asia, Latin America, and Africa.

Indeed, as this activity has developed, the Lazarsfeld-Merton formulation has been stretched so that the joint effects of personal and media communication have been tested not only in relationships where personal communication supplemented the media but also where the media served to supplement personal communicators and where an effort was made to use the two channels as equal partners in bringing about change. Very rarely have either media or personal communicators been depended upon to do the entire job alone. One notable exception was India's experimental year with the ATS-6 direct broadcasting satellite, when, with the exception of a small subexperiment, the satellite carried the whole responsibility; but this was as much a function of the lack of time to plan a fully rounded program as it was an attempt to find out what the satellite could do by itself. In general, wherever radio, television, or films were available, they were used, and few countries tried to bring about changes without field workers and/or extension services.

Three examples will illustrate how this social change model evolved. The cradle was probably the agricultural extension service in the United States, where county agricultural colleges and demonstration farms were responsible for contacts with the people and for demonstrating new techniques and materials to them. The media—radio at first, later television—were used to stir the interest of the farm people, to let them hear experts who were not readily available in their home areas, and to see more elaborate demonstrations and examples than could be provided nearby. The second example was the Rural Radio Forum, which was developed in Canada, tried out in 150 villages near Poona, India, and then used in half a dozen countries in Latin America and Africa. This pattern was built around a village group of 12 to 20 farmers who came together, usually twice a week, to hear a broadcast whose major purpose was to describe a new crop or method that might be of interest to the area that received the broadcast. Each of the forum groups then discussed the suggested innovation and decided whether to adopt it. Still a third pattern has

recently, in which special responsibilities are
n and action groups. In countries like China and
e, the local groups in communes or villages are
at crops should be grown and what innovations
io supplements them, rather than the reverse.
..., and especially in the third one, a most delicate
balance must be maintained between the media and the interpersonal
activity, but the trend has been for responsibility to shift from central
toward local direction and planning, so that increasingly the changes
are in the hands of the local people and the media are there to help
and encourage them.

The familiar five-step model of the "adoption process" was formulated by a committee of U.S. rural sociologists in 1955, drawing heavily
on studies by Ryan, Gross, and others at the Iowa State College on
the adoption of hybrid corn.[18] The five stages in this process were
conceived as:

1. *The stage of awareness*, when the individual learns of the new idea
   or practice, but has little specific information about it.
2. *The stage of interest*. The individual develops interest in the
   innovation and seeks additional information.
3. *The stage of evaluation*. The individual considers the new idea in
   relation to his needs and resources and decides whether to try it.
4. *The stage of trial*. The individual tries out the new idea on a small
   scale to find out how it fits his situation.
5. *The stage of adoption*. The individual introduces the new idea on a
   full scale with the intention of continuing it.[19]

It was assumed that the chief burden of supplying information in
Stage 1 would be carried by the mass media; that is, the farmer would
be most likely to hear about the innovation first on a program like the
"National Farm and Home Hour" or read about it in magazines or
the farm pages of newspapers. After that, interpersonal communication would be depended upon more than the media—expert information from agricultural field workers, advice and encouragement from
friends and neighbors, and so forth.

As larger amounts of empirical evidence accumulated in the 1950s
and 1960s, many exceptions were found to the neat five-stage outline.
The stages do not always occur in the order given above, and evaluation tends to go on throughout all stages. The process does not always
end with "adoption," as the outline implies, but may often result in
rejection; and even after adoption, the individual may continue to
seek additional encouragement or discouragement, leading to a change

in decision. Everett Rogers, after reviewing the exceptions, proposed a four-stage model:

1. *Knowledge.* The individual is exposed to the innovation's existence and gains some understanding of how it works.
2. *Persuasion.* The individual forms a favorable or unfavorable attitude toward the innovation.
3. *Decision.* The individual engages in additional thought, discussion, and information-seeking, which lead to a decision whether to adopt the new idea.
4. *Confirmation.* The individual seeks reinforcement for the decision he has made concerning the innovation. He may reverse his previous decision if he receives conflicting information or advice.[20]

This model, in turn, has been modified by various observers to describe the situation in which basic decision and initiative rests with local groups rather than central planners. The alternative plan takes a form something like this:

1. *Need assessment.* Local decision makers canvass their priority needs and resources.
2. *Knowledge.* Either during or after the first stage, they seek out information on new practices that might help to meet these needs within their resources.
3. *Consideration.* By discussion, by seeking advice, by investigating the experience of others, and perhaps by small scale trial, they decide which of the new ideas is sufficiently promising to be tried on a large scale.
4. *Trial.* One or more of the new ideas is put into use on a sufficiently large scale to see whether it fits the local situation.

All these are in a sense ideal types, and any of them, observed in the field, will be seen to be subject to many exceptions. However, some confirmation comes from the field of marketing, where sales agencies have long been in the business of persuading people to change buying habits and where the model used has been given the acronym AIDA, for Awareness, Interest, Desire, Action.[21]

At least two conclusions derived from experience with adoption-diffusion models promise to stand up. One is that in general the mass media are more influential in the earlier than the later part of the process. The second is that the process of diffusion, in countries at any stage of development, may usually be described as an S-curve. For example, the coming into use of any of the new electronic media or any of the new farm practices, when plotted over time, takes this form (Figure 8):

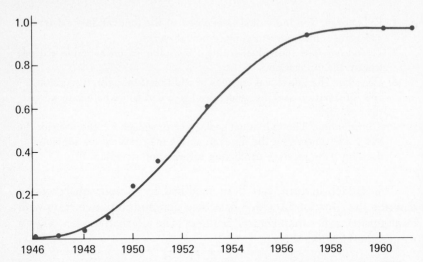

Figure 8   Percentage of U.S. households owning television sets, 1946–1960.

Thus adoption is relatively slow at first, but proceeds very rapidly as it approaches half of the population, then gradually slows again as it approaches a maximum saturation (which is, for a medium like television, somewhere around 95 percent). We read this as evidence for the cumulative effect of social example and personal influence. For example, as Rogers says, "if the first adopter of an innovation discusses it with two other members of the social system, and these two adopters each pass the idea along to two peers, the resulting distribution follows a binomial expansion."[22] And it is not always necessary to pass the idea along by personal communication; the growing number of antennas on houses, the observation of more and more families sitting around the receiver in the evening, the increasing attention in media to new developments—all these would help to encourage the S-curve of innovation in society.

For Further Consideration

Suggested questions for this chapter are included with those in Chapter 12.

References

On the theory of limited effects: P. F. Lazarsfeld, B. Berelson, and H. Gaudet, *The People's Choice* (New York: Duell, Sloan and Pearce, 1944); B. Berelson, P. F. Lazarsfeld, and W. N. McPhee, *Voting* (Chicago: University of Chicago Press, 1954); J. Klapper, *The Effects of Mass Communication* (New York: Free Press, 1960); E. Katz and P. F. Lazarsfeld, *Personal Influence: The Part Played by People in the Flow of Mass Communications* (New York: Free Press, 1955).

On uses and gratifications, the best summary is J. G. Blumler and E. Katz, (eds.), *The Uses of Mass Communication: Current Perspectives on Gratification Research* (Beverly Hills, Calif.: Sage, 1972).

Probably the best summary book on the Adoption-Diffusion model is E. M. Rogers and F. F. Shoemaker, *Communication of Innovations: A Cross-Cultural Approach* (New York: Free Press, 1971).

The most useful general references for Chapters 11 and 12 are: I. Pool et al., (eds.), *Handbook of Communication* (Skokie, Ill.: Rand McNally, 1973); and G. Lindzey et al., (eds.), *Handbook of Social Psychology* (Reading, Mass.: Addison-Wesley, 1969).

1. R. Bauer. "The Obstinate Audience." *American Psychologist*, 1964, *19*, 319–328.
2. This paper by P. F. Lazarsfeld and R. K. Merton was originally published in L. Bryson, (ed.), *The Communication of Ideas*. New York: Harper & Row, 1948. It is now available in W. Schramm and D. F. Roberts, *The Process and Effects of Mass Communication*, rev. ed. Urbana: University of Illinois Press, 1971, pp. 554–578.
3. *Ibid.*, pp. 555–556.
4. P. F. Lazarsfeld, B. Berelson, and H. Gaudet. *The People's Choice.* New York: Duell, Sloan, and Pearce, 1944. B. Berelson, P. Lazarsfeld, and W. N. McPhee. *Voting.* Chicago: University of Chicago Press, 1955.
5. J. Klapper. *The Effects of Mass Communication.* New York: Free Press, 1960. E. Katz and P. Lazarsfeld. *Personal Influence: The Part Played by People in the Flow of Mass Communications.* New York: Free Press, 1956.
6. P. F. Lazarsfeld and R. K. Merton. "Mass Communication, Popular Taste, and Organized Social Action," *op. cit.*, p. 567.
7. *Ibid.*
8. *Ibid.*, p. 566.
9. Katz and Lazarsfeld, *op. cit.*
10. Klapper, *op. cit.*, p. 8.
11. *Ibid.*, p. 8.
12. *Ibid.*, p. 10.
13. H. Cantril. *The Invasion from Mars.* Princeton, N.J.: Princeton University Press, 1940.
14. In P. F. Lazarsfeld and F. Stanton. *Radio Research, 1942–43.* New York: Duell, Sloan and Pearce, 1943, pp. 27 ff.
15. In P. F. Lazarsfeld and F. Stanton. *Communications Research, 1948–49.* New York: Harper & Row, 1949, pp. 111–129.
16. J. G. Blumler and E. Katz, (eds.). *The Uses of Mass Communication: Current Perspectives on Gratification Research.* Beverley Hills, Calif.: Sage, 1972, p. 5.

17. W. Schramm, J. Lyle, and E. B. Parker. *Television in the Lives of Our Children.* Stanford, Calif.: Stanford University Press, 1961, p. 27.
18. E. M. Rogers and F. F. Shoemaker. *Communication of Innovations: A Cross-Cultural Approach.* New York: Free Press, 1971, p. 100.
19. *Ibid.,* pp. 100–101.
20. *Ibid.,* p. 103.
21. A. Zaltman. *Marketing Contributions for the Behavioral Sciences.* New York: Harcourt Brace Jovanovich, 1964.
22. Rogers and Shoemaker, *op. cit.,* pp. 178–179.

12/
HOW COMMUNICATION HAS AN EFFECT, II

5/The Persuasion Model

From Aristotle's time to the present, the communication process has been most often studied in terms of its ability to persuade.

ARISTOTLE'S MODEL

Twenty-three hundred years ago, Aristotle wrote in his treatise on *Rhetoric*, "A speech is to be judged by its effect upon someone."[1] That long ago, he was nearer the target than were the Silver Bullet people later, for he saw the effect of persuasive oratory as nothing magical, but rather as the result of careful planning and high skill. It is interesting to find him, more than two millennia ago, emphasizing the credibility of the communicator, the use of emotional appeals, and the need to understand an audience, all topics that Carl Hovland and his Yale group were studying in the 1950s. In his *Poetics* (as we shall see later in this chapter), Aristotle anticipated by some thousands of years the theory of the uses and gratifications of communication that is so popular today. A remarkable man!

Rhetoric, he said in his treatise on that subject, can "be defined as the faculty to discover in the particular case what are the available means of persuasion."[2] If he had lived somewhat later, we can imagine him studying the mass media, but there were no such media in his time, so he turned to the most powerful channel of communication at hand—rhetoric and oratory.

The available means of persuasion are of two kinds, he said—evidence that has to be presented outside the speech, and the speech itself. No modern persuader would argue with him on this; any lawyer trying to convince a jury that a murder has taken place knows he or she must prove that there is a body and connect the accused person with it by what witnesses have seen, by fingerprints, by a weapon, or by some of the other tools available to modern jurisprudence. But what interested Aristotle most, and what sounds most modern to us, is what he believed could be accomplished by communication—the rhetoric of the persuader. Here, he said, three means of persuasion are available: "the character of the speaker . . . [the opportunity to] nurture a certain attitude in the hearer, and [proofs] carried by the argument itself."

The speech must be so given as to make the speaker seem "worthy of belief," he said; "for as a rule we trust men of probity more, and more quickly, about things in general, while on points outside the realm of exact knowledge, where opinion is divided, we trust them absolutely." The character of the speaker, he insisted, "is the most potent of all the means to persuasion." However, we must not let it depend entirely upon the previous impression of the speaker; the speech itself must be given in such a way as to build trust in the speaker.[3]

The first requirement, then, is to try to get the audience to trust the communicator. Secondly, "persuasion is effected through the audience when they are brought by the speech into a state of emotion; for we give very different decisions under the sway of pain or joy, or liking or hatred." And thirdly, "persuasion is effected by the arguments themselves, when we demonstrate the truth, real or apparent (of the desired point of view by logical proof or such other means as are suitable for a given case)."

"Such being the instruments of persuasion," he said, "to master all of them obviously calls for a man who can [appear trustworthy], who can reason logically, can analyze the types of human character, along with the virtues, and can analyze the emotions—the nature and quality of each emotion, with the means by which, and the manner in which, it is excited."

Aristotle analyzed each of these elements of persuasion at length, but perhaps this sample will show how modern an ancient approach can be, how good the advice still is after so many centuries, and how many of the essentials of communication have been agreed upon by wise persons in many ages.

THE CARTWRIGHT MODEL

What happened between the fourth century B.C. and the late 1940s, when the next model we are going to present took shape, was not that people lived who were any wiser or more analytical than Aristotle, but rather that public attention had been turned much more than before toward communication by the development of the mass media, the scientific method had been applied to the study of communication processes and effects, and a mass of empirical evidence had come into existence on which scholars could build and generalize. The Cartwright model, for example, came from studies of war bond campaigns during World War II.[4]

An enormous amount of effort had been expended between 1941 and 1945 to persuade Americans to buy these bonds, which helped finance the war. Thousands of individuals and most of the available mass media had participated in the campaign. Dorwin Cartwright, a pupil of Kurt Lewin and later a social psychologist at the University of Michigan, himself had been a scholar-volunteer in the activity. He could hardly have helped reflecting on that experience: Why had some people bought and others not? Why had the approach and the arguments been successful in some cases but not in others? He did more than reflect, however; he conducted a large number of open-ended interviews with people who had been solicited—some of them successfully, others not—and on the basis of those set down what appeared to be the conditions of success, what had to take place within an individual before a sales pitch had the desired effect. This is his model of effect.

1. The "message" (information, facts, etc.) must reach the sense organs of the persons who are to be influenced.
   1a. Total stimulus situations are accepted or rejected on the basis of an impression of their general characteristics.
   1b. The categories employed by a person in characterizing stimulus situations tend to protect him from unwanted changes in his cognitive structure.

2. Having reached the sense organs, the "message" must be accepted as part of a person's cognitive structure.

    2a. Once a given "message" is received it will tend to be accepted or rejected on the basis of more general categories to which it appears to belong.

    2b. The categories employed by a person in characterizing "messages" tend to protect him from unwanted changes in his cognitive structure.

    2c. When a "message" is inconsistent with a person's prevailing cognitive structure it will either (a) be rejected, (b) be distorted so as to fit, or (c) produce changes in the cognitive structure.

3. To induce a given action by mass persuasion, this action must be seen by the person as a path to some goal that he has.

    3a. A given action will be accepted as a path toward a goal only if the connections "fit" the person's larger cognitive structure.

    3b. The more goals that are seen as attainable by a single path, the more likely it is that a person will take that path.

    3c. If an action is seen as not leading to a desired goal or as leading to an undesired end, it will not be chosen.

    3d. If an action is seen as leading to a desired goal, it will tend not to be chosen to the extent that easier, cheaper, or otherwise more desirable actions are also seen as leading to the same goal.

4. To induce a given action, an appropriate cognitive and motivational system must gain control of the person's behavior at a particular point in time.

    4a. The more specifically defined the path of action to a goal (in an accepted motivational structure), the more likely it is that the structure will gain control of behavior.

    4b. The more specifically a path of action is located in time, the more likely it is that the structure will gain control of behavior.

    4c. A given motivational structure may be set in control of behavior by placing the person in a situation requiring a decision to take, or not to take, a step of action that is a part of the structure.[5]

Suppose we analyze the elements of that model:

• *Attention.* The message must capture attention before it can make anything else happen. We sometimes forget how fragmented our attention is in modern life. When we drive down the street we look relatively seldom at the houses, lawns, trees, people, dogs, even the other automobiles, that we pass. We see a car going the opposite way, far over on the other side of the road, and conclude it needs no special attention. In the rearview mirror we see an automobile coming up to pass. We notice it is in its own lane, and so turn our attention to other things. On a certain corner we are careful to glance at a magnolia tree that shows signs of blooming; have the blossoms yet appeared? Out of the corner of an eye we see a movement of something light colored on the lawn near us, and look at it quickly to make sure it is not a child running into the road or a puppy beginning to chase the car. We flip on the radio, and quickly change stations because the first voice is unpromising. And so it goes. Obviously we are more likely to give attention to a solicitor at the door asking us to perform a patriotic duty by buying war bonds, but attention is still a formidable barrier to any persuasive communication.

· *Evaluation in terms of "fit."* Does the message fit comfortably with what we know and believe? If not, can it be reinterpreted so that it does fit? Is it important enough so that we should modify our beliefs or values to include it, or should we reject it? If most rejections occur at the stage of gaining or not gaining attention, then certainly the next largest casualty toll is at the stage we are talking about.

· *Evaluation in terms of opportunity.* What is there in it for us? What can we gain by doing the thing we are being persuaded to do? Is there something else we could do that would be a better investment, not necessarily of money, but of effort and time? Is this really the time to buy a bond, or a new car, or whatever we are being urged to do? What is the reward for doing this rather than something else?

· *Decision to act or not to act.* Once there is a favorable response to Step 3, then the chief requirement is to make the desired action easy and pleasant. The solicitor at the door may offer the prospective buyer a pen and a card to sign. The mail order sales pitch will probably say: Don't pay now; we'll bill you later—thus putting off the least pleasant action. A war bond campaign might offer all sorts of additional rewards—a card to display in the window, a certificate, the chance to hear your name read on a local station. And all of us have read, "These prices will be offered this week only!"

This is a simple and a useful model, which makes sense both practically and theoretically. You will want to compare it with the Adoption-Diffusion model, to which there are many resemblances. It is interesting to see that, contrary to Aristotle, who devoted most of his attention to what the communicator had to do to persuade someone, both Cartwright and the architects of the Adoption model, although their models have many implications for the persuader, nevertheless are centrally interested in what has to go on *within the receivers* before they can be persuaded to take the desired action.

THE HOVLAND APPROACH

Perhaps the favorite way of thinking about communication effects and studying them, ever since Carl Hovland and his research group did it this way at Yale,[6] has been to identify key variables in the communication process and then test each one in a careful experiment against related variables. For example, the effect of a given kind of communicator presenting a given kind of message, the effect of a particular kind of message for a particular kind of audience, and so forth. From this kind of study have come tentative conclusions of great practical as well as theoretical usefulness, some of which we shall set down here.

Who makes the best communicator?

One of the most likely ways to change the effect of a communication is to vary the audience's picture of the communicator. Is the communicator prestigious? Likable? "Your" kind of person? Long before the Yale program began, Irving Lorge tested the effect of identical messages attributed in one case to Nicolai Lenin, in another to Thomas Jefferson. With American subjects the message had much more effect when attributed to Jefferson; supposedly, the opposite result would have come about with Russian subjects.[7] Hovland and Weiss presented identical articles on the atomic bomb attributed in one set of cases to a distinguished American atomic scientist, in the other to the Soviet newspaper *Pravda*. They found four times as many attitudinal changes (among American readers) agreeing with the article when it was attributed to the American source.[8] Kelman and Hovland studied the result of having the same speech on delinquency given by an individual who was introduced in one case as a judge, in another as a lay member of the studio audience, and in a third as a layman who was alleged to have certain shady chapters in his record. These communicators were rated by the audience as positive, neutral, and negative, respectively, and the amount of attitude change was proportional to the differences in rating.[9] This kind of thing has been done literally dozens of times, and the general result has always been that sources who are seen as prestigious in the field they are talking about will have more attitudinal effect than low-prestige sources.

However, as this area has developed, it has been possible to identify components of prestige: notably, expertise and disinterestedness. If communicators are seen as experts in what they are talking about or as not in a position to profit from the change they are advocating, they are more likely to have an effect than communicators who are not perceived as expert or objective. The greatest effect comes when communicators are perceived as having both of those characteristics— as being both credible and trustworthy. Especially with involved and rather suspicious people, it is sometimes more effective to arrange to have a message *overheard* so as to do away with the suspicion that the communicator is trying to manipulate the listener.

As far as they have been tested, the suggestions advanced earlier in this book about "contractual relationships" brought about by the roles people in the communication relationship see themselves as playing—for example, the relationship of teacher to student or salesperson to prospective buyer—are supported. For example, the negative effect of introducing a communicator as someone who stands to gain by "selling" an idea to the receiver and the positive effect of introducing a communicator as an authority on the subject indicate that in one case the receiver comes to the relationship with defenses up, in the other, prepared to listen and learn.

Suppose a person is confronted with conflicting messages from authorities and from peers; for example, a physician tells the school assembly that cigarette smoking is bad for one's health, whereas one's friends later laugh at that viewpoint and offer a cigarette. What happens? In general, laboratory experiments show an advantage to the expert source; field studies show an advantage to the peer group. This is another case in which there are serious doubts that the laboratory situation can be used to predict naturalistic effects. The controlled situation is often perceived as somewhat contrived, and the full pressure of peer group influence as it operates in real life can seldom be reproduced.

Either in the laboratory or in the field, however, an audience is more likely to be persuaded if it *likes* the communicator. This is aided if the source of the message is perceived by the receiver as a person similar to herself or himself—the quality Rogers calls *homophily*. Other things being equal, the receiver is likely to be influenced more by a person seen as similar. This leads to the persuasive strategy that Kenneth Burke calls "the strategy of identification," in which a persuader tries to convince the audience that he or she is "their kind of person."[10] But it makes a difference whether the subject is one in which expertise is required; if the "similar" communicator knows no more about it than the receiver, the communicator is not likely to be persuasive. As McGuire says, "Paraphrasing Groucho Marx's comment, that he would not want to belong to a club that would let a person like him in, the average person might not care to listen to a source who knows no more about the topic than he himself does."[11]

Liking interacts with similarity. It is a two-way street; a feeling of real similarity produces liking, and liking tends to increase the feeling of similarity. The more the source is liked, the more effect the message will probably have. However, Zimbardo has found that this too is subject to qualification.[12] For example, if a person will commit himself or herself to listen to a communicator he or she dislikes, that is likely to encourage some change on his or her part because of the need to get rid of his or her dissonance—contradictory feelings—by arguing internally that the message is *worth listening to*.

What makes the most effective message?

All of us know that we like to read or hear some messages more than others, yet one of the surprising things about this kind of research is how few experiments have been able to show any large effects due to what is generally considered "good rhetoric."

Whatever the reason, the general skill of a speaker has not been experimentally proved to be a very powerful determinant of persuasion. Lewin, for example, found little difference in the effectiveness of trained and untrained speakers in bringing about group decision.[13] Thistlethwaite, deHaan, and Kamenetzky found that well-organized messages affected comprehension rather than opinion change.[14] Humor, in general, has been found to affect liking for the speaker or the communication experience, but there is not much evidence of its contribution to attitude change. Repetition of a point (preferably with some variation) contributes to learning and change, but the limit of its persuasive effect seems to be reached rather quickly.

"Dynamic" style has not proved to have as much effect as one might expect. Dietrich found no significant differences in attitude change brought about by dynamic versus conversational style.[15] Hovland, Lumsdaine, and Shieffield found no significant difference in attitude effect between a radio commentator and a dramatic version of the same material.[16] McGuire reports only a slight effect produced by a dynamic "hard sell."[17] One of the key points seems to be how a high-key style is perceived. For example, a low-key presentation may be interpreted as low expertise, negating any advantage gained from its being interpreted as objective. A high-key style may be interpreted either as "propaganda" or as vigor and expertise. Depending on which interpretation is held, it might accomplish *more* change by attracting closer attention or *less* change by encouraging rejection.

What are the most effective appeals? Here the research has been able to turn up very few solid guidelines. There has been some research (for instance, that of Menefee and Granneberg in 1940[18]) and a great deal of experiential lore to indicate that emotional appeals are more likely to change attitudes than are logical ones. However, in practice it is uncommon to separate the two kinds of appeals entirely. Aristotle, as we have seen, advised *both* emotional appeals and logical arguments. Trial lawyers argue as logically as possible from the law but are not averse to calling upon emotion where they can.

However, one area of emotional appeals has generated some very interesting research that promises to lay bare some of the underlying processes of change. In the early 1950s Janis and Feshbach conducted a study on the effectiveness of fear appeal in persuading people to brush their teeth. They presented arguments at several levels of fearsomeness. The most fearsome had gruesome pictures of the results of gum disease. They found that these strongest appeals tended to be rejected and that the minimum appeals actually accomplished the most change.[19]

Replications of their experiment did not obtain precisely the same results, and later studies of fear appeal have complicated rather than simplified the relationship. An experiment by Chu showed that it makes a difference how easily a person can do something about the thing the person is being encouraged to fear. If the solution is relatively easy and simple, and consequently the message can be simple and clear, then the stronger the appeal the more effect it is likely to have. If, on the other hand, the solution is difficult and complicated or the result in doubt, the strongest messages tend to be rejected.[20] McGuire, in reviewing this literature, suggests that there is probably an interaction between the degree of fear arousal and the subject's level of anxiety, leading to a relationship that is not consistent in all cases.[21]

Questions like these have obvious practical importance. Whenever we make a decision on how to try to affect attitudes and behavior on health problems like cigarette smoking, policy problems like pollution, or population problems like family planning, we must decide what appeals to us and how high to key them. Yet on many such questions communication theory is not yet able to provide simple and practical guides. The best guidance is to examine the situation and the audience as deeply as possible and try to decide how best to stimulate the process that must operate. And then pretest!

Should a message draw its conclusions explicitly or let the receiver decide what they are?

Here we have another contrast between laboratory and field results. The laboratory experiments typically find that more change occurs and more desired points are learned when the conclusions are stated explicitly. On the other hand, many psychotherapists, especially followers of Freud, are committed from their experience to letting patients discover the conclusions for themselves.

How should one handle the opposition's arguments?

In general it seems that mentioning and refuting the opposition's arguments works better (1) when the audience is initially hostile to one's own view, (2) is highly educated and accustomed to hearing both sides of an argument, (3) is likely to hear the other side anyway. In any of these cases it is better to introduce the opposing arguments oneself than to seem to ignore them.

Should the main points be placed first or last? Does the first speaker or writer have an advantage over the second? The results do not entirely agree. For example, in 1925 Lund obtained results that led him to proclaim a "law of primacy in persuasion."[22] Cromwell, in 1950, found an advantage in recency.[23] Hovland and Mandell, in 1952, found no advantage in either primacy or recency.[24] As the matter has been further studied, however, the relationships have been found to be more complex than originally believed, and a number of other variables have had to be introduced in order to give any very useful advice about primacy and recency. Perhaps the most general statement is that arguments placed first have some advantage in attracting attention; arguments placed last have some advantage in being remembered. But even this is not enough. If one has arguments that are likely to be well accepted by an audience, there is some reason to present them first and establish attention and a favorable climate for later arguments that may not be so easily accepted. If contradictory and possibly confusing information is being presented, that presented first has a better chance of dominating what is finally accepted. If one is presenting information that arouses needs and other information that suggests a way to satisfy them, it is clearly better to arouse the needs first.

What are the effects of group membership?

Among the shadowy figures in every communication relationship are certain groups to which the participants belong or aspire to belong, whose norms they share and will defend. These memberships and loyalties must be considered in planning any kind of persuasive appeal. Whether we are dealing with family, work, social class, professional, political, or other groups, it helps greatly to know what groups people value and what are the norms they will consequently defend against change.

An experiment by Kelley and Volkart demonstrated that such norms are not influential unless the particular membership is brought to mind at the moment when the information leading to change is being processed.[25] For example, if an individual is led to see the relationship of a persuasive argument to his or her membership in, let us say, the Catholic Church or the Republican party or the Rotary Club, he or she will probably test the persuasion against the beliefs shared with those groups. If the relationship is not seen, he or she will probably not call upon whatever defenses or support might derive from such group norms. Therefore it has always been considered good tactics not to attack frontally any group loyalties or valued group memberships.

When a major change is achieved in one's values and behavior, it usually has to be accompanied by a change in one's valued groups. For example, it was reported that one principle of Chinese and North Korean "brainwashing" at the time of the Korean War was to remove the POW as far as possible from the group support to which he was accustomed. Officers were separated from enlisted men and often from one another. Mail from home was not delivered. Publications and news reflecting the norms of old groups were cut off. The POW was put into new discussion groups, and every attempt was made to build up new friendships and dependencies. Similarly, after "conversion" takes place during a religious campaign, one of the first steps in any well-planned revival is to put the converts into a group of believers who will support them in their moments of dissonance and reinforce them in their new values.

Background groups thus blend into active, foreground groups. A series of experiments by Asch, Sherif, and others have been conducted to measure the effect of social pressures on an individual. Asch put an individual into a group that had the task of judging which of three lines was the longest. The experimental subject did not know that all his fellow group members were stooges in the pay of the experimenter. They went around the circle, the stooges speaking first, each giving the opinion that Line B was the longest. Obviously it was not. But by the time the poor experimental subject had his turn, he was beginning to wonder about his own judgment. And the pressure to conform was so strong that more than 30 percent of the experimental subjects went along with the stooges and said that Line B was indeed the longest—though the answer was patently wrong. However, if even one of the stooges gave the right answer, the experimental subject was reinforced in his own judgment and much less likely to yield to the example around him.[26] This effect has been demonstrated a number of times. Sherif, for example, did it with a different stimulus, the autokinetic effect—the circumstance that a point of light in a dark room seems to move—and the participants were required to judge the direction and distance of the apparent movement.[27]

Can group decision be used to affect individual decisions?

Lewin was one of the first to study the effect of group decision on individual attitudes and behavior. He found that a group of housewives who came together in wartime, when the best meat was being shipped to the troops, to discuss the possibility of cooking unpopular cuts of meat were much more likely actually to use such meat than if they merely read about it or heard a talk about the need of doing so. In particular, they were more likely to change their practice if they made a public commitment in the group to do so.[28] This has been tested in different experimental situations and has been used practically in successful change programs like that of the Radio Rural Forum, whose use in India and other developing countries has often resulted in an increased rate of adoption of new practices.

What is the underlying process in group decision? Partly, it must be the experience of talking over the proposed change and learning about it. More important, it must represent the promise of social support and approval if one decides to change. And when we commit ourselves in public, we are risking some uncomfortable dissonance, along with loss of public credibility, if we do not bring our behavior into line with our promises and then bring our viewpoints into line with our behavior.

It hardly needs saying that many other elements of the situation may, under suitable circumstances, enter into the effect. To take one example out of many, consider the effect on an evangelistic group of singing together, the effect of linking arms and swaying bodies, the effect on a protest group of marching together, the effect of "touching" as it is done in some encounter groups. These are suggestive devices and, other things being equal, make it easier for a member of the group to accept a suggestion in accord with the shared norms of the group. The range of suggestive devices like these is very wide, from background music to hypnotism.

Does role playing help persuade?

There are interesting studies on role playing in public. For example, subjects are induced or paid to improvise a talk or write a paper in support of a viewpoint with which they do not agree. Merely improvising arguments for the other position will tend to influence their attitudes in the direction of the position they have been led to take. There are two ways of explaining this. One is that their act has roused some dissonance in them that they have to get rid of by bringing their private feelings more into accord with their performance—consequently deciding that there is something to this other viewpoint after all, and therefore some justification for doing what they did. The other explanation is that the act of improvising the talk led them to find out more about the other side than they had known before and that in so doing they learned and stored some of the arguments they used. But it was the act of *improvising* that made the difference. Improvising the talk or the paper had more effect than merely reading the same kind of material aloud or silently. If the subjects were praised for their performance or given a high grade by the instructor, that made them feel happier but did not change their attitudes any more. The key part of the change mechanism was their creative activity, which necessarily had to be done in empathy with opposing viewpoints.[29] If you notice any resemblance between these experiments and the long custom of giving prizes for schoolchildren's essays in support of some good cause, the resemblance is not coincidental.

Do decisions tend to change with time?

Yes, they do. We forget. People tend to forget the sources of ideas they have stored away. This was the implication of the "sleeper effect" experiments. The first experiment compared the effect of a source perceived as trustworthy with one perceived as untrustworthy. As expected, the subjects became more favorable to the idea proposed by the "trustworthy" source. But when the subjects were retested some weeks later, it was found that their attitudes toward the position of the trustworthy source had become less favorable, whereas they were more favorable toward the position espoused by the untrustworthy source, so that the original change was almost blotted out. When the experiment was done over again with suitable additions, it was concluded that they had simply forgotten where the different ideas had come from. When they were reminded of what the "trustworthy" source and the "untrustworthy" source had said, their attitudes returned to what they had been after the original exposure to the two sources. The implication of this, and of most of the other findings reported in the last few pages, is the great importance of how the source of the message—the other person in the relationship—is perceived. In effect he or she becomes part of the message, and when he or she is removed from the scene (through forgetfulness or anonymity), the message is not quite the same.[30]

Can a persuader "immunize" an audience against opposition arguments?

The reason for giving the opponent's arguments and then refuting them with one's own is to prepare the audience to resist those opposition persuasions. McGuire has reviewed, in *Handbook of Social Psychology*, a series of experiments along this line. In general, the underlying principle is that if an audience that is going to hear the opposition anyway can be given a set of counterarguments to rehearse mentally beforehand, they will be more likely to resist the later persuasion. This has long been realized by practical politicians. To take one example only, Chairman Mao decided in the 1950s to make available to selected persons in China a four-page newspaper made up entirely of news translated into Chinese from the Western news agencies—AP, UPI, Reuter, and Agence France Presse. Later he explained why he had done so.[31] Without, so far as we know, ever having read any of the Western research on this topic, he used the very term we have been talking about—immunization. If we inoculate people against dangerous diseases by exposing them to a small quantity of the disease-producing virus or bacteria, he asked, should we not do the same with dangerous ideas?

6/The Consistency Model

The effect of a communication often depends on how much it threatens the inner consistency of beliefs and attitudes, which everyone tries to preserve.

The parentage of this approach to communication effect was the cognitive psychology of the Kurt Lewin school. Heider was the first to put on paper the idea of a "strain toward cognitive balance" or "inner consistency."[32] From this came Newcomb's A–B–X model, Festinger's theory of "cognitive dissonance," and Cartwright's mathematical development of the theory. Both Festinger and Cartwright were students of Lewin at Iowa. However, Charles Osgood, who was an experimental psychologist trained at Yale, and William McGuire, who was one of Hovland's group at Yale, also have contributed substantially to the development of theory, and Hovland's last book, in 1961, also dealt with it.

We might well start with Newcomb's A–B–X model, which is now familiar to most students of communication, at least in the form of the diagrams Newcomb drew to illustrate what he called a "strain toward symmetry" in cognitive relationships.[33] If two people, A and B, have a positive feeling toward each other and also toward an object, idea, or person—X—he said, the relationship is symmetrical.

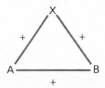

If A and B are not favorably inclined toward each other, and one is favorable toward the object X whereas the other is unfavorable—for example,

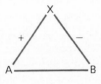

the relationship is also symmetrical. But if A and B are favorable toward each other but disagree about X, or if they are unfavorable toward each other but agree on X

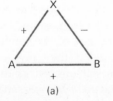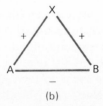

the relationships are not symmetrical, and there will be a strain to bring them somehow into balance by changing attitudes toward each other or toward X.

This, in one form or other, has been basic to all consistency theory. Cartwright and Harary generalized the model to include any number of interrelationships.[34] Leon Festinger developed a theory of "cognitive dissonance" to explain such phenomena as why people seek further supporting information even after they have made a decision between alternatives.[35] For example, why will people who have just placed an order for an expensive car read advertisements for it, or look for favorable opinions concerning it, and avoid reading about the less expensive automobile that they decided not to buy? Because, says Festinger, they are trying to reduce the dissonance they feel between the decision they made and the one they might have made. Dissonance, he said, acts like a drive to motivate such behavior as will reduce it.

This use of the concept of drive indicates the close relationship between cognitive-born Consistency theory and S → R theory. Indeed, Hovland's last book dealt with a version of the Consistency theory,[36] and Osgood developed a type of Consistency theory that he called (in a book written jointly with Suci and Tannenbaum) a theory of "congruity."[37] This was based on findings that people try to balance their attitude toward the communicator of a message with their attitude toward the message itself. For example, if we admire a certain figure and hear him or her espouse a political position with which we have been in disagreement, we feel a certain discomfort with this lack of consistency and usually try to make the two attitudes "congruent." We can reject the communication because we feel it is not an accurate quotation, or we can reconsider our position: Perhaps the policy is not wholly bad after all or the person is not so admirable as we had thought. Using his own semantic differential scales, Osgood was able to demonstrate that the change toward congruity depended on the strength and extremity of the respective attitudes toward the message and the communicator, and the distance between them. The most common result was in the direction of compromise: Both attitudes would tend to move together, with the one less strongly held moving the greater distance.

Consistency theory as developed by McGuire has come to be seen as a kind of internal process of conflict-resolution.[38] That is, receivers adjust to a new communication to take care of the conflicting demands it imposes on them: its relation to what they presently know and believe about the topic, to their own self-interest as they perceive it, to their relationships and obligations to other persons. They try to maintain a comfortable relationship among these sometimes conflicting forces. Having once achieved this, it is easier not to change it than to admit some new element of information that will force further readjustment.

Within the bounds of Consistency theory, how could one hope to make a change by means of communication? The basic requirement would be to keep the receiver from rejecting the message without considering it, for the reason that it seems threatening or irrelevant. If that can be accomplished, then it is possible to introduce an idea in an area where the receiver does not have much knowledge or hold strong opinions, and consequently that he or she feels less reason to defend. Or one could introduce an idea requiring very little change in a strongly defended area of belief and opinion. Or, on rare occasions, one could introduce an idea that is so dramatic and challenging that it simply cannot be rejected without some consideration. In either of these two latter cases, one could then hope that the receiver would readjust his or her present cognitive positive to accommodate the new idea.

It is hardly necessary to point out that Consistency theory is another approach to change in which the receiver is seen as very active in the process—very far indeed from the Silver Bullet theory.

7/The Information Model

Some scholars, following Shannon and cybernetics, prefer to think of the communication process in terms of how much information it can transmit under given conditions.

We are going to conclude our trip through this museum of models with a different kind of communication theory, one that comes out of electrical engineering and mathematics rather than out of social science. And that requires us to say a little more about the nature of information.

Information is, of course, the content of communication. On the other hand, it is necessary to remember that whereas all communication conveys information, not all information is acquired through communication. We can learn by experience or by example. For instance, we learn very quickly that when we run too fast we begin to pant, and that when we smile we are more likely to attract a friendly response than when we frown. When one of the authors was a boy, he learned to swing a bat the way he saw Babe Ruth do it (although he never learned to hit many home runs), and Japanese boys today imitate the batting style of Saduroh Oh, the great home-run hitter of the Tokyo Giants who has broken even Babe Ruth's records. Furthermore, we acquire information by secondary activity stimulated by example or experience or other communication.

When we try to list all the ways in which information comes to us we find a fuzzy area midway between those sources that are clearly communication and those that are clearly not. We can illustrate this by looking at a few homely scenarios.

Suppose that you are jogging through the park with a friend jogging beside you. The friend says, "Watch out for that tree root in front of you." You look down, see a root sticking up out of the path, turn aside, and avoid a nasty fall. No question about that: It is clearly a case of communication. Information has been offered and processed, and action resulted.

But let's imagine another version of the story. Your friend says nothing, you trip over the root and tumble embarrassingly on pine shards and wet ground. This was obviously *not* the result of communication. It might have been the result of *lack* of information or communication, but if you learned anything from it you learned from experience—to look in front of you as you run through the woods.

Still another scenario: Suppose you looked in front of you, without your friend's warning, saw the root, and avoided both it and the tumble. In this case, you acquired information, but nobody communicated it to you. What you actually did was to perform what in Chapter 3 we called a Type 3 communication act: You turned your attention to some signs, processed them, derived the information, and took some action as a result of it. But there was no Type A communication act in which somebody or something offered you signs from which to extract information.

Somebody or something. It is not difficult to accept the idea that machines can communicate information to us. The speedometers in our automobiles, for instance. Going 40 in a 25-mile zone; better slow up. That useful little machine is designed to put out informational signs that we can process and act upon if we pay attention to them. Similarly, it is not hard to think of two machines communicating with each other. A thermostat can monitor the temperature of the water in our cars, and when the temperature reaches a certain height it can tell the fan to pull in more outside air. We can tell a computer to figure out a statistical measure for us, and the machine will blink a bit, instruct its memory disc to deliver up certain data, then go through a sequence of squaring, summing, extracting roots, immeasurably faster than we could do the same thing, and finally tell its printer to give us the answer.

We have no difficulty with the idea of communicating machines. But let us pose another scenario. You rise in the morning, see a gray sky with low white clouds scudding across it, decide it is going to rain and you had better take an umbrella with you when you leave home. Information, yes, certainly; but has communication occurred? We should say it has not; there has been no intentional Type A act. The situation is like the one in which you looked down, saw the tree root, and on the basis of past experience decided you had better avoid it: On the basis of past experience you read the gray sky as likely to produce rain and decided to take an umbrella. Yet we hear arguments to the contrary on that case. If you can interpret mechanical signs as communication, some have said, can you not also accept natural signs? The answer still seems to be no, because the difference lies in intention. The speedometer is built to carry a message through certain signs; unless we personify Nature, we can hardly think of it as intentionally taking the form it does to communicate to us.

Another example of the fuzzy area is secondary or incidental learning from observation or experience. For example, you see a house newly painted, the lawn freshly mowed. You take in that information. Do the signs also communicate to you that this family cares how the neighborhood looks? One purpose of the new paint job may have been to communicate just that. And we are certainly entitled to deduce that from the appearance of the house and the lawn. Furthermore, we have no doubt that some parts of communication are unintentional; for example, a frown of annoyance may contradict polite words. But this area of incidental or secondary communication is another one that causes us trouble when we try to say just what are the boundaries between communication and information.

AN INFORMATION MODEL

From the field of Information theory, however—meaning the ideas on which the engineers, physicists, and mathematicians who work on computers and electronic communications base their thinking—has emerged a model of communication that has proved highly interesting and stimulating to social scientists as well as information scientists. Most of us first met this new model in Claude Shannon's famous article in the *Bell Telephone Laboratory Journal* in 1948, which was almost at once published as a book and circulated widely throughout the world.[39] The roots of the model, however, reach as far back as the beginnings of statistical mechanics, studies of electronic communication in the Bell Labs during the 1920s, and Wiener's pioneering work in cybernetics.[40]

The new model made such an impression on communication scholars trained in social science for two reasons: It provided analogies from the study of communication engineering and technology that illuminated many of the communication concepts from social disciplines; and secondly, it suggested a new kind of mathematics that could be applied to some parts of human as well as to electronic communication.

Like many models, the Information theory model became known first to communication scholars through a diagram—this one (Figure 9), which appeared in the Shannon article and then was reprinted many times:

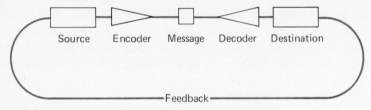

Figure 9   Shannon's diagram of Information theory.

Communication students who adopt this model must be alert to the fact that its application to human communication is mostly analogical. Information theory is actually a theory of *signal transmission*. Its users are concerned less with effect than with how accurately a signal can be carried through the system. Even the model looks a bit like the old pictures of Alexander Graham Bell speaking into the conical element of one of his first telephones to another person who holds his ear to a similar conical element. "Success" for that system was achieved when the voice coming out the receiving end sounded something like the voice going into the sending end. An example more familiar to us today is the hi-fi set that is judged by how faithfully its speakers reproduce the tapes or discs we play on it. "Communication" is defined in Information theory as what happens when the element at the destination end of the circuit assumes exactly the same state as the element at the sending end. This can happen in a telegraph or a telephone or broadcasting, but it is almost impossible to conceive of two people who can communicate exactly the same meaning to each other. Human minds and personalities are too different, and they are constantly changing. They learn. The telephones we talk over are identical and they do not learn.

So Information theory is largely an analogy to, rather than a description of, human communication. But that does not mean it has not been one of the most stimulating additions to communication study in our time. The term *feedback* was at once adopted into social science. The concepts of *encoding* and *decoding* proved to be convenient shorthand for the more complex cognitive processes that take place in making and interpreting the signs that are shared by humans. The new way of looking at information in terms of certainty and uncertainty, and the implications for human communications of engineering terms like "channel capacity"—all these were fresh and exciting for scholars who had been accustomed to looking at communication wholly in social science terms.

"Information" means to an Information theorist what is required to do away with the uncertainty in a given message system. That brings us to the key word in the vocabulary of Information theory: *entropy*. This is a famous term in modern mathematical physics, where it means the uncertainty or disorganization of a physical system. The law that "entropy always increases," Eddington said, "holds, I think, the supreme position among the laws of Nature." The measurement of entropy, he went on to say, is the only way we could tell whether a movie of the history of the universe were being run forward or backward, because the physical world through time always grows more shuffled, less organized.

Entropy was a key term to Shannon because it was the yardstick by which he could measure information. Information is necessary to eliminate uncertainty or randomness from a system. Entropy will be at a maximum when all states of a system are equally probable— meaning they will occur with equal probability. It takes less information to be able to predict whether the next toss of the coin will be heads or tails than to predict what letter of the alphabet will be selected if a blindfolded person is selecting. One fact, the answer to one question, will tell us what side of the coin will come up: We need to know only, will the next toss be heads? But it takes nearly five times as much information—five times as many questions must be asked—to predict which letter of the alphabet will be chosen.

Entropy—or to be precise, relative entropy—is the opposite of the old familiar term *redundancy*. The more redundant a language or a system is, the more easily predictable it is, but the less information it can carry at a given time. The amount of redundancy is one of great strategic decisions facing communication: How often must one repeat, at what length must one explain? Any language or any code without redundancy would be chaos; no one would learn it easily, and mistakes would begin. Shannon calculated that if the relative entropy of English were only 30 percent—meaning the units of the language were 70 percent predictable—it would be no fun to make or solve crossword puzzles. On the other hand, if the relative entropy were 70 percent—meaning that the language were only 30 percent predictable—then it would be easy to make three-dimensional crossword puzzles. You can see how linguists might be interested in Information theory, and they have indeed used it to measure readability, among other things. It has also been used to measure the exchange of information in a network, the diffusion of an idea in a population, and the amounts of information (considered abstractly rather than specifically) in a message or a channel.

This is not the place to try to teach the mathematics of Information theory. If you want to learn something about it you will find easy-to-read references at the end of this chapter. You will see that it is a binary system, like a computer, and that it measures information in *bits* (binary digits). You can figure out, if you wish, that it takes only one bit of information to be able to predict which side of a coin will turn up, but 5.4 bits of information (meaning you would have to ask, on the average, 5.4 well-chosen questions) to predict which of 42 keys of a typewriter would be struck, if the striking were completely at random. This kind of mathematics, as we have indicated, has proved useful in a number of cases, but the great impact of Information theory on human communication theory is by providing fresh views of old concepts and thus guiding thinking along new lines.

An example is channel capacity, which is one of the commonest problems communicators have. All channels, whether biological, electronic, or mechanical, can carry only so much. The optic nerve can carry only so much information to the brain; this is less than the amount of information available to the eye, and therefore it is necessary to select what one looks at. On the other hand, it is more information than the cognitive system of the brain can handle, and therefore it is important to us to know what kind of information gets through, and why. Readers can absorb more words through their eyes than through their ears in a given time, and therefore if they can spend 30 minutes on a newscast or a newspaper they can take in more information, other things being equal, from the newspaper than from the radio. Information theory has stimulated a number of experiments in the capacity of readers and listeners to absorb information from different media. Shannon has published a remarkable theorem proving that if the flow of information is kept within the maximum channel capacity of a receiver, then a maximum amount of information can get through with a minimum amount of noise (meaning competing and confusing signals). But if one tries to transmit more than the practicable capacity of the channel, then the amount of noise and the number of errors increase very rapidly. This has been tested by broadcasters who have wanted to know how many news items could be carried efficiently in a newscast of given length. They found exactly what Shannon had predicted. About 20 items could be comfortably recalled from a cast of the length they were studying with few mistakes. But as they shortened the items and included more and more of them, there was little gain in the number remembered; and if they presented more than 40 items, less information actually got through than if they kept the number under 40, because many more items were remembered incorrectly.[41] So in this case, and other cases like it, a formula from electrical engineering had proved to be both a stimulus to new thinking and a practical tool for old uses.

SUMMARY APPROACHES TO
ANALYZING COMMUNICATIONS

Let us review the seven approaches to communication we have summarized in this chapter and the last.

The Information theory approach is obviously different from all the others in that it is primarily concerned with delivering a signal. Its significance to students of human communication is less in helping to understand the effect of the signal than in providing an analogy to the process and some mathematics whereby to measure the signal itself. The now discredited Silver Bullet theory is also different from all the others in that it is concerned with one particular effect only— what propaganda can do to people—and it assumed something that no other model does: a passive recipient of communication who is like the target in a shooting gallery, ready to be knocked over by a shot from the mass media gun.

Leaving behind the Silver Bullet idea, we looked at a series of models all of which view the receiver as active and the effect as a point contribution of sender and receiver. The Limited Effects model, like the Silver Bullet concept, is concerned chiefly with the effects of mass communication, but came to an almost opposite conclusion. Far from being irresistible, the media are seen as having relatively restricted effects because they have to operate through a maze of other patterns and influences. The Uses and Gratifications model considers one of the great determinants of effect to be certain qualities of the receiver— the uses an individual makes of communication received and the gratifications derived from such use. The Adoption-Diffusion model, like the other two sociology-oriented models we have just mentioned, tends to look at what a receiver *does* with a message and the *social situation* in which he or she acts upon it; it concludes that the direct effect of the mass media on the adoption process is far less than that of personal influence and advice.

Of all the models described, Hovland's Persuasion theory took perhaps the broadest view of the entire process, although he proceeded by dissecting the entire process—communicator variables, channel variables, and receiver variables—and manipulating each variable experimentally in relation to the others in order to see how change in one affected change in another. Thus he tried to understand the whole, but in terms of its components rather than of the broad picture. The psychologists who have worked with the Consistency theory concentrated on the way a receiver tends to handle an incoming communication in such a way as to preserve the cognitive beliefs and relationships he or she has come to value.

As we indicated, these models (with the exception of the Silver Bullet) are rather more alike than different. They illustrate over time a fairly steady trend away from thinking of what a communicator can *do to* a receiver toward thinking of what a receiver *does with* a communication. Since the time of the Silver Bullet, none of the chief models has assumed the existence of a passive receiver, and the most recent models have tended to assume *two* active parties in the communication transaction, trying to affect each other.

In recent years there has been increasing interest in developing what some scholars have called a Transaction model, although the theory has not been formalized. This approach is somewhat like the one taken in Chapter 3 of this book. It assumes the presence of two relatively equal participants in the communication process, each working on a set of signs presented by one participant in terms of what he or she wants out of the transaction and interpreted by the other participants in terms of what each of them wants. Thus the communication process is seen as being in some ways analogous to trade or diplomatic or legal relationships in which both participants take action and from which each one has certain things he or she can give and certain things he or she wants to get. Rules, well understood if not always expressed, govern such a transaction, examples being the rules that direct the transaction between a pupil and a teacher, a parent and a child, a salesperson and a customer. If the transaction proceeds as hoped, each party will gain; the needs of each will be satisfied to a greater degree than before. And as the participants share information, they will probably move closer to a common understanding of the subject under discussion. Not necessarily closer to agreement, but closer at least to understanding what the other thinks and feels and knows about a given subject. And closer to knowing what each can do safely and comfortably in the situation.

This approach is a promising one, although still waiting for experiments and formalized theory to develop it.

For Further Consideration

1. What assumption does each of these models make about the function of communication? For example, the Information model seems to assume that the main role is to deliver a signal. How about the other models?
2. Recall what Lasswell named as the three basic functions of communication in society: surveillance, coordination, and socialization. Which of these models do you think he would have found most congenial to his viewpoint?
3. Which of these models seems to be concerned chiefly with communication in the individual; which ones with communication in society?

4. Hovland conducted research on communication chiefly by means of experiments; Lazarsfeld, chiefly by sample surveys. If you hadn't known that, would you have been able to predict it by looking at their models? If so, on what evidence?
5. Each of these, it has been said, is a *partial* model of communication. Would there be any way to combine some of these to make a more nearly complete communication model? Or would you have to start over again? And if the latter, where would be a good place to start?
6. Suppose you were going to try to develop the Transaction model. What are some of the questions you would try to answer? Can you think of any research projects that would help you fill out the model?

References

Chief readings on the Persuasion model, in addition to articles listed below, are these books from the Yale group: C. I. Hovland, A. A. Lumsdaine, and F. D. Sheffield, *Experiments on Mass Communication* (Princeton, N.J.: Princeton University Press, 1949); C. I. Hovland, I. L. Janis, and H. H. Kelley, *Communication and Persuasion* (New Haven, Conn.: Yale University Press, 1953); C. Hovland, (ed.), *The Order of Presentation in Persuasion* (New Haven, Conn.: Yale University Press, 1957); C. Hovland and I. L. Janis, *Personality and Persuasibility* (New Haven, Conn.: Yale University Press, 1959); and C. Hovland and C. Rosenberg, *Attitude Organization and Change* (New Haven, Conn.: Yale University Press, 1960).

On Consistency theory, see F. Heider, "Attitudes and Cognitive Organizations" (*Journal of Psychology*, 1946, *21*, 107–112); T. M. Newcomb, "An Approach to the Study of Communicative Acts" (*Psychological Review*, 1953, *60*, 393–404); C. E. Osgood, G. J. Suci, and P. H. Tannenbaum, *The Measurement of Meaning* (Urbana: University of Illinois Press, 1957); L. Festinger, *A Theory of Cognitive Dissonance* (New York: Harper & Row, 1957); and the review by W. McGuire in G. Lindzey and E. Aronson, (eds.), *Handbook of Social Psychology* (Reading, Mass.: Addison-Wesley, 1968).

For general reading on the Information theory model: C. E. Shannon and W. Weaver, *The Mathematical Theory of Communication* (Urbana: University of Illinois Press, 1949); C. Cherry, *On Human Communication* (Cambridge, Mass.: MIT Press, 1957); and an article applying the theory to some communication problems, W. Schramm, "Information Theory and Mass Communication" (*Journalism Quarterly*, 1955, *32*, 131–146).

1. *The Rhetoric of Aristotle.* Translated by Lane Cooper. Englewood Cliffs, N.J.: Prentice-Hall, 1932, Section XX.
2. *Ibid.*, p. 7
3. *Ibid.*, pp. 8–9.
4. D. Cartwright. "Some Principles of Mass Persuasion: Selected Findings of Research on the Sale of U.S. War Bonds." *Human Relations*, 1949, *2*, 253.
5. *Ibid.*

6. See the first References paragraph for a list of C. Hovland's books on his Yale studies.

7. I. Lorge. "Prestige, Suggestion and Attitudes." *Journal of Social Psychology*, 1936, *7*, 386–402.

8. C. I. Hovland and W. Weiss. "The Influence of Source Credibility on Communication Effectiveness." *Public Opinion Quarterly*, 15, 635–650.

9. H. C. Kelman and C. I. Hovland. " 'Reinstatement' of the Communicator in Delayed Measurements of Opinion Change." *Journal of Abnormal and Social Psychology*, 1953, *19*, 327–335.

10. K. Burke. *A Grammar of Motives*. Englewood Cliffs, N.J.: Prentice-Hall, 1945. K. Burke. *A Rhetoric of Motives*. Englewood Cliffs, N.J.: Prentice-Hall, 1950.

11. W. J. McGuire. "Persuasion, Resistance, and Attitude Change." In I. Pool et al. (eds.), *Handbook of Communication*. Skokie, Ill.: Rand McNally, 1973.

12. P. G. Zimbardo. "The Effect of Effort and Improvisation on Self-Persuasion Produced by Role-Playing." *Journal of Experimental Social Psychology*, 1965, *1*, 103–120.

13. K. Lewin. "Group Decision and Social Change." In E. E. Maccoby, T. M. Newcomb, and E. L. Hartley (eds.), *Readings in Social Psychology*. New York: Holt, Rinehart and Winston, 1958, pp. 197–211.

14. D. L. Thistlethwaite, H. deHaan, and J. Kamenetzky. "The Effects of 'Directive' vs. 'Non-Directive' Communication Procedures on Attitudes." *Journal of Abnormal and Social Psychology*, 1955, *51*, 107–113.

15. J. E. Dietrich. "The Relative Effectiveness of Two Modes of Radio Delivery in Influencing Attitudes." *Speech Monographs*, 1946, *13*, 58–65.

16. C. Hovland, A. A. Lumsdaine, and F. D. Sheffield. *Experiments on Mass Communication*. Princeton, N.J.: Princeton University Press, 1949.

17. W. J. McGuire. In G. Lindzey and E. Aronson, (eds.), *Handbook of Social Psychology*. Reading, Mass.: Addison-Wesley, 1968.

18. S. C. Menefee and A. G. Granneberg. "Propaganda and Opinions on Foreign Policy." *Journal of Social Psychology*, 1940, *11*, 393–404.

19. I .L. Janis and S. Feshbach. "Effects of Fear-Arousing Communication." *Journal of Abnormal and Social Psychology*, 1953, *48*, 78–92.

20. G. C. Chu. "Fear Arousal, Efficacy, and Imminency." *Journal of Personality and Social Psychology*, 1966, *5*, 517–521.

21. McGuire. *Handbook of Communication, op. cit.*

22. F. H. Lund. "The Psychology of Belief: IV. The Law of Primacy in Persuasion." *Journal of Abnormal and Social Psychology*, 1925, *20*, 183–191.

23. H. Cromwell. "The Relative Effects of Audience Attitude in the First Versus the Second Argumentative Speech of a Series." *Speech Monographs*, 1950, *17*, 105–122.

24. C. I. Hovland, and W. Mandell. "Is There a 'Law of Primacy in Persuasion'?" In C. I. Hovland, (ed.), *The Order of Presentation in Persuasion*. New Haven, Conn.: Yale University Press, 1957, pp. 13–22.

25. H. H. Kelley and E. Volkart. "The Resistance to Change of Group-Anchored Attitudes." *American Sociological Review*, 1952, *17*, 453–465.
26. S. E. Asch. "Studies of Independence and Conformity: A Minority of One Against a Unanimous Majority." *Psychological Monographs*, 1956, *70, 9.*
27. See McGuire's excellent summary in *Handbook of Social Psychology*, vol. III, pp. 235–236.
28. Lewin, *op. cit.*
29. McGuire. *Handbook of Social Psychology, op. cit.*, p. 219.
30. Kelman and Hovland, *op. cit.*
31. See *Peking Review*, November 4, 1977, *45*, for an account of Mao's statement.
32. F. Heider. "Attitudes and Cognitive Organizations." *Journal of Psychology*, 1946, *21*, 107–112.
33. T. M. Newcomb. "An Approach to the Study of Communicative Acts." *Psychological Review*, 1953, *60*, 393–404.
34. D. Cartwright and F. Harary. "Structural Balance: A Generalization of Heider's Theory." *Psychological Review*, 1956, *63*, 277–293.
35. L. Festinger. *A Theory of Cognitive Dissonance*. New York: Harper & Row, 1957.
36. C. Hovland and C. Rosenberg. *Attitude Organization and Change*. New Haven, Conn.: Yale University Press, 1960.
37. C. E. Osgood, G. J. Suci, and P. H. Tannenbaum. *The Measurement of Meaning*. Urbana: University of Illinois Press, 1957.
38. See McGuire's reviews in Lindzey and Aronson, *op. cit.*, and in Pool, et al., *op. cit.*, pp. 216–252.
39. C. E. Shannon and W. Weaver. *The Mathematical Theory of Communication*. Urbana: University of Illinois Press, 1949.
40. N. Wiener. *Cybernetics, or Control and Communication in the Animal and the Machine*. Cambridge, Mass.: MIT Press, 1961.
41. W. Schramm. "Information Theory and Mass Communication." In B. Berelson and M. Janowitz, (eds.), *Reader in Public Opinion and Communication*. New York: Free Press, 1966, pp. 723–735.

13/
MASS MEDIA—
THE QUIET EFFECTS

THE PERSONAL USES OF TIME

The term *mass media* does not appear in the great *Oxford English Dictionary*, published one volume at a time beginning in 1878, but the time the last volume appeared, in 1928, American adults were devoting almost one-fourth of their waking hours, on the average, to those same media, and the figure has continued to increase. The co-opting of so much of the time that we as individuals have at our disposal constitutes a major, even though curiously imperceptible, effect of the mass media. It is worth a careful look.

During the fall of 1979, in the 98 percent of American homes with television, the receiver was turned on for an average of seven hours a day. That is over 2500 hours per year—the equivalent of more than one hundred 24-hour days, waking or sleeping. A person who has lived in that kind of house for ten years has had the opportunity to watch nearly three solid years of television. Of course, no member of the family is likely to watch the tube all the time it is lighted. The average adult has probably watched about three hours a day; the average child, an hour more. Even these figures, multiplied by 365 days, are quite impressive.

Between 8 P.M. and 9 P.M. on an average evening between September and April about 100 million Americans are likely to be watching television (in the summer the total is about 15 percent less). On any given day about 75 percent of American adults are likely to read a newspaper, spending on the average about 30 minutes on it. In other words, Americans spend something like 70 million hours every day on newspapers. Just under 99 percent of American homes and about 90 percent of American automobiles have radios. The figures on radio listening time are not clear, but a frequent estimate is 150 million hours a day devoted to radio. Add in the time spent on magazines, books, and movies, and the truly enormous commitment of time we make to mass media will become apparent.

Still another way to look at the time commitment to mass media is the amount of intake during the growing years of children. By the time young Americans are in the twelfth grade, each of them has seen at least 15,000 hours of television—more time than they have spent in school, at play, or in any other activity except sleeping. The growing child, during those years, has seen at least 10,000 murders, knifings, shootings, and other violent acts on television. During those same years, an average American adult has seen about 300,000 commercials and has spent more time on television than on any other activity except work and sleep.

You are probably asking by now whether it is only in America that the mass media claim such huge slices of our lives. If we had comparable figures for Japan—where, as in the United States, almost every home has television and radio and one or more newspapers—we might find still higher figures. Certainly recent studies indicate that young Japanese children watch even more television than do U.S. children, although male adults are believed to watch a little less than U.S. adults. In European countries, where the time devoted to television programming is typically less than in the United States, and in Third World countries, where television receivers are less generally available and literacy is less, adults on the average devote less time to media than do Americans.

It is television that has made the most dramatic contribution to these time figures, but we should take a longer view of history than that. Five hundred years ago, when printing was just coming into use in Western Europe, the average human spent no more than a few minutes a day on mass media. Until the penny press came, in the early nineteenth century, and until the broadening of free education brought literacy and textbooks, the average time devoted to mass media was still measured in minutes a day. But literacy and prosperity encouraged reading; and then came movies, the first widely popular general entertainment medium, at the end of the nineteenth century; and in 1920 radio extended popular entertainment from the theater to the living room. Our best estimate, in the absence of accurate surveys, is that in the 1920s the average adult in the United States was spending between three and four hours per day on the media. And then came television—tentatively, experimentally, in the late 1930s; in a great avalanche after World War II.

Table 11 mirrors a study by Coffin, in 1955, of a sample of 2500 homes in Indiana that were just acquiring television and shows what happened to time allocations when the new medium arrived:

Table 11   PERSONAL USES OF TIME

| | TIME SPENT (IN MINUTES PER DAY) | | |
	Before Television Was Available	*After Purchase of a Receiver*	*Difference*
Magazines	17	10	−7
Newspapers	39	32	−7
Radio	122	52	−70
Television	12[a]	173	+161
TOTAL	190	267	+77

SOURCE: From E. Rubenstein et al. *Television and Social Behavior, Technical Report of the Surgeon General's Advisory Committee.* Washington, D.C.: U.S. Department of Health, Education, and Welfare, 1973, vol. IV, p. 411.
[a] Time spent viewing television away from home.

The important figure in that table is the 77 minutes that television added to the average viewer's total mass media time. Typically in previous years when a new medium had come into use it caused a readjustment of time allocations within about the same total time. But television actually added more than one hour to the slice of life typically given to media. It took a little away from magazine and newspaper reading, a very large amount away from radio, and, we can assume, a certain amount from movie attendance. That is the typical effect of new media; the older ones adjust to make room. But in this case it was necessary to find at least 77 minutes more from activities other than media use. In other words, television increased the time we spent on *all* media by about 40 percent.

We have spent more time studying the use we make of this mass media time than what we are *kept from doing* by giving so much time to the media. Reviewing the data, Comstock wrote:

Television accounted for a full third of all leisure time, and about 40 percent of leisure, when viewing described as secondary to some other activity, such as eating, was included. Even socializing of all kinds, including conversations at home and away, did not challenge television's domination of free time; it accounted for only about a fourth of leisure. Reading, study, and other uses of mass media accounted for only about 15 percent. Going somewhere and doing something—a hike, hunting, the opera, the Dallas Cowboys—made up only about 5 percent of leisure. Television has become the principal component of voluntary life in America.[1]

But at the cost of what? What activities are being replaced by that television time?

Two researchers at the University of Michigan, Robinson and Converse, recently compared a set of 24-hour time-use diaries filled in by a national sample of American urban adults in 1965 and 1966 with corresponding data from 30 years earlier, when television had not yet come into use. They found respondents in the 1960s reporting significantly less time sleeping, eating, reading, going to the movies, listening to the radio, participating in athletic sports and games, talking, driving for pleasure (not business), dancing, and going to church.[2]

A broader study was conducted in the 1960s for UNESCO by a Hungarian sociologist, Alexander Szalai.[3] He obtained time-use diaries in four countries of Western Europe, six of Eastern Europe, one in Latin America, and the United States. The total sample was over 25,000. Except for the United States, and East and West Germany, most of the countries were still at a fairly early stage of introducing television; one of them had only 26 percent of its homes equipped with television; another, only 35. Thus it was possible to compare the time-use diaries of users with those of nonusers in the same cultures. Robinson reanalyzed these data for the Surgeon General's study. He found that persons who had television had reduced their:

Sleeping time by an average of 13 minutes a day
Social time, away from home, by an average of 12 minutes a day
Radio time by an average of 8 minutes
Reading time by an average of 6 minutes
Housework by 7 minutes, on the average
Travel by 5 minutes average
Book reading by 6 minutes
Conversation by 5 minutes

Even at an early stage of television, then, people had cut substantially into the time they had been using for other media; they were staying home more; they were sleeping less; and they were conversing less, presumably so as not to interfere with television viewing. One wonders whether this changing pattern of social life—less going out, less talking with one's friends and neighbors, more time spent in the living room in front of the TV or the radio—has had anything to do with the changing appearance of American small towns, notably the disappearance of front porches. These porches were for conversing and for seeing one's neighbors—both competitors with the electronic neighbors in the living room.

In the past half-dozen years, two channels of American entertainment television and one channel carrying mostly public television have become available in American Samoa. In this kind of traditional society it is sometimes easier to see social impact than in an industrialized society. The program ratings in Samoa are some of the highest in the world. The result is that families now typically stay home in the evening instead of joining in village activities. They watch dancing oftener than doing their own dancing, hear singing oftener than they sing. Rather than "talk story" they tend to "hear story." Given more experience with television, their time distributions may adjust to retain more emphasis on the traditional activities of Samoan life. But in the meantime, the impact of the new medium is easy to see.[4]

The coming of television, by commandeering nearly one-third of our waking hours for the mass media, has changed not only our use of leisure but also our use of media. One way to get more time for media, when leisure time is in short supply, is to do something else while listening to or viewing one of the media. For example, one of the commonest uses of radio now is to relieve the boredom of driving an automobile; another is to provide a background for studying. One puts the television set where one can watch the early evening news while eating dinner. One reads on the plane or train. And so forth. Levy asked a large sample of individuals whether they ever did something else while watching TV news, and if so what.[5] Only 24 percent said they never did anything else during the news. Here were the percentages saying that at least occasionally they engaged in a second activity while the news was on the tube:

Eating dinner	41.2
Reading newspaper, books, etc.	25.8
Talking to people in room	23.3
Snacking, drinking	22.5
Working in kitchen	19.6
Sewing	17.1
Caring for children	15.0
Doing housework	14.2
Preparing for bed	9.6

It is hardly necessary to mention that most of these activities would draw a viewer's eyes or ears or both away from the television set. The use of radio as a secondary medium has now become familiar to us, but it is still a bit surprising to find television cast in that role, and especially to find reading and television viewing—both of which require eye concentration—going on at the same time.

Thus the effect of giving so many of our waking hours to mass media has been a silent but powerful one. It has made the living room an entertainment center and has discouraged our seeking entertainment elsewhere. It has cut into our social lives, our travel, our time for conversation. It has left us less time for sleep. It has created a series of things we might call "media holidays," like Super Bowl Sunday, and minor recurring but demanding festivals like Saturday and Sunday football, the favorite news anchorperson's program, the favorite entertainment program, the arrival of the Sunday morning newspaper. For some things that used to be popular, five hours of media time have not been good. They have nearly killed the baseball minor leagues, the local orchestras playing classical music, the Chautauquas and circuses. They have rearranged our lives more than we can realize unless we ask ourselves: Suppose all except, say, the newspaper and the book would go out of existence; once we recovered from the shock and found the television circuit was really dead, what would we do with that newly won four hours or so of leisure?

KNOWLEDGE

Still another quiet effect registers on us minute after minute during those long hours we give the mass media. To remind yourself what it is, you have only to look at a test like this:

Where did you learn what you know of these persons?
Ayatollah Rubollah Khomeini
Deng Xiaoping
Anwar Sadat
John Paul II
Kurt Waldheim
Bjorn Borg
Sanjay Gandhi
Quiz yourself a little further:

Where did you learn what you know of these events?
The fall from power of the "Gang of Four" in China
The Soviet invasion of Afghanistan

The election of a new government in Zimbabwe (Rhodesia)
The taking of American hostages in Teheran
The most recent Super Bowl game
Try one more test:

Where did you acquire the mental picture you carry of these persons and experiences?
How the moon looks when you stand on it
How the Earth looks from space
How a political demonstration looks in Iran
What the Concorde looks like
What the office of the President of the United States looks like

Most of your information on these people, scenes, and events undoubtedly came from the media. Some from television, some from print, some from elsewhere. You undoubtedly have talked about some or all of these topics with other people. You may have seen the Concorde, or seen Pope John Paul II on his visit to the United States, or seen Borg play tennis. But chances are that your main sources of knowledge were the media.

It has not always been so. A thousand years ago a typical resident of Earth knew his own village or city, and little more. A walk to the nearest hill and a long look over distant valleys was an adventure equivalent to an airplane trip today or the evening news on television. The coming of a traveler to your village with accounts of places and events perhaps 100 miles away was an experience much more powerful than the arrival of the weekly newsmagazine today. At that time, minstrels would go from village to village singing ballads about the kings and knights and their combats somewhere beyond the hills that bordered the village; and these songs were more than popular music today—they were news.

Five hundred years ago, mariners from Europe were beginning to push out into the oceans, and hand-printed books were becoming available, but the only way to learn how a distant place or person looked was to listen to a description or go to see what an artist had drawn or painted. It would be 350 years before anyone could take pictures, 400 before moving pictures would be available, 450 before people could watch pictures in "real time"—when an event was occurring.

Remember that human beings have been on Earth for at least 100,000 years. It is only in the last minutes of mankind's long day on Earth when these things have happened. For only a few years out of at least 100,000 have we depended on mass media to be our eyes and ears in far places. And only in that time have our worlds so expanded and our distances so shrunk that what happened in Vietnam a few years ago or what is happening in Teheran today or what will probably happen in Asia or Africa tomorrow seems almost as near to us as what happened only a few miles from a village a few hundred years ago.

Far from being silly, therefore, the questions we have been asking represent a basic change in our way of life and our relation to the environment. Some people have said that the television picture of Earth, the "blue planet" as seen from one of the Apollo spaceships, may be the greatest learning experience of our times. Current historians have speculated that a few notable television shots of the Vietnam war—a Vietnam officer shooting an unarmed captive, an American soldier setting fire to a thatch village with his cigarette lighter—did more than anything else to tell people at home what war is really like, and incidentally to get U.S. forces out of Indochina. Furthermore, there is no doubt that media coverage and commentary have brought about a fundamental change in world viewpoint: a realization that Earth resources are finite and must be shared and that in one way or other the destiny of one group of Earth's people is common to all other groups, and the big problems must be solved in common.

What kinds of knowledge do we get from media, what kinds from other people and personal experience? Obviously, the farther an event or a person is from us, the more likely we are to have to depend on media. We are more likely to have seen or spoken to the mayor of our city than our member congress, more likely to have seen or spoken to him or her than the President of the United States, more likely to have seen our own President than the leader of a foreign country. We often are eyewitnesses to a fire in our own city or an accident in our neighborhood, but still there are many occasions when we turn to television for a picture of local events or to the newspaper for a fuller account of what happened.

For a number of years, scholars have been studying where people get their information on elections. In Table 12 such results were put together after the 1976 elections.

People were asked in each survey what had been their primary source of information for the election just completed. Viewed in that way, it is apparent that "other people" were significant sources of information (and probably advice) chiefly for local elections and newspapers were the main media source only for local elections. Television was slightly more important than newspapers for state elections, considerably more important in national elections. In other words, the

Table 12 RESULTS OF SURVEYS MEASURING MEDIA SOURCES OF INFORMATION TO THE PUBLIC FOR LOCAL, STATE, AND NATIONAL ELECTIONS, 1952–1976

	ALL ELECTIONS	LOCAL ELECTIONS				STATE ELECTIONS				NATIONAL ELECTIONS			
	1952	1964	1968	1972	1976	1964	1968	1972	1976	1964	1968	1972	1976
Newspapers	22%	42%	40%	41%	44%	41%	37%	39%	35%	36%	24%	26%	20%
Television	31	27	26	31	34	43	42	49	53	64	65	66	75
Radio	27	10	6	7	7	10	6	7	5	9	4	6	4
People	—	18	23	23	12	8	9	9	6	4	4	5	3
Magazines	5	1	1	2	1	1	1	1	1	6	5	5	5
Other	—	7	4	5	6	4	4	3	3	3	2	2	1
TOTAL		105%	100%	109%	104%	107%	99%	108%	103%	122%	104%	110%	108%

SOURCE: C. J. Sterling and T. R. Haight. *The Mass Media: Aspen Institute Guide to Communication Industry Trends*. New York: Praeger, 1978, p. 277.
NOTE: Some columns add to more than 100 percent because of double answers.

223

closer at hand the event, the more people depended on newspapers and on their friends and neighbors; the farther away it was, the more they depended on television.

A time trend also begins to show up in the table we have just reproduced: The dependence on newspapers in state and national elections seems to be slowly declining; the use of television, rising. This is supported by other results. In 1961, for the first time, national surveys reported that television was "the most believable news medium" in the opinions of a national sample. Since that time, the percentage who feel newspapers are "most believable" has remained approximately the same, while the percentage naming television as most believable has increased from 39 to 51 percent.[6] Similarly, between 1965 and 1975, total television viewing time increased an average of about five hours a week, while newspaper reading time fell about one hour per week. These same changes have taken place in every age group—the 20s, 30s, 40s, and 50s—but the larger changes have been among older people.[7]

Why have people come to depend on newspapers rather than television as a source of information about public affairs and major news? Robinson and Converse suggest that when television came into wide use it was first considered almost wholly a source of entertainment-fantasy content.[8] As television matured, however, it matured also as a news source. Its news coverage expanded and drew pictures from ever widening sources. Its Vietnam coverage, its coverage of the moonshots, its coverage of events of national elections and events of national importance like the assassination of President John Kennedy, and the appearance of serious and highly professional news programs like "60 Minutes"—all these demonstrated to audiences that it was more than an entertainment medium. Robinson and Converse point out that there was no very noticeable effect of television on newspapers, news reading, or book reading until the 1970s, when this new image of television had become apparent.

Yet we should not assume from this trend that television has captured the news function, even in the case of very faraway or very pictorial events. Television is clearly the best window on events as they happen: The impact of the moon scenes could never have been duplicated in newspapers. Except in rare cases, however, television news is a headline service, and for more facts, more interpretations, we are more likely to go to print. Similarly, as we said elsewhere, television is very good at covering science politics, but if we want to learn more about *science* we usually turn to print. The extraordinary thing about television is the vividness of its coverage and the extent to which people have come to trust it.

One more question: What kind of knowledge of our environment typically comes to us from other people, what kind from media? Greenberg, whom we have already quoted and whose diagram we have reproduced, has the best answer to that.[9] Only the news interesting to the smallest numbers and the very largest numbers of people is likely to come to us by word of mouth. Thus, if there is a case of measles in the neighborhood, we are likely to hear about it from a neighbor, not from the newspaper, certainly not from television. On the other hand, an event of the greatest national interest—a shocking event like the assassination of President Kennedy—is also likely to be passed around in the first hours by word of mouth. Those of us who were old enough to be media users in 1963 when the President was killed remember very well how we heard that news, and surveys have shown that about half of us heard it first from an excited individual who in turn had heard it from someone else or from radio or television. That news was so traumatic that people felt they had to tell others. Similarly, a case of measles is of such purely local interest that neighbors tell neighbors rather than calling a reporter. Everything between these two extremes—the bulk of the news—typically comes to us from news media. In other words, we have turned over the bulk of the responsibility for informing us to the mass media and asked them to cover the entire world for our information. This is a remarkable development in human history—as becomes apparent when we look back a few hundred years—but it also has its dangers. It requires us to put a gatekeeper between us and what happens everywhere in the world beyond our immediate experience. How well this gatekeeper functions, how clear the news window is between us and faraway events, is a matter of concern both to us and to the media.

SOCIALIZATION

All television is educational TV; the only difference is what it is teaching.

There is some question as to who first said this, but little doubt concerning the idea itself. The effectiveness of television in the classroom has long been recognized; the more we see it in action, the more inclined we are to respect what it teaches, intentionally or not, *outside* the classroom. What we have said about television can also be applied, in greater or lesser measure, to all the other media. People learn from them even when they do not realize they are learning. And no better example can be found of the incidental, unintended, often unexpected learning from the media than what they contribute to the skills, values, and beliefs that go to make up human socialization.

Socialization means growing up into a society. We have to learn the rules of society, what to expect and what is expected of us, what is possible and what is forbidden, who and what are important, and what kind of behavior is rewarded.

Socialization goes on through life, but the great years are the first 20 or so, during which, as Roberts describes it, a totally dependent baby turns into an independent adult.[10] The child begins with a relatively empty field of information to fill. That field very quickly begins to fill up. Information is stored on which to base decisions and judge other information. The child develops new and more efficient ways to process information, new ways of choosing friends and interacting with them, new physical abilities to do things a child wants to do. He or she learns both by trial and error and by internalizing values and standards. Almost as though by magic the child turns into an adult, no longer dependent upon parents, beginning to think of a spouse's and a parent's role for himself or herself.

It has long been recognized that the media play an important part in this process, but, of course, not the only part. Parents, especially in the early years, are perhaps the most important factors. Then brothers and sisters, friends, school when the child is old enough to go to school, church if the child is brought up to go to church, early experience with jobs and career building, competitive activities like athletics, social experiences with the other sex, and so forth. Almost all a young person's experiences enter into the socialized product.

And TV. It is generally agreed that television is the most influential of the media in socialization, even though it does not deliberately set out to socialize us, as do parents and schoolteachers, for example. And even though the principal motive for all a child's viewing of television is entertainment, let us not underestimate the amount of incidental learning that goes with entertainment. Marshall McLuhan once said to a researcher, "You are wasting your time studying ETV in schools; the real education is out here, out here with the networks and the picture tubes." In one sense, the fact that children use TV as a source of entertainment makes it more powerful as a teacher. It does not pose as a teacher. It does not make assignments or check assignments or give tests. Therefore it arouses no resistance. Children do not come expecting to work. They expect to be pleased, not taught. And so hour after hour important interpretations of life pass across the picture tube, and the viewers absorb a high proportion of them, without realizing they are learning.

For example, on the picture tube they see:

How skilled and apparently successful young people act toward the opposite sex

What clothes they wear
Who is important in the society
What makes them important
How they get that way, and how they act when they are important
What are the desirable jobs in the society
How rich people live
What the society thinks of minorities
How they can expect to be treated—for instance, by taxi drivers, waiters, hiring offices—when they go away from their own town or neighborhood
How violent people in the society are
Can a criminal get away with breaking the law
How police and detectives act
What qualities make a person admirable, and the reverse, in our society

Let us say again that this kind of information on television, or in other media, does not come from systematic teaching. What a young person gets is merely fallout from the tremendous parade of television programs going past viewers for three to four hours a day. TV doesn't specifically tell children the answer to any of the questions we asked. They see. They see examples of what works and what doesn't, how people of different kinds act, dress, and look, how the important and successful are distinguished from the unimportant and the failures. In other words, children are watching life, and a picture of life they increasingly tend to believe.

Jack Lyle and Heidi Hoffman, two communication researchers, queried several hundred Los Angeles children and found that about three-fourths of those of elementary school age believed that "If you saw it on TV news" it was certain to be true.[11]

Talking about this finding Comstock said:

> By high school, the credibility of television coverage is far more
> frequently questioned. But there is something more to television news
> than simply the exposure to events, the enlarged vicarious exposure to
> politics, or the trust it inspires. The schools emphasize in their treatment
> of public events consensual symbols—the office of the presidency, the
> role of Congress and the Supreme Court, and such abstract questions as
> the relative merits of bi- and unicameral legislatures. Television, like
> all news media, emphasizes the dissensual—protests, riots, strikes, the
> tearful congressman contemplating an embezzler's cell, the disgraced
> President stepping into a helicopter. . . . Television is not redundant to
> what children learn elsewhere, and what it portrays is a world of
> conflict and dishonesty that often may leave them uncomfortable with
> their vaguely formulated convictions. Cynicism, skepticism, the belief

that not all is right or just—television inevitably encourages such reactions among the young.[12]

Many observers have hazarded the guess that television and (secondarily, perhaps) the other media are especially important in the socialization process today because families have less influence than they had a generation ago. They tend now to be more permissive. They maintain less intimate and frequent relationships with other branches of the family and especially the older members. They tend to adhere less faithfully to one political party and switch allegiances and votes more often. Fewer families seem to be faithful churchgoers. Consequently less stability is passed on to the young people. And therefore the media, as Comstock says, "come to play a greater role [in socialization], both indirectly through the information and impressions they bring to parents and directly by what they convey to children."[13]

We are not trying to give the impression that mass media contributions to socialization are necessarily undesirable. Quite the contrary. It is not necessarily bad that television, for example, takes children outside the limits of their lives and their neighborhoods and shows them other kinds of life and other places. It is not bad to stretch young people's ideas by showing them different kinds of models and challenging them with unfamiliar points of view. It is not necessarily bad to show them patterns of behavior they can imitate.

The question is not whether young people are having experiences like these—we know they *are*—or even whether they *should* have. The real question is, What kind of view of the world and its people are they being shown? What models are they being given to imitate? What expectations are they being encouraged to hold concerning jobs and living conditions? We have no reason to worry that they are being shown a violent world; we know the world is full of violence. Rather, we should be concerned whether and how often they are shown that violence is rewarded or that people can "get away with it." We should be concerned if women are shown chiefly in subservient roles; for example, if we continue to find, as did a 1971 study, that of 299 central figures in commercials 70 percent of the males were portrayed as authorities, but only 14 percent of the women.[14] We should be concerned whether blacks, Chicanos, and other minority groups are being presented fairly; for example, if the situation has not changed since a 1972 study showed no blacks at all in 60 percent of the Saturday morning children's programs.[15]

On the one hand, we can be grateful that children have these hours with the media to broaden their experiences and their outlook, to show them far places and far people they might never otherwise see.

On the other hand, we can afford to worry over the kind of world, the kind of behavior, the kind of standards, they are being shown— not primarily in the news, but rather in the entertainment programs from which they derive vicarious experience and in which they see a picture of the world different from what they see at home or learn in school. We really don't know enough about it to say just what the effects of these experiences are, but we do know that children and young people are being socialized, contributions are being made to their adult lives, hour by hour, day by day, as they sit in front of the television set, or read, or listen to the radio.

We call these the quiet effects because they happen without our seeking them and without results that can be immediately or dramatically seen. Nevertheless, we can hardly doubt that they are powerful. We commit a fourth to a third of our waking hours—a fourth to a third of our active lives!—to the media, and thereby give up the chance to do anything else with a segment of living we can never recapture. We let media gatekeepers—unknown to us, persons whom we shall probably never meet—decide what we shall see and hear of the distant world. We give the media, especially television, a major part of the task of helping our children grow into adults. Although we may never be able to point to the specific effect of any particular program of any particular hour, still the long-term effects will be with us all the days of our lives.

For Further Consideration

1. If you could use television for the kind of information you think it could most effectively provide, what kinds of events and people would you want it to cover for you?
2. You probably have had the experience of doing something else while you view television or listen to radio. When you do that, how much of the program do you fail to take in? What aspects of the program do you fail to get?
3. If you have seen television in another country, what has been your impression of it? Do you find it better or worse, more or less pleasurable, more or less informative than television at home? And in what respects?
4. The Surgeon General's Scientific Advisory Committee had a hard time deciding whether the research they commissioned really did or did not prove that violent television caused violent behavior. What kind of proof would you want before deciding that violence on television really does cause violence in life?

References

For general reading: see the five volumes of the Surgeon General's study reports, E. Rubenstein et al., (eds.), *Television and Social Behavior* (Washington, D.C.: U.S. Department of Health, Education, and Welfare, 1973) especially J. Lyle, (ed.), *Day-to-Day Life Patterns of Children.* Also G. Comstock et al., *Television and Human Behavior* (New York: Columbia University Press, 1978); and G. Comstock, *Television in America* (Beverly Hills, Calif.: Sage, 1980). Also the biennial reports of the Roper Organization on *Changing Attitudes Toward Television and Other Mass Media* (New York: Television Information Office, the most recent volume being 1979). The most complete compilation of tabular data on the media is C. J. Sterling and T. R. Haight, *The Mass Media: Aspen Institute Guide to Communication Industry Trends* (New York: Praeger, 1978).

1. G. Comstock et al. *Television and Human Behavior.* New York: Columbia University Press, 1978, pp. 32–33.
2. J. P. Robinson and P. E. Converse. "The Impact of Television on Mass Media Use." In A. Szalai, (ed.), *The Use of Time: Daily Activities of Urban and Suburban Populations in Twelve Countries.* The Hague: Mouton, 1972, pp. 197–212.
3. Also summarized in J. P. Robinson, "TV's Impact on Everyday Life." In E. Rubenstein, et al., (eds.) *Television and Social Behavior, Technical Report of the Surgeon General's Scientific Advisory Committee.* Washington, D.C.: U.S. Department of Health, Education, and Welfare, 1973, vol. IV, pp. 410–431.
4. W. Schramm, L. Nelson, and M. Betham. *Bold Adventure: The Story of ETV in American Samoa.* Stanford, Calif.: Stanford University Press, 1980.
5. M. R. Levy. "The Audience Experience with Television News." *Journalism Monographs,* 1978, 55.
6. The Roper Organization. *Changing Attitudes Toward Television and Other Mass Media, 1959–1978.* New York: Roper, 1979.
7. Robinson and Converse, *op. cit.,* p. 429.
8. *Ibid.,* p. 424.
9. B. S. Greenberg and E. B. Parker. *The Kennedy Assassination and the American Public: Social Communication in Crisis.* Stanford, Calif.: Stanford University Press, 1965, p. 17.
10. D. F. Roberts. In Rubenstein et al., *op. cit.,* "Children's Responses to TV Violence," vol. II, p. 178.
11. J. Lyle and H. Hoffman. "Explorations in Patterns of Television Viewing by Pre-School Age Children." In Rubenstein et al., *op. cit.,* vol. IV, pp. 129 ff.
12. Comstock et al., *op. cit.,* p. 121.
13. *Ibid.,* p. 125.
14. *Ibid.*
15. B. S. Greenberg. "Children's Reactions to TV Blacks." *Journalism Quarterly,* 1972, 49, 5–14.

14/
MASS MEDIA
—THE LESS QUIET
EFFECTS

PUBLIC OPINION

Both politicians and scholars are likely to agree with the judgment of *Television and Human Behavior*[1] that "television has drastically altered American politics." Yet television is not the first medium that has influenced the political process. It was not television that made possible democratic elections and created public opinion as a force in political life; that was done by the first media—news and opinion sheets and newspapers, which preceded television by more than three centuries. Similarly, the kinds of changes that television has made were begun by film and radio. Television has changed politics not so much by originating new practices as by the size of the differences it has made. That is what the head of one party's national committee meant when he reflected on the effect of television by calling politics "now a whole new ball game."

Some observers have commented that post-TV politics has actually taken on some of the characteristics of a "ball game." The nominating conventions are treated, by political parties and networks alike as show business; the candidates are reported like sports heroes and spend as much effort projecting an attractive personality as do the great stars of entertainment. The comment has also been frequently made that television can't win elections, although one 20-minute speech—the famous television talk in which Richard Nixon in 1952 defended himself against the charge of accepting private expense money by invoking his wife's "plain cloth" coat, his mortgage, and his dog Checkers—did keep a prominent figure from passing out of national politics. Without that talk he very probably would never have become Vice-President or President. So television has not so much changed the rules of the game as the way points are scored.

Perhaps we can make some of this effect clear by saying something about media personalities, media events, and media agenda-setting.

MEDIA PERSONALITIES

Long before television, the media had proved their extraordinary ability to create characters who could tug at the hearts and minds of audiences.

In the time of Dickens, whose novels were published in weekly installments and sent by ship from England across the Atlantic, people used to rent small boats to meet the incoming oceangoing ships at the entrance to New York harbor, in order to get an early report on what had happened to some favorite character in the latest installment. They would shout up at the people on the ship's deck questions like, "Did little Nell die?"

When silent movies came in, they created a long line of sex symbols, from Rudolph Valentino ("The Sheik") to Mary Pickford ("America's sweetheart") to Marilyn Monroe, a few really beloved characters like Charlie Chaplin as the little tramp, a long line of adventure heroes from flamboyant types like Douglas Fairbanks to strong cowboys like John Wayne, and even a herd of animal heroes like Lassie.

Radio's galaxy of personalities was hard to equal: Jack Benny, Fred Allen, Bob Hope, George Burns and Gracie Allen, and many others. Even announcers like Graham McNamee for sports and Milton Cross for the Saturday afternoon operas became national figures. For more than 20 years people laughed and cried every week over the well-known, well-loved members of "One Man's Family."

When television came along it took over many of the characters of radio and film, and developed new personalities of its own. Among other things it transferred some of the magic of radio and film actors to newsmen and political figures. Radio had already made a start at

this. In the years of the Great Depression, Frankin D. Roosevelt, because of his "fireside chats," became the best-known radio voice in
America; in World War II, the voice of Winston Churchill rallied
Britain as FDR had rallied the United States. Some of the remarkable
group of American correspondents who reported the coming of war
to Europe—Edward R. Murrow and William Shirer, for instance—
won only slightly less trust. As a matter of fact, it was this trust in
radio news that made it possible for a Halloween spoof by Orson
Welles—a dramatization of H. G. Wells's *War of the Worlds*, de-
picting in radio news style a supposed Martian invasion of New Jersey—to be accepted by many people as fact and to cause a widespread
panic.[2] Another personality built by radio was Father Coughlin, whose
weekly radio talks, combining politics with religion, drew a record
audience and frightened some social analysts into wondering what a
skilled demagogue might accomplish with the new medium. (Hitler
helped answer that question.) And an evening newscaster on Iowa's
most powerful radio station, with an impressive speaking manner but
no political experience, came within a few thousand votes of being
elected governor of Iowa, then ran for Congress and was elected and
reelected, time after time.

Parties began to look for a good voice, and then for a good television personality, in their candidates. John F. Kennedy based no
small part of his 1960 Presidential campaign on what could be accomplished with television, which projected admirably his youth and
vigor. It was not television alone that elected him, but the first television debate of that campaign was clearly the turning point and succeeded in proving something that people who did not know him personally could hardly have come to believe otherwise: that he was a
worthy opponent of the Vice-President, despite comparative lack of
age and experience. He found also that he could meet effectively one
of the most damaging attacks on his candidacy—fear of electing
America's first Catholic President—by rebroadcasting his interview
on that subject with a group of Protestant clergymen. Television, as we
have said, was only one factor in his election, but without it he would
have had far less chance.

For a long time media experts have been a part of the staff of
national and state candidates, although originally most of them were
press rather than broadcasting representatives. James Hagerty, Eisen-
hower's press representative, undoubtedly played a considerable part
in prolonging the political career of his employer by frank and skillful handling of the news of the President's heart attack during his
first term. Since 1960 candidates have redoubled their efforts to prepare themselves to be seen and heard on television and have sought

the help of experts as needed. Let there be no more such haggard pictures as Nixon projected in the first debate with Kennedy in 1960. Let there be no more such accidents as President Ford's stumbling when he got out of an airplane in the 1976 campaign. Let there be no speaking that projects anything less than confidence and authority.[3]

Polls, computers, and television, as countless commentators have noted, have now become essentials of national campaigning. The pollsters find out the issues voters want to hear about, computers process the information almost overnight for the candiates and their advisers, and television lets the candidates speak to those key issues almost before the voters themselves know what they are. "Packaging the candidate"—unpleasant though the phrase is—thus becomes no more insidious than helping candidates present themselves and their ideas in the most favorable way possible. It is probably true that in most elections media coverage does not change many votes. Yet it changes some, and these may be key ones. It reinforces existing political loyalties. In the case of a new candidate, a little-known political figure, the media help to set the public image of the candidate.

And what kind of image are they looking for? A kind of "political hero," says Don Nimmo, political scientist and long-time student of public opinion.[4] They look for qualifications such as maturity, honesty, sincerity, strength, activity, energy, ability to lead. They look for candidates they can admire and whose ideas and plans they feel they can share. Jimmy Carter, running against Watergate rather than Gerald Ford, got himself elected by presenting himself throughout the country as a fresh and honest man, saying over and over, "I just want to see this country once again as pure, honest, and decent, and truthful, and fair, and confident, and idealistic, and compassionate, as filled with love, as are the American people."

Gene Wyckoff, who has served as adviser to a number of candidates, says:

> All television viewers would seem to have mental picture galleries in their heads, the walls of which are hung with the portraits of heroes, lovers, villains, stooges, fathers, statesmen, politicians, comedians, and other stereotyped characters in television's commedia dell'arte. With little conscious effort—or perhaps in spite of conscious effort—viewers probably match the pictures in their mental picture galleries against the images of the candidates' character accordingly.[5]

We have talked mostly about candidates as media personalities. The media have also built political trust in some of their own people. For example, Walter Cronkite was for years found by pollsters to be one of the most trusted persons in the country. That raises the question of what the media have done to build such admiration and trust. A similar status comes harder to persons who have risen to the top of business and industrial organizations, to positions of religious or academic excellence, or to high political office. Roper polls show government standing rather low among "admired organizations," but television at the very top.[6] Thus it seems likely that media coverage has contributed to reordering the standing of American popular heroes.

Media coverage has apparently contributed also to a shorter time-span of political loyalty; one is not necessarily a lifelong Republican or a lifelong Democrat anymore, nor an unswerving supporter of Politician X, but tends to judge X as X looks now rather than in the past, the person and the current viewpoint rather than membership in a party. This opens the door wider to the winds of change than in the past, to the currents of news and the projections of political personalities. And needless to say, to new personalities when they fit the requirements.

MEDIA EVENTS

Daniel J. Boorstin, looking at contemporary life with a historian's eye, perceived some years ago that current history was beginning to fill up with what he called "pseudo-events"—happenings created chiefly for media coverage. In other words, rather than moving with the currents of news, skillful persons were learning how to move the news itself.[7]

This practice, of course, is far older than television. In the days when newspapers were the only major news medium, news management was the occupation of "press agents." These persons were expert in getting special news attention for circuses, prizefights, and other events to which it was desired to attract people. For example, when the circus came to town it was typically covered with a six-inch ad and/or a three-paragraph story. But the skillful press agent would dream up other pseudo-events to interest prospective customers. It was possible to plant a story of a "talking horse," or a new species of animal, or a wild elephant, or a quarrel between trapeze artists, or a lion tamer who was a candidate for the Miss America title—or any one of countless other topics that might give reporters something unusual to write about and encourage audiences to come to see the excitement.

Most press conferences were pseudo-events, intended to get attention for an author of a new book, or a political candidate, or some other client. When radio came in, media representatives arranged radio interviews. Radio, of course, had some advantage because audiences could hear, and to that extent participate, in an event or a pseudo-event. It was immensely more exciting to hear the voting on the floor of a nominating convention than to read about it next day in the newspaper, Consequently, political events were built up with a maximum of excitement and suspense. No one who heard the broadcast of one of Hitler's mass meetings will ever forget that excitement. The audiences who listened to the first broadcasts of an election night felt similarly caught up in the excitement and suspense of the choice of a President. The broadcast media made it possible to experience events in "real time" rather than next day. It was like being there, as radio recognized when it introduced a series of programs reenacting great events of history and called the series, "You Are There."

But television, as usual, opened a still more dramatic door. Election night let the audience see the hot news coming in and the votes being totaled, the computers forecasting results, the pollsters trying to explain them. Well-known newscasters and political figures passed across the screen to be seen rather than merely listened to or read.

After 1960, parties and candidates began to put a notably higher proportion of their campaign funds into paid media time and space—the greater part of it into television. The hour-long political addresses and torchlight parades were fine for local audiences, but not very effective on TV. Therefore the patterns of presentation had to be changed. Thirty- or sixty-second commercials, expertly made with a candidate answering a question supposedly asked by a voter, or a well-known person endorsing the candidate, proved as effective for politics as for purchases. Governor Nelson Rockefeller of New York built his final gubernatorial campaign largely on such commercials.

However, the media managers came to prefer news exposure to commercial time. This invited all the ingenuity of candidates and advisers to make events that would draw coverage. The President, of course, had the advantage. He was the incumbent. All it was necessary to do was announce a news conference, and three networks and all the Washington press corps would be present. The President could greet a visitor in the White House rose garden, present a medal or a certificate, sit at the desk with a foreign diplomat, climb into a helicopter on the White House lawn, attend church or a funeral or a wedding or a dinner, and be sure of news coverage and probably pictures. President Nixon in 1972, President Carter in 1980 demonstrated how much an incumbent could do on the news media without ever leaving the White House.

Other political figures, of course, usually have to work harder to gain news coverage. Strangely enough, the pseudo-events of the pretelevision era—the campaign travels, handshaking visits, the babies to be patted or kissed, the trips through factories and over farms, the brief talks to organizations or working people or even street crowds, which used to be the *only* way political candidates could be seen by the voters—did not go out of style when television came to be important, but now they are planned always with an eye to media coverage. A candidate could shake 40 or 50 hands in a shopping center and be seen by perhaps 100 people, but if the media were tipped off he or she might get a few seconds on television and be seen by 20,000 persons. The candidate could lay a wreath on a local monument or visit a local hero, and appear in the paper or on the evening news. Any experienced media consultant could devise reasons to invite cameramen to be present. In other words, a whole new generation of media events grew out of what had been merely personal campaigning.

Most of these events, it is true, have been aimed at letting the electorate see the candidate, get some sense of the personality, hear or read a well-prepared, well-spoken sentence or two. They are not settings in which the great issues of the election can be discussed at length. As such, they doubtless contribute to choosing a candidate rather than choosing sides on an issue. But there is no doubt that far more people than half a century ago have had some vicarious experience with a national election and know what a national political candidate actually looks like, acts like, sounds like. Whether that makes for deeper acquaintance or better choice remains to be proved.

Television, because of the kind of medium it is, has led in the process of magnifying minor or pseudo-events. Television is basically an entertainment medium. News has to compete with drama, comedy, variety. Therefore, newscasters have come to feel that it is well for them to provide a bit of fun, and as much excitement as possible, along with the serious content of the news. Thus it is the most exciting, the most dramatic, or the funniest picture that is likely to be chosen from what is available.

An example of this can be found in the illuminating study by Kurt and Gladys Lang of the Chicago parade when General Douglas MacArthur returned from Korea in 1951. The Langs assigned a group of observers to watch the television coverage of the parade and stationed other observers at frequent intervals along the parade route. The face-to-face observers were rather disappointed. They had to wait a long time, and then the motorcade sped past so quickly that they barely caught a glimpse of the famous general. They had time only to give one cheer, and then for them the event was over. They were neither very excited nor impressed. But the television picture was quite different. The cameras were in an automobile directly in back of General MacArthur's car. They focused on the (momentarily) cheering crowds, turned back to the smiling general, turned to the next cheering crowd, and so forth. In other words, television gave the impression of a triumphant parade through cheering multitudes. The multitudes themselves were rather bored by the experience; TV viewers were thrilled. Thus, as the Langs pointed out, the viewer's selective perception may have less to do with the effect of television coverage than the selectivity of the camera and its operator.[8]

MEDIA AGENDA-SETTING

We have pointed out the difficulty of pinning down the specific effect of the mass media on public opinion. This has discouraged most researchers who have tried to find out exactly what television has to do with political attitudes and votes. On the one hand, it is clear that television has made a great change in politics. On the other hand, studying two Presidential elections, the researchers at the Columbia Bureau of Applied Social Research concluded that they could find no evidence that more than a few votes were changed by broadcasts.[9] Trying to explain some of the effects that seemed to be attributable to the media, the Columbia researchers developed the so-called Two-Step Flow hypothesis, which said that opinion leaders passed along to others in the community the ideas and attitudes they (the opinion leaders) derived from the media. Unfortunately, as we have noted, this hypothesis has not tested well in practice, and it is no longer regarded as a major key to political effect.

Neither practical politicians nor journalists, however, have been willing to accept either the idea that the media have little effect on public opinion or that their chief impact comes through a two-step flow from opinion leaders. Walter Lippman, journalist and long-time student of public opinion, entitled the first chapter of his pioneering book on *Public Opinion*, "The World Outside and the Pictures in Our Heads." He concluded that it was chiefly the news media that transferred pictures of the political universe to the minds of voters.[10] Theodore White, whose books on *The Making of the President* have been perhaps the best summaries and interpretations of recent campaigns, wrote this in his 1972 volume:

> The power of the press in America is a primordial one. It sets the agenda of public discussion; and this sweeping power is unrestrained by any law. It determines what people will talk and think about—an authority that in other nations is reserved for tyrants, priests, parties and mandarins.

No major act of the American Congress, no foreign adventure, no act of diplomacy, no great social reform can succeed in the United States unless the press prepares the public mind. And when the press seizes a great issue to thrust onto the agenda of talk, it moves action on its own—the cause of the environment, the cause of civil rights, the liquidation of the war in Vietnam, and, as climax, the Watergate affair were all set on the agenda, in first instance, by press.[11]

By coincidence or perhaps because it was an idea whose time had come, White's phrase "sets the agenda of public discussion" was very much on the minds of some communication researchers and some political scientists in the early 1970s. A political scientist, Bernard Cohen, expressed the thought in the simplest terms when he wrote that whereas the media might not be successful much of the time in telling people what to think, they are highly successful in telling people what to think *about*. Communication researchers tested the concept of agenda-setting in practical campaign studies. An article by McCombs and Shaw in 1972 was the first empirical report on agenda-setting.[12] They found good evidence that the political electorate, at a given time and in a given place, were concerned with and were discussing the major issues that were salient in the chief news media at that time and place. Throughout the 1970s McCombs and his colleagues continued to test the idea, trying to find out the conditions under which it works and where it does not work. A new theory of Agenda-Setting began to emerge which, on the whole, seems to be more useful than the idea of Two-Step Flow.

The theory of Agenda-Setting is based on two ideas—that the media are necessarily gatekeepers for reporting the news of the world (they can't possibly carry the news without rigorously selecting from an enormous mass of stories), and, secondly, that people feel a continuing need for orientation to the complex world of politics. That is to say, they need help in deciding what events and what issues, among those outside their own limited experience, are worth being concerned about and paying attention to.

The news media—news wires, newspapers, newsmagazines, radio, and television—have gatekeepers at every stage of the news process contributing to selection: local reporters, wire news editors, telegraph editors, and so forth. Each one must make a choice from among more news than can possibly be carried. Each of them must make a decision that ultimately will have some impact on the political agenda presented to reading, listening, viewing audiences. Thus each news agency, each newspaper, each radio or television newsroom, ultimately arrives at its own agenda, which it then offers its audiences. McCombs points out that these news media agendas are necessarily closely related to the agenda of their news sources: The President's spokesman tells reporters *his* idea of the current agenda; the candidates communicate their agenda by deciding what to talk about; the bureaucracy, the large business organization, the labor union, each will have its own agenda of news it feels belongs on the agenda of the news media.

And within limits, the news media reflect these prior agendas. Within limits, but not completely. They still must choose. They still have the opportunity to dig out events of their own choice and decide upon issues that the public should know about. One dramatic example of local media initiative of this kind was the story of Watergate. Against the bitter opposition of almost every source that could have contributed to that story, one newspaper (the *Washington Post*) doggedly pursued a dim trail, and over the space of months practically forced the story onto the agenda of other news media and ultimately of the public. Two reporters for that one newspaper (Bernstein and Woodward) were so determined to run the story down to its source that finally other papers, and radio and television newsrooms, had to pick it up and help develop what became the big political story of the year, perhaps of the decade.[13]

The general opinion of scholars who have worked on Agenda-Setting is that newspapers have more to do with the process than television. This is because they come earlier in the process of news development and are able to carry more detail. In fact, newspapers often serve as gatekeepers for television news departments, which can make an evaluation of a story's potential before sending out an expensive three—or more—person crew and a quarter-million dollars' worth of equipment. But when a story reaches the point where it produces exciting pictures, then television's coverage becomes extremely vivid, and television itself becomes an effective gatekeeper for the public agenda.

One further note on Agenda-Setting: The familiarity of the topic makes a difference in the extent to which media have anything to do with setting the agenda. On issues like inflation or taxes, McCombs points out,

> . . . there is no need to look to the media for cues as to the importance
> of these topics. Everyday life provides sufficient experience and
> information. But for the more distant and abstract issues like [new
> developments in the case of] the hostages in Iran, the Soviet invasion of
> Afghanistan, or nuclear proliferation, the media are our limited window
> on the world.[14]

ADVERTISING

For a second example of the less quiet media effects let us take advertising.

If media advertising has no effect, then America's businessmen are wasting between $20 billion and $30 billion a year. The last complete set of figures available to us (1977) shows about $10 billion of advertising money going to newspapers, $7 billion to television, roughly $2.5 billion to radio, and the rest scattered through magazines and other media channels.

But suppose it *were* shown, contrary to all research and all conclusions of advertisers themselves, that media advertising is ineffective. Then, almost overnight, a most remarkable change would take place in American mass media. Television would go out of existence, except for public television, which would presumably keep its government and private support but lose its program grants from business and industry. Radio would go out of existence. Newspapers would shrink from their present plumpness to a new average of four to eight pages each. Of course, both television and radio could continue to the extent that audiences were willing to pay for them. To support television in the fashion to which it has become accustomed would average out at something over $100 per home; radio, about $30 per home. These are not impossible charges; but it is not easy to think of the American public rushing to make up for the lost support from advertising. And it is very hard, indeed, to think of an arrangement that, without advertising, would keep the Sunday *New York Times* weighing three to five pounds.

Some viewers and readers would not regret the loss of advertising. Television audiences, especially, do not like to have their programs interrupted by commercials, and many feel that there are too many commercials in proportion to news and entertainment. Nevertheless, 78 percent of a national sample said in 1978 that they felt "having commercials on TV is a fair price to pay for being able to watch it." Parents, who see their children watching an average of 20,000 commercials a year—equivalent to three hours total commercial viewing a week—are somewhat less willing to pay that price. One-third of the sample said in 1978 that they would prefer to have commercials totally eliminated from children's programs, and half said they would be willing to have commercials eliminated even if it meant considerably reducing the number of children's programs.[15] For the most part there has been no such dissatisfaction with advertisements in newspapers. The situation is different. Audiences can avoid television or radio commercials only by turning off the set or turning themselves off, whereas readers can pick and choose among the printed ads and read many or few as they choose. They do not object to Sunday papers crammed with ads and weighing several pounds, because news, editorial comments, and features come with the ads.

Because the media are so different, the ads are necessarily different. Newspaper ads follow the model of the news: They report new bargains, new sales, new products. Housewives scan the grocery ads as they scan the headlines on a news page, and many people read the classified pages as news about something they wish to buy. Television advertisers have 30 to 60 seconds (because commercial time is so expensive) to plant a name or an idea or an interest in the minds of their viewers. The name of a soft drink or a cigarette. The name of a store. The name of a product. The time of a coming program. The memory of the good smell of pizza or the good taste of cold beer. And so that the memory will be as pleasant and vivid as possible, the advertisers try to associate it with something pleasant or exciting. That is why pretty girls or handsome young men are seen so often in TV ads. That is why a brand of paint is shown in association with pictures of beautiful houses of famous people like George Washington or Thomas Edison. That is why catchy songs, jingles, or slogans are attached whenever possible to commercials.

Of course TV advertisers are not content merely to have viewers recall a name or a fact or a taste; they want the audience to buy. The purpose of all advertising is to stimulate purchases. However, what they can do well in a few seconds, with a not-very-deeply involved audience, with a commercial surrounded by other commercials, with a message that may be resented because it pulls viewers away from an entertaining program—what they can do with what they have is simply to help the viewer take a first step toward buying. If they can remind the audience that cold beer tastes good in hot weather (or in cold weather in front of a fire, or wherever), there is a chance the viewers will buy Brand X beer when they buy. If, in addition, they can implant the name of Brand X, there is a good chance that buyers will ask for that brand rather than other names less familiar. If they can pique the interest of viewers in an automobile or a calculator or a new piece of furniture or a new pair of running shoes, there is a reasonable chance that the viewers will turn that idea over in their heads, and if they go far enough along the purchasing road to go into a store, they may buy their brand. If advertisers can implant in an audience the picture of a candidate, and some favorable impression of his or her personality, character, and acumen—that is enough to try to accomplish in 30 seconds.

The television commercial has become a kind of art form. It is likely to be the most expensively and carefully produced, the most carefully researched, the most fully pretested part of the day's program. Michael Arlen published in 1980 a little book called *Thirty Seconds*,[16] on the making of such a commercial. This one was being made for the American Telephone and Telegraph Company, which wanted to encourage long-distance telephone calls. The task was in charge of a large advertising agency, which worked more than a year on the theme and content before turning over the actual work of creating the commercial to a specialized production organization. The idea was to get rid of some of the unpleasant connotations of long-distance calling—high cost, bad news to report, and so forth—and substitute a casual posture toward long distance: "It's fun, it's easy, it's cheap. The agency decided to build the commercial around a catchy song, "Reach out, reach out and touch some one" (translation: Make a long-distance call), "Reach out and just say Hi!" A composer was hired to do the song, and an orchestra and a soloist to record it. The visual part of the commercial was a series of tiny vignettes: a soldier in barracks calling his mother at home; two girls—one black, one white—talking long distance while they did yoga headstands; a famous hockey player, who had lost his front teeth in combat and was sitting in the locker room grinning a toothless grin, talking by phone to his small boy at home, who was at the stage of losing his baby teeth and also was grinning a toothless grin; these and others— ten characters, five little scenes of people "reaching out" by long-distance telephone to communicate affection rather than bad news. When the time came to record, the production agency devoted as much time to choosing a person who would be on the screen four or five seconds as they might to choosing the main character in a TV series of a feature film. To select two girls to do yoga headstands, they auditioned more than 200 candidates. They were careful to frame each of the vignettes in an attractive manner, whether in a locker room or a New York apartment. To add an extra touch to one of the headstand scenes, a trained cat was hired. The animal was supposed to walk across the screen while the girl was talking, but it was balky, and they shot the scene over and over until finally the cat appeared at just the right time in just the right place. And so the process of making a 30-second message went. It is not surprising that half a minute of effective commercial production may cost $50,000, whereas an entire prime-time program may be made for, say, $100,000, and BBC can produce documentaries for the "Open University" for $20,000.

The most often quoted model of "how television advertising works" is a sort of idealized pattern, suggested by Lavidge and Steiner in 1961.[17] It resembles many of the other Persuasion models, notably the Adoption-Diffusion and the Cartwright models that we have already illustrated. Although, as we have pointed out, a 30-second commercial can do little more than start a viewer along this process, the model shows the whole progression from awareness of the product, through development of a favorable attitude toward it, to the stimulation of a desire to buy. This is the Lavidge-Steiner model:

Types of Effects	*Movement Toward Purchase*
COGNITIVE—the realm of thoughts. Ads provide information and facts.	AWARENESS ↓ KNOWLEDGE ↓
AFFECTIVE—the realm of emotions. Ads change attitudes and feelings.	LINKING ↓ PREFERENCE ↓ CONVICTION ↓
CONATIVE—the realm of motives. Ads stimulate or direct desires.	PURCHASE

When this model has been tested in advertising campaigns, the results have usually been less elegant than the model. Many people did not pass through the stages as indicated. Some bought without acquiring much information; some without much evidence of attitude change; some almost casually, with no great conviction that this was *the* product to buy. Certainly the "Reach Out" commercials made no attempt to take viewers through all the stages of the model, but rather to plant a seed. The commercial itself was only a starter for the process.

In some ways a better example of the process comes not from commercial advertising but rather from a study of what would be called "public service." This is the analysis by the sociologist Robert K. Merton of a wartime "marathon" broadcast by the popular singer Kate Smith.[18] Like any commercial advertising campaign, the broadcast was designed to stimulate purchase, in this case the purchase of government war bonds. The program was a "marathon" that lasted 24 hours, although Miss Smith was onstage only at frequent intervals, not the whole time. But the program was long enough to cater to the audience at each stage of the progression toward buying.

The program was planned with meticulous care to accomplish

exactly what it did. The choice of Miss Smith herself was well thought out. Some campaigners might have chosen a sex symbol or a beauty queen. Miss Smith was not glamorous. She was, to put it impolitely, fat. She was middle-aged. But, as the planners believed and Merton confirmed in later interviews, she projected a most unusual image of sincerity. The reason for wanting this kind of image is easy to understand: It distinguished her message from that of the commercial pitchmen and the fast-talking salesmen, and consequently kept the communication relationship from being one that required the buyer to "beware."

Moreover, she was a very popular performer. Millions of Americans tuned in her program each week and hummed her theme song, "When the Moon Comes over the Mountain." She was therefore assured of a large audience for any radio appearance.

The style of the program was planned to take advantage of these things. It was a mixture of entertainment and "amateur" salesmanship. It was designed to keep Miss Smith on the air so long that it was a challenge to her strength and endurance, and many people actually stayed with the program out of sympathy for Kate Smith and because they wondered how long she could last.

This type of program fitted ideally into the main theme decided on for the message: Sacrifice. Miss Smith was "sacrificing": She received no money for the program; she was putting herself to a great physical strain for a patriotic motive; people who bought bonds could feel that they were sacrificing along with her.

Many of her messages made use of the *sacrifice* appeal. Many others used the theme of common effort: Forget private differences and work together for America! But listeners could hardly forget that they were being asked to work together with Kate Smith. Sacrifice. Work together. Help bring the boys home. Surprisingly little attention was paid to the economics of bond buying; rather than trying to prove it was a good investment, the designers of the program preferred to keep the arguments emotional.

In the wartime situation they were unlikely to strike great cognitive opposition; patriotic values ranked high. And many listeners already had planned to buy bonds anyway; 38 out of 75 who were interviewed after they had telephoned pledges to station WABC, New York, proved to have been emotionally involved and to have planned even before the broadcast to buy bonds. The program's effect on them was merely to catalyze an action already decided upon. Of the group of 75, 28 more already were involved but had not decided to buy. In these cases, it appeared that Miss Smith succeeded in arousing them emotionally, creating enough dissonance between their feelings and

decision to lead them to act. There was another small
were rather indifferent to the ideas expressed but had
buy. The effect of the program on them was simply to
provide a suitable and easy way of carrying out the intention. These
people were more likely than others to consider economic reasons
important. They were also likely to be admirers of Miss Smith and
susceptible to her pleas. We can assume that the mechanism working
here was a kind of identification with the star rather than an arousal
of conscience or a change of mind.

Finally, there was a still smaller group—3 out of 75, or 4 percent—
who before the program had not been deeply involved nor had intended to buy. These people apparently went through a real change
of mind and heart. The program introduced enough inconsistency
between their former position and the new ideas they were absorbing,
the emotions they were made to feel, to bring about a reorganization
and an action. This was the nearest thing to a real change, or "conversion," that the program accomplished. The other 72 people were
merely directed into paths of action that were not really incongruent
with their previous ideas and feelings.

Great care was taken not only with the themes and with the pro-
jection of Miss Smith's personality but also to make the path of action
easy and direct. Purchasers had merely to telephone the radio station,
give name and address, and pledge a certain amount. They stood a
chance of earning an additional bonus by having Miss Smith read
their names and thank them on the air. Or, if they preferred, they
could write a letter. It was not even necessary at the time to send
money.

Furthermore, action was put into the context of time. How many
pledges could Miss Smith win during her marathon? By pledging that
night, it was possible to contribute to her effort—to break the record,
to do honor to Kate who was doing honor to them.

Looked at with hindsight (which is often 20–20), the Smith campaign seems to have been carried out with great skill and care. But
it is noteworthy that, spectacular as the effect was, most of the changes
themselves were not spectacular. They were changes of a few degrees
rather than 180 degrees.

ECONOMIC AND SOCIAL DEVELOPMENT

The most dramatic chapter of social change in which the mass media
have been asked to participate in recent years has been the economic
and social development of the approximately 50 nations that are currently described as the "less developed countries."

These are national states or large territories where the average per capita income, in 1971 dollars, is still under $300 per year, in many of them under $100. Compare this with the approximate $2500 income per person in developed countries. In the less developed countries the life expectancy at birth averages 15 years less than in the other countries; the food intake in calories is about 80 percent of what it is in developed countries; about two-thirds of the people are still working in agriculture as compared to perhaps one-fifth in developed countries (and less than 10 percent in the United States). And 50 percent of the people, on the average, in LDCs are unable to read and write, as compared to less than 10 percent in the developed nations.[19]

Twenty years ago the industrialized West, and industrialized non-Western countries like Japan, looked upon these less fortunate countries with high hopes. The more fortunate countries would share their experience, export some of their most potent technology—industrial, agricultural, communication—and help the LDCs take the same giant leap that the industrialized nations had already taken, but this time in a few decades rather than the several centuries needed in the West. Development banks were created to provide a source of capital. Well-financed assistance agencies (like the Agency for International Development in the United States) were established to supervise the transfer of technology.

An international meeting of scholars and development specialists was held at the East-West Center in Honolulu, in the mid-1960s. At this meeting, a series of early successes were reported and only a few failures, and the mood was highly optimistic. When a similar meeting was held at the same location ten years later, the mood was quite different. The conferees were distinctly more somber. The transfer of Western technology had not worked as well as anticipated. The Western model of capital-intensive development into an industrial society had not worked as well as in the West. Although the average gross national product in many of the LDCs had risen about as expected and exports from the developing world had about doubled, still very little of the economic improvement had "trickled down," as it had been expected to do, to the poor and landless in the developing countries. Furthermore, the rapid increase in population in LDCs had absorbed most of the average growth in income. The *percentage* of literacy had risen, but because of the growth in population, there were actually *more illiterates* in the developing regions than there had been ten years earlier.

The reports on projects were also less favorable than in the previous decade. A generous United States government had built six open-circuit TV channels to bring master teachers to the approximately 7000 schoolchildren of American Samoa, but after some initial success, teacher resistance and bureaucratic problems had caused TV to be taken out of the higher grades, and the territory's chief interest turned to another kind of TV—three channels crammed every evening with American network programs for highly appreciative audiences. The Rural Radio Forum, a radio-fed system of discussion groups first developed in Canada, worked beautifully in the pilot project in 150 villages of India, but when India tried to expand it to 25,000 villages, the problems of expansion proved quite different from the problems of a pilot project, and the innovation gradually faded out. The Green Revolution was highly promising at first and developed well in certain areas like the Punjab of northern India, but many farmers found they did not have the resources or the land to implement it. A few states, most of which had already passed through their agricultural revolution—Korea, Taiwan, Singapore, Hong Kong—moved into an industrial stage and resulting prosperity. But for most of the LDCs, it had become apparent in that decade that (1) there was no "Western" model of development that would fit all developing countries, and actually what each country needed was a model of its own; (2) rather than Western capital-intensive development, the LDCs typically saw more hope in a *labor*-intensive strategy, centered on the farm rather than in the cities; (3) no transfer of technology was working very well unless it was anchored in local activity and local desires, rather than in outside encouragement; (4) therefore a communication system designed to speed guidance and direction from the capital city to the villages was not enough—there needed to be good channels, a communication upward as well as downward, and, above all, horizontal channels among the people who were supposed to be "developing"; (5) and beyond that, no communication, no matter how skillful, would speed development unless it was integrated into a system providing expertise, resources, and equipment to help do what had to be done.

Therefore, by the middle 1970s, both the developed and the developing countries were taking a second look at development. The LDCs were asking, What do we really want to develop into, and what is the best road toward that goal? The industrialized countries were asking, Given a record of far less than complete success, what is the best help we can provide? And as one Third World spokesman said at the 1975 conference: "We need your help, but we have to develop along the route of our own choice, and mostly with our own efforts."

This frustrating and often disappointing experience, however, has given us a chance to see what the mass media can be expected to do toward social change and what they cannot. These are some of the conclusions that seem to be emerging:

1. The media can do very little by themselves to bring about social change unless they are intertwined with a program of economic, technical, and social support. They can implant some facts, suggest some ideas, "set the agenda" for thinking about the problem, but to carry on a program of change they must have the kind of support that will encourage people to learn new practices and help them to put these practices into effect.

2. However, given the assurance of this kind of support they can serve as a "big microphone" to spread the word from the center to the village (where otherwise the voice of the center might not be so easily heard), advertise and help to organize campaigns, focus attention on needs and opportunities—in other words, expand the reach and speed of communication.

3. They can reach out where personal services are scarce—supply distant teachers where there are no teachers, supply expert advice and information where paramedics or slightly trained agricultural advisers need it. Even where health and agricultural services are available, they can in many cases assist and support those services by supplying special information. Even in countries like the United States where agriculture extension services are strong, the media have supported these services with the broadcast "National Farm and Home Hour" and the farm page in local newspapers.

4. Even in the situations just described, however, a considerable amount of local activity is required to make effective use of media support. Many countries have organized systems of distant teaching to teach basic education where there are no schools, but in order to make it work they have had first to organize local study groups, with chairmen or supervisors. Radio has been used effectively to serve Radio Rural Forum discussion groups, but it is necessary first for an extension agent or a local village worker to organize the group; and someone usually has to be in charge of it. In Australia, where radio is used to teach elementary schoolchildren in remote regions that have no schools, parents usually cooperate in bringing the children together to study, to listen to the radio lessons and discuss them. In Britain, where adults take courses at home in the evening or early morning from the "Open University," they find they must work very hard in order to get much good out of the printed and broadcast materials, and as often as possible they avail themselves of the chance to study together or consult a tutor. Mass media can do relatively little by themselves to organize the kinds of local activity that most successful programs of social change require, although they can support and encourage such activities when they have been organized.

5. As development programs have become increasingly aware of their dependence on local activity, they have come to make more and

more use of small rather than large media—that is, radio, rather than television; slides, filmstrips, printed or drawn pictures, rather than moving pictures; mimeographed or blackboard newspapers, rather than printed ones; transceivers or citizen-band radios, rather than radio stations; where appropriate, folk media—puppet shows, story-telling dances, ballads, and the like—rather than formal media. Radio is still the chief channel of information, except for word of mouth, within developing countries. The smaller media are especially well suited for fitting the differing needs of different regions and for horizontal communication within the regions. Another development along this line is the use of large media for small purposes—for example, satellite channels for two-way communication between paramedics in remote parts of Alaska with doctors in city hospitals hundreds or thousands of miles away.

6. As point-to-point communication becomes an increasingly important part of development programs, two-way communication also becomes more desirable. The Australian Flying Doctors, for example, use two-way radio communication between Sydney and the "outback." The University of the South Pacific uses two-way voice communication via the ATS-1 satellite for tutorial sessions with its students on distant Pacific Islands.

7. It is difficult to use large media (e.g., television, movies) for two-way communication, but they can be used effectively to confer status, reward accomplishment, and focus attention. To take a few examples, it enhances the status of a local agricultural adviser to have that person on television or radio. It is a considerable reward to have a local program praised in the media for its accomplishments. And media announcements can be used to introduce a new campaign, a new clinic, a new opportunity to market farm products, and so forth.

8. By presenting a common viewpoint and national figures or symbols, the media can help to build solidarity and cooperation in new countries and countries where social, political, or religious interests are diverse.

9. Developing countries, and, indeed, all countries concerned with social change, have long seen the need of feedback from their campaign communications. They now feel also the need of "feedforward" from their campaigns—meaning not a report back on how the campaign is going, but a report on what the needs are. The means of getting feedback are well enough known that no experienced communicator designs a campaign without making sure there is a provision for it. Feedforward takes more ingenuity. Some of the ways to obtain it through the media are discussion groups on local activities and

needs; pictorial or oral reports on local programs, along with comments by local observers; letters to the editors of newspapers; and the like.

For Further Consideration

1. It has been said that people trust television news because they themselves *see* the events it reports. Is this justified?
2. What do you learn about a political candidate by talking to people as compared to what you learn about the candidate from the media?
3. Why do people after attending a game often read the newspaper account of it?
4. Do you find advertising more irritating in one medium than in another? If so, which one is most, which one is least, irritating? Any suggestions as to how it might be made *less* irritating?
5. People now think that *local* activity—in a village or a commune—is very important to the success of a development program. Why?

References

In addition to the books listed in Chapter 13, let us suggest D. Boorstin, *The Image—A Guide to Pseudo-Events in America* (New York: Harper & Row, 1961); W. Lippmann, *Public Opinion* (New York: Macmillan, 1922); and D. Nimmo, *Political Communication and Public Opinion* (Pacific Palisades, Calif.: Goodyear, 1978); also the reviews by D. O. Sears in the two Handbooks listed in the References for Chapter 11.

For a start on the very extensive literature on advertising, try H. E. Krugman, "The Impact of Television Advertising: Learning Without Involvement," in W. Schramm and D. F. Roberts, (eds.), *The Process and Effects of Mass Communication* (Urbana: University of Illinois Press, 1971) pp. 485–515.

1. G. Comstock et al. *Television and Human Behavior.* New York: Columbia University Press, 1978, p. 311.
2. See H. Cantril, *The Invasion from Mars.* Princeton, N.J.: Princeton University Press, 1940.
3. For an entertaining account of this process, see D. Nimmo, *The Political Persuaders.* Englewood Cliffs, N.J.: Prentice-Hall, 1970.
4. D. Nimmo. *Political Communication and Public Opinion.* Pacific Palisades, Calif.: Goodyear, 1978, p. 378.
5. *Ibid.*, pp. 377–378.
6. The Roper Organization. *Changing Public Attitudes Toward Television and Other Mass Media, 1959–1978,* New York: Television Information Office, 1979.

7. D. Boorstin. *The Image—A Guide to Pseudo-Events in America.* New York: Harper & Row, 1961.

8. G. E. Lang and K. Lang. "The Unique Perspective of Television: A Pilot Study." *American Sociological Review,* 1953, *18,* 3–12.

9. See Lazarsfeld et al., *The People's Choice;* Berelson et al., *Voting;* Klapper, *The Effects of Mass Communication.* Cited in References in Chapter 11.

10. W. Lippmann. *Public Opinion.* New York: Macmillan, 1922.

11. T. White. *The Making of the President, 1972.* New York: Macmillan, 1973, p. 327.

12. M. McCombs and D. Shaw. "The Agenda-Setting Function of Mass Media." *Public Opinion Quarterly,* 1972, *32,* 176–187.

13. See C. Bernstein and B. Woodward, *All the President's Men.* New York: Simon & Schuster, 1974.

14. M. McCombs and D. Shaw. "An Up-to-Date Report on the Agenda-Setting Function." Paper for International Communication Association meeting at Acapulco, May 1980, p. 25.

15. Roper Organization, *op. cit.*

16. M. Arlen. *Thirty Seconds.* New York: Random House, 1980.

17. R. J. Lavidge and G. A. Steiner. "A Model for Predicting Measurement of Advertising Effectiveness." *Journal of Marketing,* 1961, *25,* 59–62.

18. R. K. Merton. *Mass Persuasion.* New York: Harper & Row, 1946.

19. See W. Schramm and D. Lerner, (eds.), *Communication and Change in the Last Ten Years—and the Next.* Honolulu: University Press of Hawaii, 1976, pp. 6–14 and passim.

15/
THE INFORMATION
REVOLUTION

Most of the nations that have arrived at the stage of development we call postindustrial civilization—the countries of Europe and North America, Japan, and a few others—have got there by passing through four social revolutions in the past few centuries. They have had

a *political* revolution, which has distributed power more widely than within a few families or a small privileged class, and in some cases liberated the country from a colonial government;

an *educational* revolution, which has made it possible for most persons to learn to read and write, and for a high proportion of those to go as far in school as their abilities justify;

an *agricultural* revolution, which has divided land in economically efficient units, introduced new agricultural technology, and thus produced more calories for more people and released the majority of farm workers to industry and business; and

an *industrial* revolution, which has substituted new sources of energy for manual labor, speeded up production by use of machines, and created fast transportation and long-range communications.

For the most part, these revolutions were neither violent nor bloody, but all of them brought about spectacular changes in the way human beings live and the kind of society they live in.

Now we find ourselves entering another social revolution, or so we believe. Some current historians call it an Information Revolution, others an Age of Information. But more and more observers are beginning to see the dimensions of change as revolutionary and information as the chief source of power within the postindustrial period, in the same way that land, energy, and machines were the chief resources of the last two revolutions.

In the preceding chapters we have talked about human communication as it exists, a system with which we have lived long enough to be able to talk about models of how it works, the nature of social controls upon it, the audiences it has, and its effects. What we must now understand is that all this past we have been talking about is prologue to a new age in which the basic nature of human communication will not change, to be sure, but in which the social system of communication itself is likely to be considerably different from the ages of communication we have known.

We have always tended to underestimate the effects of new communication technology. Not long before he retired to his home in Sri Lanka, Arthur Clarke, father of the communication satellite, made a talk in which he quoted an anecdote relayed to him by Sir Anthony Wedgewood Benn, who was at that time Postmaster of Great Britain. The chief engineer of the Post Office was called to testify before a parliamentary commission a century ago (Sir Anthony said) and was asked whether he had any comments on the latest American invention, the telephone. "No, Sir," he replied. "The Americans have need of the telephone—but we do not. We have plenty of messenger boys." To this Clarke added that if a committee had been set up in 1450 to discuss whether it was worth developing Gutenberg's ingenious invention, the committee would probably have decided, on entirely logical grounds, not to commit further funds. The printing press with movable metal type was a clever idea, they would have conceded, but it would have no large-scale application—because so few of the population could read.[1]

Living in the midst of modern communication technology as we do, it is hard for us to realize how new this technology is in the experience of man. Clarke gave this illustration:

> If you showed a modern diesel engine, an automobile, a steam turbine, or a helicopter to Benjamin Franklin, Galileo, Leonardo da Vinci, and Archimedes—a list spanning two thousand years in time—not one

of them would have had any difficulty in understanding how these machines worked. Leonardo, in fact, would recognize several from his notebooks. All four men would be astonished at the materials and the workmanship, which would have seemed magical in its precision, but once they got over that surprise they would feel quite at home—as long as they did not delve too deeply into the auxiliary control and electrical systems.

But now suppose they were confronted by a television set, an electronic computer, a nuclear reactor, a radar installation. Quite apart from the complexity of these devices, the individual elements of which they are composed would be incomprehensible to any man born before this century. Whatever his degree of education or intelligence, he would not possess the mental framework that could accommodate electron beams, transistors, atomic fission, wave guides, and cathode-ray tubes.[2]

So we are face to face with something new in the world, which we suspect is likely to bring us into a new and different age. What are the signs of it?

SIGNS OF THE NEW AGE

For one thing, *an explosion of new communication technology.*

We are living in the shadow of three remarkable years in the 1940s. Nineteen forty-five saw the publication of Clarke's four-page article in the British radio journal, *Wireless World*, entitled "Extra-Terrestrial Relays," which set forth, with amazing foresight, the idea and potential of the communication satellite. Nineteen forty-six saw the appearance of Von Neumann's historic monograph on the theory of the modern computer; every computer built since that time has followed Von Neumann's pattern. Nineteen forty-seven saw the invention, at the Bell Telephone Laboratories, of the transistor by three physicist-engineers—Bardeen, Brattain, and Shockley. They won the Nobel Prize for it.

These prophets themselves were too conservative in estimating the future of their ideas. Clarke wrote to the editor of *Wireless World* that the communication satellite was an idea whose time might come in perhaps 50 years—say, 1995. Actually, the first Sputnik was in orbit in 1957, just 12 years after the pioneering article; in less than ten more years a worldwide satellite communication system was in use. The first large computers were being built within a year after Von Neumann's ideas became known. The transistor began to miniaturize all electronic equipment the minute it was available.

It is sometimes hard to realize how fast communication technology has developed. In 1945, an article. In October 1957, a tiny satellite.

Between 1957 and 1980, about 25,000 artificial satellites and space probes have been launched. In 1980 there were two international satellite communication systems, six regional systems, six military systems, eight national systems, and a great number of satellites and satellite systems for special purposes such as aeronautical navigation, weather forecasting, and data relay. One hundred and two nations had signed the agreement to cooperate in the use of the largest system, Intelsat.

Computer development has proceeded at a similar rate. The first large electronic computer was built in the same year as Von Neumann's monograph was published. Compared to a modern computer, an analyst said, that first machine was "an abacus."[3] A National Academy of Science study estimated in 1970 that for a man working without a calculator to make 125 million multiplications would cost about $12.5 million. Give the man a hand calculator, and the same job would cost $2.5 million. On the first large electronic computer, 126 million multiplications would have cost about $130,000; on the fastest computer available in 1970, $4! And for modern computers, even that seems a turtle's pace.

The developments in solid-state technology following upon the transistor are everywhere around us, from the transistor radio to the communication satellite. Transistors are tiny things themselves and therefore, by replacing vacuum tubes, have miniaturized much of electronic equipment. Silicon chips, another solid-state device about as big as a fingernail, can now serve as memories for small computers and provide the circuits for calculation. Chips are now available that will store as many as 64,000 bits of information; by 1985 they are expected to have a capacity of one million bits. Ten years ago, the Marquardt Corporation's Astro Division estimated that with solid-state electronics, *all information recorded within the past 10,000 years* could be stored, if desired, inside a six-foot cube. This means, said Clarke, marveling at the announcement, that "not every book ever printed, *everything* ever written in *any* language on paper, papyrus, parchment, or stone."[4] In a six-foot cube, only 216 cubic feet. Is it any wonder that information scientists can now think of storing whole libraries in such a way as to be available on command, of communicating with individuals anywhere in the world by means of wristwatch radios (the comic strips were prophetic!), and of designing machines smart enough to reproduce themselves and perhaps challenge humankind itself in intelligence?

The second signal of the new age is *the enormous increase in production of information.*

It is rather hard to come upon figures representing the total flow of information, because so many channels and users are included. Furthermore, the existence of multiple connections and the distribution of the same message to so many receivers make for an accounting problem quite different from totaling salaries or satellites.

But for perspective, let us look back to the year 1844, when the telegraph was invented. With that new instrument it was possible to transmit information at the hitherto unheard-of rate of ten bits per second—about two English letters. Now, with the availability of wave guides, it is possible to plan for a channel that will carry one *billion* bits per second. The speed with which one generation of communication technology succeeds another shows why such changes are coming about in our time. We have seen five generations of communication satellites in 20 years; a new generation of major computer every four years; four generations of video display in five years and the same rate of change for semiconductor memories; three generations of microprocessors in five years; and so forth.

As technology has speeded up, so has communication. Libraries—the great libraries have been doubling in size about every 14 years: 14,000 percent per century. In the early fourteenth century, the library at the Sorbonne in Paris contained 1338 books and was the largest in Europe; now half a dozen libraries in the world have more than eight million books. Books—in 50 years the number of books sold in this country per year has increased by about 600 percent. Journals—there are now estimated to be about 100,000 scholarly and technical journals in the world, and this number is thought to have increased 50 percent in the past ten years.[5] Cable systems—the expansion of television cable systems may be seen as one measure of public willingness to bring in new sources of information; the number of cable subscribers has been multiplying by a factor of approximately five every ten years. Telephone—the number of telephone conversations in the United States increased by a factor of nearly 100 between 1970 and 1980; between 1960 and 1978, telephone traffic between the United States and Europe grew from less than one million to about 50 million calls per year, and during this time the cost per minute was approximately halved.[6] Telex—international Telex has been growing at a rate of about 25 percent per year. Desktop computers—the number of small computers in use in the United States increased by about 50 percent between 1978 and 1980 alone.[7] Data base use—the number of searches of computer-based data files is estimated to have increased from about 2.9 million to about 9 million in the years following 1973.[8]

Parallel to the growth of technology and the production of information has been a striking change in investment. Between 1968 and 1978, money spent on mass communication in the United States rose from about $16 million to about $37 million.[9] Fritz Machlup, the Princeton economist, calculated that the production and distribution of information already accounted for 15 percent of the gross national product in 1958, and that the "knowledge industry" was growing at about 10 percent. This trend is not limited to the United States.[10] Japan has been putting about 6 percent of its gross national product into telecommunications and computers. The Canadian Science Council estimated that about 5 percent of Canada's GNP went into computers alone, in 1980. And in France the computer industry passed the automobile industry in size several years ago.

The third signal is *a significant change in the work force.*

Just as the mechanization of agriculture released the majority of agricultural workers to industry and the installation of servo-mechanisms to control machines released a large number of factory workers to service and business jobs, so now a larger and larger proportion of service and business jobs are concerned with information. Daniel Bell predicted that knowledge would be the main factor in economic growth in postindustrial society, and Peter Drucker forecast that knowledge rather than capital would become respectively the primary "industry" and the essential productive resource of postindustrial society. Machlup, however, surprised everyone with his 1958 calculation that about 29 percent of the compensation of the U.S. labor force was going to information services. In a Stanford dissertation in 1976, using Bureau of Labor Statistics records, Marc Porat estimated that 53 percent of total U.S. compensation (in 1976) was being paid for information services.[11]

These figures should not be over-interpreted, because a high proportion of all the workers in education are obviously dealing with information services, as are many telephone, post office, and mass media employees, and, in at least a considerable proportion of their duties, so are lawyers, accountants, and many classes of government bureaucrats. But the fact that half the work force of a country can now be described as working in information services is a striking fact that would have been hard to envisage in any previous century.

It is developments like these that have led historians and futurologists to say—depending on their style and vocabulary—either that we are in the first decades of an Information Revolution or of an Age of Information. Projecting these trends forward, we can say with some confidence that whatever we decide to call the period we are entering, these will be some of its characteristics:

1. *More information* will flow, with consequent chance of an overload.

2. *Information will come faster,* forcing us to create mechanisms and institutions to scan and sort and process it more efficiently.
3. A higher proportion of the *information will come from farther away.* The big electronic window on the world and the ability to get in touch directly with almost any person and place on earth are likely to readjust relationships and offer both individuals and governments a different perspective on their world.
4. More of this flow of information than at any time since the introduction of radio is likely to be *point-to-point rather than point-to-mass.* This will require a review of media systems.
5. *Information is likely to be a source of power* to those who have quick access to it and can process it efficiently.

Supposing that something like this turns out to really be the shape of things to come in human communication, what is it going to mean to us? We can ask the question, but hardly pretend to know the answers.

THE SETTINGS FOR OVERLOAD

Look at my own situation, At the moment, I feel it necessary to be familiar with the contents of about 50 scholarly journals. Those are the ones I *know* I should be familiar with; how many of the hundred thousand I do *not* know, but should be familiar with, I am not prepared to say. To keep up professionally, I should read several hundred new books each year, and a very large number of duplicated drafts or preprints that circulate among scholars. I should also keep in touch with 50 or more scholars who are working on problems that interest me, and answer the letters of another 50 to 100 who ask information from me. In addition to these things, I must work on my own articles and books. What I have listed is already an impossible task, even if I had no other work to do, had no need of sleep or relaxation, and could read and write 24 hours a day. But it illustrates what the information explosion means to a communication scholar. In some natural science fields the task is still more formidable.

The only feasible solution anyone has found for this sort of problem is to share the task. This is why scholarly fields develop reviews, abstracts, indexes. These are far less desirable than reading everything yourself, but at least they enable scholars to help other scholars learn what is in the new literature and decide what they *must* read themselves. In the decades ahead, some persons may find it both helpful and rewarding to make scanning and summarizing one of their chief scholarly tasks. Ultimately such a system will be on the computer line. In any case, it must be supported by well-stocked libraries, because no individual scholar could afford to buy all the new literature even if he or she were sure he or she could read all of it.

Let us take another example. The cable installation in a home has 36 channels, about half of which are presently occupied. Five of the channels are taken up by local stations. Others are "super stations," all-news stations, movie services of different kinds, religious stations, security cameras, and so forth. One channel is for local groups and organizations to present programs of their own. Ultimately we expect all the channels to be in use. In fact, we rather anticipate that someday we shall have about 80 channels, many of them providing two-way communication—an opportunity for us to order up computerized study courses, ask for certain kinds of information, search at least a few data sources, or shop by mail.

Looking forward to a choice of 80 channels in one's home is a mind-boggling experience. Even now we have more than we can use; even when we have the time to look at one channel, 16 or 17 will always be unused. In such a situation any viewer is likely to change viewing habits. It is hard to think of leaving the receiver on one station for an evening or a day, as some persons do when they have only a few station choices. We are much more likely even now to program our viewing in advance, with the aid of weekly or monthly program guides, rather than take potluck by flipping the dial. Suppose there is more than one program we should like to watch at a given hour. One solution is to buy a videocassette recorder and record the second program while we view the first choice. That leaves only 15 or 16 channels that we are unable to cover; it is rather awesome to think that if and when we have 80 channels we shall have to leave 78 unused! If the average channel carries 18 hours a day, that will mean that 1440 hours of televised material of some kind, sixty 24-hour days, will be coming into a home every day. At present the average adult in the United States devotes about three hours per day to television. Given 1440 hours from which to choose, will we assign more time to television? Or simply become frustrated?

Suppose now that someone really wants to understand the complex and changing world we live in. That well-meaning person will have available not only the usual television and radio newscasts but also the shortwave radio to bring news from at least 20 other countries. There will be the newspapers, the newsmagazines, the new books, of which at least one thousand per year have something important to say about the present world. The cable will almost certainly offer additional services, of which the currently available 24-hour news is a precursor. These services may very well include some wire service news, a sampling of editorial comments, and special interpretive services, corresponding, say, to the *London Observer* foreign service, or public affairs columns from the *New York Times*, the *Washington Post*, the *Los Angeles Times*, and so forth. Before long, we shall probably be able to have any of this material printed out for us in our homes by some photo facsimile process, if we want to pay for it. We shall have newspaper indexes, like the *New York Times* Index, readily available to send us microfilm pages we feel we ought to read. We shall be able to hear a passing parade of diplomats, correspondents, pundits, scholars, and travelers from far places. How will we feel about a situation like that, if we *really* want to find out what is happening in the far world? Will we be grateful to have so much choice of information for the few hours we can devote to it, or will we look back fondly to the quiet time when two newspapers a day, two magazines a month, an annual speech in town by our member of Congress, a ten-minute stop every four years by one of the two Presidential campaign trains, and a week of lectures every year at summer Chautauqua were our windows on the world?

We have been looking at a few homely little examples of overload. Now let us put some figures next to them. George R. White, the Xerox engineer, has estimated with some rather fancy mathematics that a human being's total cerebral store of information probably increased about one order of magnitude after printing and another order of magnitude after the electronic revolution—in other words, an increase of 100 times. At the same time, he calculated, the total data *available* increased *two* orders of magnitude as a result of printing and *another two* orders since the coming of electronics—10,000 times![12]

It isn't necessary to review White's mathematics; what if he is wrong by an order of magnitude, so that only 1000 rather than 10,000 times as much information is available to us now as we would have had in 1400? The practical question is, What is a concerned citizen to do? Sample the available feast—perhaps read a daily newspaper, a newsmagazine, an occasional book, tune in the evening news, go to a lecture when possible—and be frustrated? Give all waking hours to the pursuit of information—and still be frustrated? Or curse the Information Revolution and tune in an entertainment program or play golf?

We mentioned earlier that the pace of information is likely to change markedly. In 1805 it took Nelson's flagship crew *11 minutes* to put out the flags that passed a brief but historic message from the admiral to the rest of the English fleet preparing to fight the battle of Trafalgar: "England expects every man to do his duty!" Eleven minutes. Until the middle of the nineteenth century distant messages could travel only as fast as transportation. In the time of the Mongol emperors, China had an excellent courier system that covered about 100 miles a day. Until sometime in the nineteenth century the fastest carriers of news were the pigeons that Baron Reuter used to carry bulletins across the English Channel. They could fly, at their swiftest, 60 miles an hour for a short distance.

Then, of course, came the telegraph, and 40 years later the telephone, and then the other electronic media, and news began to move around the globe, and between the moon and the Earth, at the speed of light. If you take this for granted, sit down some afternoon with some of your colleagues and calculate for fun how long it would take to move the entire contents of the Biblioteque Nationale from Paris to London—given the equipment likely to be available. If one could put the contents on computers and obtain sufficient circuits to another computer across the Channel, it would take between 7 and 17 minutes, depending on conditions.

Furthermore, it will make a difference that so much information will come from faraway. Distance will be relatively unimportant a few decades from now when rates are based on satellite rather than cable transmission. When an electronic message goes 23,000 miles up to a satellite and 23,000 down, it is a matter of little importance whether it comes down 100, 1000, or even 10,000 miles from its starting point. We have already found that this makes for a different world. It makes a difference when three-fourths of all Americans can gather together by television, as they did in 1963, for the funeral of a murdered President. It makes a difference when Vietnam is brought so close that we can see the war in our living room and when information comes so swiftly over a quarter of a million miles that we can see what our astronauts are seeing on the moon, at almost exactly the same time as they do.

In fact, all the developments we have been describing are going to make a difference. Some are worrisome, some are hopeful. Some are individual, some societal.

Alvin Toffler said that information overload is one of the conditions of "future shock." "Man has limited capacity to process information," he said. "Overloading the system leads to serious back down of performance. By bombarding humans with an excess of information, by impressing them with the *need* to know, "without understanding its potential impact," he continued,

we are accelerating the generalized rate of change in society. We are forcing people to adapt to a new life pace, to confront novel situations and master them in ever shorter intervals. We are forcing them to choose among fast-multiplying options. We are, in other words, forcing them to process information at a far more rapid pace than was necessary in slowly evolving societies. There can be little doubt that we are subjecting at least some of them to cognitive overstimulation.[13]

How many people will come to terms with this problem? How many of them will learn to use the indexing devices, learn to sample, learn to take in as much as they can and satisfy themselves by that accomplishment, learn to stand up to the rising tide of information and take from it what they can—without too much regret that they can't take it all? We can guess that the people who will have the hardest time will be those who feel very deeply the need and obligation to know but do not have the skills and self-command to take what they can get and feel no guilt for not taking more. The people who will have the least psychological trouble and will make the least societal contribution will be those who do not feel the need or obligation to know.

The question is, do we, overloaded with information, cope or withdraw? Do we gain a broader basis for opinions and decisions, or do we accept a broader basis for fantasy? How many in the audience of tomorrow will simply retreat from the mass of information and gradually confuse a too copious reality with a make-believe reality? Toffler gives an example of what he feels this latter reaction to be like: the climax of the film *Blow-Up,* in which the hero joins in a tennis game with players hitting a nonexistent ball back and forth over the net—unable any longer to distinguish between illusion and reality. "Millions of viewers identified with the hero in that moment," Toffler commented.[14]

SOCIETAL EXTENSIONS OF THE PROBLEM

The individual problems of an Information Revolution blend into the societal problems. For example, we wonder how much better informed the average person will be as a result of the flood tide of information. Will people retreat from it, as Toffler predicts, or ignore it and let it roll past while they watch *Dallas?* This, at least, we can be fairly confident of: that there will be a great difference in how much different people profit from it. Unfortunately those people who learn the most are likely to be the ones who already have the most information, for in knowledge, as in economics, it seems to be a sad fact that the rich grow richer and the poor relatively poorer. Typically, the students who come to school knowing more learn more quickly than others. Will the great tide of information therefore help to create a two-class society of haves and have-nots in information?

There have been recent examples of this. "Sesame Street," one of the most skillful programs ever made for children, seems to have widened rather than narrowed the gap between the children who already know more and the others.[15] Will the Information Revolution simply widen the knowledge gap? Very likely it will do so at first, because the information haves will be likely to gain access to the new information more quickly than the have-nots. On the other hand, an increase of information in the past has usually resulted in raising the average of information in the population—for both haves and have-nots. This certainly happened when printing came into use. The coming tide of information should make it easier for the information poor to reduce the gap because there is some ceiling in the amount of information anyone can acquire; and as the information rich approach that ceiling, those with less information should find it easier to catch up. Without pretending to know how a situation like this will turn out, it would seem that whether we are able to reduce the knowledge gap will depend in great part upon the effort we make to do so. If we want to make it a major policy to raise the knowledge level of the less-well-informed people faster than might otherwise happen, we have the tools to do it.

We now can deliver information almost anywhere—home, school, library, office, factory, village, island, or igloo. The stage is set for lifelong education, to move more schooling out of school, to bring schools to the people rather than people to schools. Furthermore, by methods like computerized instruction education can be individualized, with more responsibility as well as more freedom in the hands of the learner. In other words, we can offer more help than any time in the past to people who have been bypassed by education and other opportunities to learn. The "Open Universities" throughout the world, projects like the Tanzania self-managed schools and the Mexican *telesecundaria*, and the "School without Walls," all utilizing television broadcasting, have shown how this can be done. If any society really wants to distribute knowledge and skills more widely, there are ways to do it.

One trend in this revolutionary Age of Information will transfer to individuals more of the responsibility for what they get from the flow of information. This is the tendency toward emphasizing point-to-point rather than point-to-mass communication, and the growing ability of individuals to "use" the media rather than being used by them. In a sense, the telephone may be seen as a more modern medium than television, because it is two-way and point-to-point, and the users are in charge of programming it. The greater part of information flow today is this kind of pattern—data, telephone, telex, et cetera. Cable television is a kind of point-to-point service, widening the choices available to viewers, and it will be far more in the hands of its users when some of its channels become two-way and viewers can order up programs or information they want, or shop over visual channels, or express their opinions in real time. Beyond that, the ordinary person has gained an amount of access to mass media that would startle a modern Rip Van Winkle who had slept for a few decades and just come back to look around. The typewriter and the photocopy machine have, in a sense, made it possible for every one to be a publisher. Tape recorders, walkie-talkies, transceivers, citizen-band radios, have made it possible for all of us to play a part in broadcasting. Movie cameras have become relatively cheap and so simple that home movies are becoming a device for communicating as well as a record of what has happened. Video recorders and players enable us not only to order television programs to suit us and preserve those we want to see again but also, when equipped with a camera, to let us make our own video. Even beyond that, open channels are becoming available for individuals and groups who want to broadcast their own programs to their own audiences. Microcomputers, now becoming so readily available, are making it possible for individuals to share some of the data-processing capabilities of the great machines that are in the hands of large academic and scientific organizations. In other words, the day of Big Media and Little Man seems to be drawing to a close. The media may not be so unapproachable or unfathomable, after all.

One special problem will have to be faced by national governments as a result of the new pace of information. Information will come so fast and so fully that the traditional lead time of diplomacy may be reduced almost to nothing. The general public will know what is happening almost as soon as their leaders do, and this will be exaggerated by the new tendency of governments to speak directly to other countries through the media—for example, as Iran chose to address the United States through television rather than diplomatic notes during the hostage crisis. This makes an awkward situation for foreign offices, which traditionally have relied on a period of secrecy during which to read the cables, canvass the situation, and work out a policy recommendation before they have to go public. If their usual lead time disappears, they will have to invent some new mechanisms for reality testing in order to decide quickly whether unofficial "messages" are true or false, rumor or fact, serious or incidental, As a matter of fact, all of us will have to develop quicker means of reality testing, in a time of very fast and very large communication flow, in order to know what in that flow is worth our attention and concern.

Another problem that will have to be shared by the government and its citizens is the matter of privacy. Increasingly, all the details of our lives are being recorded in computer memories. Our financial dealings are being taken over by computer systems, so that a cashless society is not beyond possibility in the future. Our merchandise and service orders are more and more being handled by computers, which write us carefully formalized letters in answer to inquiries. This leaves most of us a little uneasy. We are not sure that we want machines transferring money in and out of our accounts, and we are profoundly dissatisfied by the way computers answer our questions about a missing article or a missing ten dollars.

More important is the question of the extent to which personal records may become public. It is doubtless a good idea, in some cases necessary for good government, to have a great deal of information on file about each of its citizens. It is doubtless good business for credit bureaus, banks, and retail stores to have on hand a considerable amount of information about our business dealings. But any computer code can be cracked, and in most cases it is not necessary to crack the code: The contents are made available to "qualified" organizations— other government departments; businesses that want to know about our credit or our health or our police record, if any, or that simply want to send us direct mail advertising; or in some cases to news organizations whose lawyers can use the law to get information out of files. Once again, this makes us feel a little uneasy—not particularly because one mercantile organization sells our address to others (although that is sometimes irritating) or because a credit bureau tells another organization whether we have any overdue bills, but rather because of the amount to which the details of our life can be paraded in front of people who really have no need to know: that parking ticket in 1978, that little operation we had in 1950, the organization that gave us $500 for consulting in 1961, how much money we made in 1970, what we said a few years later about legalizing "pot," and so forth. This problem is likely to get worse before it gets better, and some basic law about the storage and availability of personal information may be needed.

THE SPECIAL IMPORTANCE OF THE COMPUTER

This new ability to store almost endless amount of information and retrieve it on demand brings us to consider the computer, which may well become the great communicating machine of the Information Revolution because of its ability to sort and process the mass of information. The computer, despite its undoubted usefulness, raises two questions that, though largely theoretical at the moment, may become very practical in the years ahead. One is how to think about the economics of information, of which the computer is the chief custodian. There is a rather extraordinary quality of information. If I give you an apple or a book or ten dollars, you have more and I have less. If I sell you my automobile, you pay me something, and I have more money but no automobile. Therefore the transaction can be evaluated in economic terms. But if I give you a piece of information, you have more of it and I have just as much as I had before. In other words, the value can be multiplied, not subtracted. There can be no completely private ownership of information, once it is communicated. Therefore the value of information is something that presents an unusual economic problem. Some information is more valuable, the fewer people who own it—for example, how to make a neutron bomb. Other information is more valuable the more people who own it—for example, the news that a tidal wave or a typhoon will strike within the hour. This requires us, therefore, to think of it in economic terms somewhat differently from what we think of most kinds of property.

In the second place, the Information Revolution requires us to think, and most seriously, about the future of a "thinking machine" in human society.

For the next page or so we shall be walking a very narrow line between science and science fiction, as one almost inevitably must do if one writes of the long-time future of computers. Therefore, sit back and prepare to be skeptical.

Is the computer really a "thinking machine"? *Can* it think?

The usual argument is that no machine can be more intelligent than its designers and builders. No machine can be expected to be original or creative. These are "human" qualities.

"Fallacious!" says Arthur Clarke. He quotes this paragraph by the guru of cybernetics, Dr. Norbert Wiener:

> It is my thesis that machines can and do transcend some of the limitations of their designers [he is speaking of computing machines]. . . . It may well be that in principle we cannot make any machine, the elements of whose behavior we cannot comprehend sooner or later. This does not mean in any way that we shall be able to comprehend them in substantially less time than the operation of the machine, nor even within any given number of years or generations. . . . This means that though they are theoretically subject to human criticism, such criticism may be ineffective until a time long after it is relevant.[16]

This means, comments Clarke, "that even machines *less* intelligent than men might escape from our control by sheer speed of operation. And in fact there is every reason to suppose that machines will become much more intelligent than their builders, as well as incomparably faster."

Wiener is a mathematician and a scientist. Clarke is an engineer and a futurologist, although his contribution to the communication satellite indicates that his futurology is more than fiction. These men and numerous others tend to agree on these points:

> Today's computers are "morons" in intelligence, although gifted with phenomenal speed in performing calculations and other operations with data.
>
> Some computers have been built that can learn from their mistakes and never repeat them. (The first of these qualities is human, say some writers on the subject; the second is *super*human!)
>
> Some computers have been built to search for proofs of logical theorems and have been reported to sometimes come up with proofs that had not occurred to their designers.
>
> Several machines that have been built for the study of artificial intelligence are capable of revising their wiring to adapt to new requirements.
>
> They can play a fairly good game of chess and compose a fairly good piece of music.

These are but "glimmerings" of intelligence, it is true. Enthusiasts insist, however, that computers are still in their stone age of development and soon will be quite different. The principles have been worked out by which computers can design other computers and even build them. This is perilously close to the idea of reproducing the species, which has been thought to be a monopoly of "living" things. J. R. Licklider in an article entitled "The Computer as a Communicating Machine" described an artificial intelligence machine identified by the acronym OLIVER, which some computers were trying to build to help human beings overcome the decision overload. OLIVER, in its perfected form, would be a personal computer, programmed to make lesser decisions and provide its owner with needed information. It would thus be a companion or a helper more than a business machine. In the present stage of design it would be able to "store information about his friends' preference for Manhattans or Martinis, data about traffic routes, the weather, stock prices, etc., remind him of his wife's birthday, renew magazine subscriptions, pay the rent on time, . . . tap into a worldwide pool of data . . . thus become a kind of universal question-answerer for him." Some computer scientists, however, "see much beyond that. It is theoretically possible to construct an OLIVER that would analyze the content of its owner's words, scrutinize his choice, deduce his value systems, update its own programs to reflect changes in his values, and ultimately handle larger and larger decisions for him."[17]

The next step in bringing the computer out of its stone age may well be to create personal computers like OLIVER (at least the first-stage OLIVER) designed and programmed to make life easier for a specific owner. The next step, if it is ever taken, would be to produce a computer that would work more on its own. A. M. Turing, an English mathematician, posited a game in which two Telex or teleprinter operators would be seated in adjoining rooms. They would be unable to see or hear each other, and neither would know whether the other was human or a machine. Suppose now, said Turing, that each were allowed to ask the other any questions desired. If, at the end of an hour or two, one of them could not tell from the other's answers and questions whether the other was a human being or a machine—and if one of them were a machine—then, asked Turing, could the human operator say that the machine was not intelligent, not "thinking"? Such a machine has not yet been built, but Turing put down some principles for it, and Clarke says flatly it will be built, "within decades —not centuries."[18]

The computer has certain great advantages over humans. Its "brain cells" operate much more swiftly, for example. One can build into it more and better sense organs, if desired—senses that would allow it to detect radio waves, eyes that would see far better. Its brain is much less complex than the ten-million-neuron human brain, but even a brain of that complexity is conceivable for a thinking machine, although it would have to be built by other computers, not by human engineers. An artificial intelligence machine of the kind we are talking about would also have the advantage of being less subject to such human problems as the need to eat, sleep, breathe air, and see the doctor or dentist occasionally.

We are on the edge of science fiction at this point. A personal computer, a more complex, more versatile computer, a computer programmed to do more difficult, more nearly "human" things—these are within the bounds of planning, if not in sight. But one step farther along this path sits the artificial intelligence machine that can talk as though thinking (like Turing's machine), that can design and build another computer, that can identify problems of its own to solve. When we reach that stage, I am afraid we are in science fiction, for a computer at that point would be, in effect, an organism. It would be able to compete with man and, as half a dozen writers of fiction and drama (like Karol Capek, in *R.U.R.*, and Clarke himself in his script for *2001*) and a few quite competent scientists have predicted, might "take over" from man. To quote Clarke once again, because he has a way of saying things more vividly than most other people: "The tools the ape-men invented caused them to evolve into their successor, Homo sapiens. The tool we have invented *is* our successor."

You need not follow the scenario that far, and you certainly are not required to believe that Homo sapiens has created his successor, Machine sapiens. But you should be aware that the computer has a special importance in the Information Revolution. It is not only perhaps the most powerful communication machine ever built; it represents also the first result of scaling the supposedly unscalable barrier between thinking man and machine. The results are still in doubt.

The next years of the Information Revolution are likely to be exciting ones. In one sense, the most promising; in another, the most threatening. The best of times, the worst of times. The men and women at the beginning of the Industrial Revolution must have had some of this same sense of uncertain destiny. Unlike them, however, we shall have something to say about what happens.

For Further Consideration

1. This chapter discusses probable technological changes in communication in the relatively near future. What developments do you foresee beyond these? What new technologies, in terms of the quality of human life, would be most helpful 50 years from now?
2. There has been mention in this book of the possibility that major television networks will disappear as the capacity for specialization in the mass media increases, just as general consumer magazines have largely been replaced by special interest magazines. Do you think this is necessarily true? What are the significant differences between the position of general magazines in, say, 1960, and that of the major TV networks today?
3. Do you feel that international relations will be managed with more or less difficulty in the developing age of instantaneous information? In addition to those discussed here, what factors are operating in each direction?
4. The new Age of Information will bring many problems, one of which is set out in the question above; this chapter identifies some others, but many obviously remain. What are some of these?

References

It is hard to conceive of a book that we could confidently recommend to you as an authoritative introduction to the future. But some of the books mentioned in this chapter will stimulate your thinking—for example, Arthur C.

Clarke's *Profiles of the Future* and Alvin Toffler's *Future Shock*. Some articles are also mentioned in this chapter, and other articles appear frequently that deal with the shape of things to come.

1. A. C. Clarke. "Beyond Babel." In W. Schramm and D. F. Roberts, (eds.), *The Process and Effects of Mass Communication*. Urbana: University of Illinois Press, 1971, pp. 453–454.
2. *Ibid.*
3. H. Goldhamer. "Effects of Communication Technology." In Schramm and Roberts, *ibid.*, p. 902.
4. A. C. Clarke. *Profiles of the Future: An Inquiry into the Limits of the Possible*. New York: Harper & Row, 1958, p. 221.
5. Adapted from J. Martin, *Faster Development of Telecommunication*. 1976. Quoted in R. J. Solomon. *World Communication Facts: A Handbook for an International Conference on World Communications—Decisions for the 80's*. Philadelphia, Pa.: Annenberg School of Communications, 1980.
6. Quoted by Solomon, *ibid.* From Hough and Associates, Ltd., report for Canadian Department of Communication, 1979.
7. Quoted by Solomon, *ibid.* From report by International Data Corporation in CDP Industry Report, January 1980.
8. P. B. Silverman. "International Television as a Tool for Technology Transfer." Paper for Technology Exchange 1978, Atlanta, Georgia, February 9, 1978.
9. Quoted by Solomon, *op. cit.* Citing *Journal of Communication*, 1980.
10. F. Machlup. *The Production and Distribution of Knowledge in the United States*. Princeton, N.J.: Princeton University Press, 1962.
11. M. Porat. *The Information Economy*. Stanford University Ph.D. dissertation, Stanford, California, 1976.
12. G. R. White. "Graphics Systems." In G. Gerbner et al., (eds.), *Communications Technology and Social Policy*. New York: Wiley, 1973, pp. 49–50.
13. A. Toffler. *Future Shock*. New York: Bantam Books, 1971, pp. 354–355.
14. *Ibid.*, p. 365.
15. See T. Cook. *Sesame Street Revisited*. New York: Russell Sage Foundation, 1975.
16. Quoted by Clarke, *Profiles of the Future*, p. 218.
17. Toffler, *op. cit.*, pp. 434–435.
18. Clarke, *Profiles of the Future*, p. 217.

NAME INDEX

SUBJECT INDEX